THE TWILIGHT
of
IMPERIAL RUSSIA

Richard Charques

D1344037

OXFORD UNIVERSITY PRESS

LONDON   OXFORD   NEW YORK

First published 1958
First issued as an Oxford University Press paperback, 1965

printing, last digit: 10

Printed in the United States of America

Contents

Maps

To H. B.

in memory

Preface

Since the reign of the last of the Romanov tsars is a classic testing-ground of Marxist theory, it is more than ordinarily vain to look to Soviet historians for the objective account of the period which, counsel of perfection though it may be, still represents the normal ideal of western historiography. In this narrative history of the reign I have pursued no special thesis nor subscribed to any particular doctrine of historical causation. I have kept to the limits of the reign, adding only by way of balance to the introductory survey of the condition of Russia at the accession a short epilogue on the logic of events between the fall of the monarchy and the Bolshevik seizure of power. I have not attempted to describe in any detail that crucial period of eight months between February and October 1917 since it appears to me to belong to a phase of Russian history that properly takes in the civil war which followed. This I propose to make the subject of a later work.

I have had in mind three main points of emphasis. The Bolsheviks contributed little or nothing to the revolution which overthrew the autocracy of the tsars and swept away the dynasty. Until 1917, indeed, their prospects appeared to be no better than those of several rival groups of conspirators or propagandists in exile. I have therefore tried to chart the tides and currents represented by all the other factions and parties, legal and underground, which swelled the revolutionary cataclysm.

I have further indicated some of the 'ifs' of the reign which still exercise the imagination. Amid the revolutionary momentum of events during those twenty-three years there was an astonishing element, as perhaps there always is at periods of social crisis, of the fortuitous. What might have happened is not history, but in retrospect the Russian scene between 1894 and 1917 is strewn with the remains of things hypothetical. Though in the last resort the shaping forces of history are no doubt impersonal, the personal equation in politics is never negligible. No law of Russian historical development compelled Nicholas to accept the advice of Pobedonostsev or to reject the opportunity of coming to terms with the Duma even as late as 1915.

The confusion of the Russian liberals provides a third and leading point of emphasis in *The Twilight of Imperial Russia*. In itself it presents a remarkable study of politics as the art of the impossible and at the same time lights up a principal cause of the Bolshevik triumph. The prospects of liberalism of any sort in Russia were admittedly slender, since the authoritarian bias of Russian political tradition was deep-rooted. But the familiar argument that liberalism was doomed in the absence of a powerful middle class is valid only if Russian liberalism is identified with the forms of liberalism in the west. Russian liberalism of this borrowed variety, which is specially associated with the name of Miliukov and which stood for complete parliamentary democracy in an empire more than three parts illiterate and held together for centuries only by an unqualified absolutism, undoubtedly invited defeat. But there was also a native form of Russian liberalism which had sprung from practical reform, however rudimentary, and taken firm root in a system, however cramped and inhibited, of local self-government. And it was this liberalism 'from within', which was more concerned with the substance of local needs in the peasant vastness of Russia than with the shadow of popular sovereignty, that was absorbed into an alien and doctrinal liberalism evolved jointly from western practice and a vestigial 'legal' Marxism. In 1905, at what might indeed have proved a turning point in the history of tsarist Russia, in the interval before the first Duma and in the first Duma itself, the titular liberals were in effect revolutionaries. As such they were easily outbidden in the course of events by those of more extreme purpose, whose dialectical distinction between a bourgeois and a proletarian revolution they had all too blindly accepted.

Is it far-fetched to suggest that the error of Russian liberalism before 1917 may have some relevance to conditions in Russia today? If the absolutism of the Stalin period is beyond recall, the hope of a more liberal regime in Russia, and with it of avoiding final catastrophe in the relations of Russia and the west, must surely lie in a process of internal reform that is both cautious and conservative. To look for more than that, it seems to me, is doctrinaire folly.

Except for the attempt to avoid over-simplification on the one hand and narrative confusion on the other in presenting so intricate a pattern of events, the problem that more than any other has vexed me in this short history of the reign is one of proportion. Most studies of the decay of tsarism have concentrated on the phase of administrative collapse in the world war and on the history and doctrine of Bolshevism. These, of course, are central aspects of the present work. But unless it was to fill the greater part of the book there was no choice but to condense rather severely the war period. The origins and the ideological controversies of Bolshevism I have sketched only in passing, since detailed accounts are available elsewhere. On the admittedly academic issue of whether or not the Bolshevik accession to power was inevitable it may be worth while making the simple point that the idea of inevitability in history seems essentially anti-historic. 'Surely to no nation', wrote Winston Churchill in *The World Crisis: The Aftermath*, 'has Fate been more malignant than to Russia. Her ship went down in sight of port. She had actually weathered the storm when all was cast away.' That Churchillian image of the Russian events of 1917 bears no close correspondence to the truth. But it is a degree less false, I think, than the notion that the stars in their courses moved in sympathy with the industrial proletariat.

A word on dates. Russia did not adopt the western calendar until February 1918, and the 'Old Style' of Russian chronology, twelve days earlier than ours in the nineteenth century, thirteen days earlier in the twentieth, is a perpetual source of confusion. I have thought it best, however, to keep to the Old Style, though for international and other notable occasions I have given the date in both the Old and the New.

I have listed in the bibliography the principal sources I have used. Not a great deal of fresh documentary material of major interest has been brought to light in recent years, but among new volumes of memoirs or newly collected reminiscences of the period that I have used are those by Miliukov (1955) and Chernov (1953). For their kindness and help I owe much to the staff of the London Library, to those in charge of the Russian Union Catalogue of the National Central Library and not least to the staff of the Harpenden branch of the Hertfordshire County Library.

1. Russia at the Accession of Nicholas II

An emergent power in Europe in the early years of the eighteenth century, when Peter the Great stretched the frontier of Muscovy to the Baltic and raised a ponderous structure of empire upon the needs of war, Russia became a Great Power in defeating Napoleon's Grand Army in 1812. Yet even towards the close of the nineteenth century she was still almost a world apart from Europe. Peter had opened a window on the west, but in the deceiving mists of St Petersburg the view on either side was distorted and for the nations of the west nineteenth-century Russia remained an enigmatic and cruel land with a rank flavour of barbarism. The foreigner entered it, as foreigners had entered Russia in earlier ages and as they would do again in later and more unquiet years, with some difficulty, and almost always with a sense of pursuing mystery. The mystery was seldom dissipated within Russia itself, but amid all that was impenetrably strange the impression which the western traveller habitually took away with him was of a continuing isolation from the life of the west and an agelong material backwardness. It was, as events proved, a peculiar isolation and a peculiar backwardness, and what in both instances was out of the ordinary affords a key to the history of the twenty-three years of the reign of the last of the Romanov tsars.

Part of the mystery, of course, lay in the vastness of Russia. The empire to which Nicholas II succeeded as ruler in 1894 was much the largest that had ever been known. From the Arctic circle to the Black Sea, from the Baltic and the Carpathians to the Pacific and the borders of China and India, it covered an area of eight and a half million square miles. It was an empire won for the most part in peace by centuries of migration across the illimitable and almost unpeopled Eurasian plain, though always in the last resort the advancing frontier had been secured by war. But more than two-thirds of the empire lay east of the Ural Mountains, and in the remote wilds of forest or steppe between the scattered townships that had sprung up on the eastern plain the land was still all but untrodden. Peasant colonization of Siberia on any considerable scale had scarcely begun at the accession of Nicholas II, and the sense of its infinite and empty spaces lent what was almost an extra dimension to the continental vastness of Russia.

The density of population in Russia west of the Urals was lower than that of any country in western Europe. But in 1897, the year of the earliest official Russian census, the total population of the Russian empire was no less than 129.4 million.[1] This was not far short of the combined population of England, France and Germany. Three significant things should be noted in connexion with the Russian figure of population. First, more than five-sixths represented those listed in the category of peasants, and of these all but a few million were engaged in peasant agriculture. Next, the total population was almost double the population of Russia a half-century before. That rate of growth, though assisted by the absorption into the empire during the period of new territory, was largely through natural increase. As such it projected the worsening problem of peasant 'over-population' which dominated both society and the state during the half-century and which was carried over into the twentieth century. Finally, the national and racial composition of the total figure was of the utmost diversity.

Of the hundred and twenty-nine million people no more than fifty-five million were of Great Russian stock. Appreciably less than half of the inhabitants of the Russian empire, that is, were Russians—people whose mother tongue was Russian. In an empire comprising in all some eighty or more nationalities and ethnic groups there were, in 1897, twenty-two million Ukrainians, six million White Russians, eight million Poles, four million Balts, three and a half million Georgians, Armenians and other Caucasian peoples, more than twice as many Kazakhs, Uzbeks, Turkmens and other peoples of central Asia, four million Tatars, nearly two million Germans, half a million Mongols, together with smaller numbers of nomadic or semi-nomadic tribesmen in the Far East and the Far North. There were also five million Jews. As the most notable statesman of the reign put it, 'there was, strictly speaking, no Russia, only a Russian empire'.

The principle of government in this multinational Eurasian empire

[1]This figure includes a population of three million in the autonomous duchy of Finland.

The provinces of European Russia.

was an unqualified monarchical absolutism. The restraints upon the tsar and autocrat were those of mortality only. In every sphere of Russian life law derived from his will alone, power and policy were concentrated in his person. In the contentious phrase of the English seventeenth century, the prerogative of the sovereign was a prerogative absolute. This was a dispensation which on the threshold of the twentieth century had behind it all the logic or seeming logic of Russian historical development. The tradition of Russian autocracy had sprung from Byzantium and had been fostered by the impulse of centuries towards national unity. It had been reinforced by the claims of order and security in an expanding and undeveloped empire. And it had withstood change not only because the very nature of autocracy implies the rejection of even the smallest encroachment upon it but because of the weight and mass of the social edifice constructed on so narrow a base. Disturb the political foundation and would not the whole vast and ordered structure collapse in anarchy? It was that spectre of dissolution which evoked from the reigning tsar throughout the nineteenth century the repeated warning that the principle of autocracy was 'inviolable' and 'immutable'. And indeed the perils of attempting to modify by autocratic decree the supreme prerogative of the Russian autocrat were in no way imaginary, and are still too commonly slighted by the foreign historian bred in a liberal tradition. The fatality of absolutism, no doubt, is that it normally requires a revolution to unseat it, but that is all the more reason for recognizing both the irrelevance of western liberal standards to Russian history and the peculiar dilemma of the conservative reformer in Russia.

For, strangely enough, autocracy represented in some degree a faith and a hope for the masses. The Byzantine theocratic origins of the state were still reflected in the sentiment of the Russian village. For the peasantry the tsar was indeed an anointed ruler. Supreme judge and lawgiver, raised above all the appointed 'estates' of the realm, he was the father of his people who felt for them as a father should. It was not the tsar, the peasantry were convinced, but the tsar's servants who had laid upon them an age-long burden of injustice. *Do Boga vysoko, a do tsaria daleko*— 'Heaven is high and the tsar is far off', they said, but they still looked to the throne, however uncertainly, for protection.

From the marriage of the divine order of autocracy with Great Russian supremacy in the empire came the messianic character of Russian nationalism. For good and ill nationalism has been for centuries the shaping influence in the political life of the west, as today it is the creative force in the politics of the east. Russia, between east and west, nourished a sense of the distinctive inheritance she had acquired from Byzantium and Greek Orthodoxy. Through the force of nationalist assertion, the contrast she presented with Europe carried with it a feeling of superiority to Europe. Amid every appearance of material disadvantage or cultural inferiority the Russian people were encouraged to believe that they had a special destiny among the nations, even a mission to the rest of the world.

The duties of the Russian throne, stretching into the most recondite departments of policy, were inexhaustible. Only a ruler of prodigal strength of body and mind could seek to discharge them in detail, and none could attempt to discharge them all in person. The system of administration, therefore, was one of extreme centralization. The autocrat was all-powerful, but he was also the hub of a formidable apparatus of bureaucracy: Russia was, indeed, an absolutist-bureaucratic state. Yet in a wholly unconstitutional regime it is seldom possible to establish beyond doubt the source of delegated authority, and one of the commonplaces of Russian autocracy is that it bred an oriental system of place and power near the throne. The members of the always numerous imperial family caught a dazzling gleam of authority from the crown. The atmosphere of a court which was the scene of a struggle for influence at the highest level was necessarily Byzantine. Throughout the nineteenth century, too, the imperial practice was maintained of appointing special commissions of enquiry, either vested with official powers or expressly designated 'private' commissions, to report to the tsar in person. As supreme arbiter of the empire's affairs he was in no way bound by the advice that might be tendered to him.

The appointed machinery of government functioned in strict and narrow grooves. It was commonly remarked that the country had ministries but no government. As departments of the central authority, the ministries—for foreign affairs, finance, the interior, war, the navy, justice, and so on—were instruments of the supreme executive will in precisely the same way as was the Ministry of the Court. The ministers were appointed directly by the crown. For purposes of joint consultation they met in committee, but it was left to each individual minister, who made his 'most loyal report' separately in audience with the tsar, to decide whether the affairs of his department required such consultation. The committee served no other purpose; its chairman, who had no departmental responsibilities, enjoyed no special powers. In these conditions ministers were rivals rather than colleagues and were constantly engaged in intrigue against one another. Much the most influential ministry, since it controlled the entire police system of the empire, was the Ministry of the Interior.

Though the right to make laws belonged absolutely to the throne, an advisory function in legislation was exercised by the State Council (*Gosudarstvenny Soviet*). This body consisted as a rule of between forty and sixty persons; all the ministers were members and the rest, similarly, were appointed directly by the crown. They were chosen for the most part from among ex-ministers, former ambassadors and governors-general of provinces; appointed for life at the end as a rule of a long period of state service, they were generally over-ripe in years and rigidly conservative in their bias. At the same time, at periods of extreme reaction there were almost always among them, as among the higher bureaucracy generally, some who favoured moderation as a course in better keeping with the times. The State Council had no powers of initiative; it merely submitted to the tsar at his command drafts of laws which in outline had usually been projected elsewhere, most often in narrow palace circles. The tsar might accept or reject as he pleased whatever proposals were made to him. The State Council, staffed by expert officials, was organized in three sections, dealing respectively with general legislative affairs, the civil and ecclesiastical administration, and the state economy (one of its principal tasks was to examine the annual budget). In 1899, five years after Nicholas II came to the throne, a fourth section was instituted for industry, science and commerce. Subservient in status and cramped in style though it was, as a government institution the State Council came nearest to exercising a tacit constitutional function in the scheme of tsarist absolutism.

A more shadowy quasi-constitutional function fell to the Senate, originally devised by Peter the Great to keep watch over both the civil administration and the law courts, and afterwards reorganized as the highest court of appeal in civil and criminal cases. Its members were likewise appointed directly by the tsar, as a rule from the ranks of the higher aristocracy in state service. Though in theory it had the right to pronounce upon the legal propriety of new measures, the Senate could only make recommendations in the framing of laws.

The local apparatus of central government was vast, cumbrous and notoriously inefficient. Though it left great gaps in the provision of the most elementary local needs, it also obtruded upon most private activities. Nowhere was the hand of officialdom more ubiquitous or more arbitrary than in Russia. The rigid centralization of authority in the capital left room for an all but unlimited local despotism. European Russia was divided into fifty provinces, each headed by a governor or, more importantly, a governor-general, on whom was laid the duty of sending annual reports to the emperor. A similar charge was laid upon the viceroy or other representative of the sovereign in territories farther afield. By this means the emperor was informed of local conditions throughout the realm. The reports were seldom, in fact, very informative, since governors were ordinarily chosen not for their disinterestedness or ability but because of their connexions at court, and since also they were under constant pressure from the Minister of the Interior, to whom they were subordinate, to put the best face on even the worst of all possible worlds. They executed his instructions and those of the other ministries in St Petersburg with the aid of collegiate boards of officials. In theory, the separation of powers was strictly observed in the formal scheme of provincial government; in point of fact, the politics of the local representatives of the Ministry of the Interior rode roughshod over the due processes of law. So, in greater or less degree, did almost every other agency of provincial government. For, except in police matters, the writ of St Petersburg did not easily run across poor communications a thousand or more miles away. The farther the scene from the centre the more tyrannical as a rule was the exercise of the powers of officialdom, above all of the police.

The police, indeed, were very nearly masters of the human situation in Russia. They controlled the individual rights and liberties of the population. They supervised the internal passport system, by which all movement in Russia was regulated. They were the appointed agents for the collection of all state taxes and local dues. Their permissive powers lay at the root of the universal corruption in the lower reaches of authority; almost nothing could be attempted, nothing could be achieved, without the giving and taking of bribes. And beyond the civil police, and strictly separated from it, stretched the network of the political police—the *gen-*

darmerie—functioning independently of the governors, supported
by secret agents, spies and informers and vested with summary
administrative powers.

In much that concerned the everyday welfare of the masses,
government at the centre mattered appreciably less than local
administration. Throughout the country the same types of official
worked under identical conditions of service. The higher ranks of
the bureaucracy, among whom the governors afforded a principal
source of recruitment to ministerial appointments, seldom failed to
include men of ability and conscience; the best examples, conservative almost to a man though they were, belonged to the former
German nobility of the Baltic provinces, the so-called 'Baltic
barons'. But the general level of energy or competence was low.
The inertia, the indifference, the pedantry and the delaying
punctilio of the Russian bureaucracy as a whole were indeed
notorious. These qualities owed not a little to the system of grading
in the state service which Peter the Great had introduced as a
means of opening a career to talent, and which endured for two
centuries after him. All entrants to the civil administration began
on an equal footing in the lowest of the fourteen established ranks;
promotion, which carried with it a Germanic style of honorifics
like 'excellency' and 'high excellency' and even included the
privilege of ennoblement, personal or hereditary, was ostensibly
by individual merit. The effect of this hierarchical system, far from
harnessing energy and ambition to the service of the state, was to
encourage in the body of officialdom a vicious paralysis of will and
servility of spirit. Only the form of things mattered; paper work
was everything. All ranks of officials, together with numerous
other sections of society, including the body of students, had their
own distinctive and obligatory uniform. The absence of public
initiative in nineteenth-century Russia, it has frequently been
observed, was attested all too vividly by the prevalence of uniforms.

For public initiative ran counter to the medieval principles of
the absolutist-bureaucratic state. There was no place in this order
of government and society for independent political activity; the
existence of organized parties or the declaration of public programmes would have infringed the prerogative. Yet on the eve of
the twentieth century the absolutism of the tsar, whatever its
historical justification, was the most flagrant anomaly of Russian
life. It was maintained as an immutable principle in face of a record
of Russian achievement during three generations in literature,

learning and science which was comparable with that of any nation in the west, of the demonstrable ambition of the Russian educated classes to share in the tasks of government, and of the growing complexity of the problems of society as its fabric was transformed in the developing process of a belated industrial revolution.

At the time of the accession of Nicholas II the desire for political freedom in Russia lay very close, as always, to the sense of human dignity. Almost the only Russian voices raised in protest against the existing order were of those in political exile from their native land. But the overtones in the common use of a word like *proizvol*, a barely translatable word signifying the pervasive arbitrariness of authority in Russia—the absence of legality or indeed of defined law—echoed in the mind and heart of all who heard it. The word *vlast*, meaning power or dominion, was habitually substituted for the word *pravitelstvo*, meaning government, thus conveying a similar sense of the exercise of authority unhindered by law. The very word for 'society'—*obshchestvo*—ordinarily stood for the body of opinion in opposition to the prevailing order of government, the quite untranslatable word *obshchestvennost* ('society-ness', or the mind of society) for hostility to the basic assumptions of autocratic rule. The title of a volume of reminiscences by one of the sanest and most practical-minded liberals of the reign of Nicholas II, V. A. Maklakov, in which the words *vlast* and *obshchestvennost* are used, would make no sense in English except in some such long-winded translation as *The Structure of Autocracy and the Liberal Opposition of Educated Society in the Closing Period of Old Russia*. That, in point of fact, illustrates a central theme of the reign of Nicholas II. Its most fateful aspect is the unremitting struggle of crown and opposition for the support of Russia's peasant masses, the real arbiters of Russia's destiny.

The Russian peasantry were not a social class; they were a legal 'estate' (*sostoyanie* or *soslovie*). Right up to the revolution of 1917 the population of Russia continued to be rigorously divided into separate estates of the realm: the nobility; the urban classes, consisting of the petty burghers (*meshchane*), the merchant class, and those legally styled personal or hereditary honorary citizens; and the peasants. (The Cossacks, a military class, formed a separate estate of their own.) Every member of each estate was registered as such with an appropriate local body or institution. Each estate enjoyed different and unequal rights. A peasant continued in the estate in which it had pleased a Russian providence to call him unless, by education or state service or by recognized transfer to trade or industry, he stepped out of it. A gulf yawned between one estate and the next. The widest gulf of all, the chasm which separated the peasant masses from the ruling classes, determined the fate of tsarist Russia.

When Nicholas II came to the throne a generation had passed since the abolition of serfdom. The evil which had for so long stultified Russian life had become only a memory. Yet the memory was kept passionately alive by all the daily circumstances of peasant existence. For the emancipation of 1861, immense achievement though it was, had come too late and conferred too little. The peasantry had gained their freedom only on terms which substituted a new form of economic servitude for the old and perpetuated their isolation from the rest of society.

The economic settlement effected by the acts of 1861 and the following years was of extraordinary complexity. Broadly speaking, the peasant on the private estate had acquired with his freedom the right to purchase a holding of about half the amount of land he had formerly cultivated—less than half in precisely those central and southern black-earth regions where peasant poverty had been most acute and peasant unrest most endemic. For this holding he was required to make annual redemption payments, representing the value of the land surrendered to him by the landowner (who had received immediate compensation from the state), over a period of forty-nine years. The entire economic scheme of emancipation had foundered almost as soon as it was introduced. For the peasant's allotment of land has been reduced to a disastrously uneconomic size and the scale of redemption payments, small though it might seem, had been based upon a gross over-valuation of the land and imposed upon him a crushing burden of indebtedness.[1]

The failure of this economic dispensation had become progressively plainer as rising figures of population pressed upon peasant standards which were often already at the barest subsistence level. But the failure of the scheme of liberation was not economic only; more disturbingly, perhaps, it was also psychological. Increasingly the peasant had become aware that his liberty was only half-

[1]It should be made clear that the peasants on state land emerged from the emancipation with a larger holding than the majority of peasants on the private estates. In most cases, indeed, it was originally sufficient to provide a livelihood.

liberty. The emancipated serf was still a world apart from those who had never known serfdom, cut off from them by an insurmountable barrier of legal disability. For the first time, it is true, he now enjoyed the right to marry as he pleased, to go to law, even to own property. But his rights otherwise were undefined and were all too often in doubt. Worse, he still suffered penalties and restrictions that were laid upon no other class. For a quarter of a century after 1861 he alone continued to pay poll-tax. Under the jurisdiction of special lower courts for peasant affairs, he, and he alone, was still subject to corporal punishment. And, finally, as a peasant he was less an individual than a registered member of a particular village community, bound by the decisions of the *mir*, or commune, the assembly of all the male heads of households. The village commune had long discharged collective responsibility for the payment of taxes and all other obligations, and it continued to do so now. But it had also acquired formidable powers of coercion and restraint. In almost every practical sense, indeed, it had stepped into the place of the serf-owning squire as the peasant's master.

For what had been established in rural Russia in no way resembled a western system of peasant proprietorship. The peasant's allotment of land was not his private property; not for a moment was he at liberty to make what use of it he wished. Possession of peasant land was vested in the village community, and the management of the land thus held in common fell to the commune and its elected elders. Over much the greater part of European Russia the commune continued to observe the practice of periodically repartitioning the land—'taking land from the dead', in the peasants' own phrase, 'and giving it to the living'— as numbers varied among the families working in the fields.[1] The commune controlled the rotation of crops and agricultural operations generally; the elders, to whom each peasant owed obedience, controlled the fortunes of members of households. For a primary interest of the impoverished community was not to increase the burden of collective dues and taxes by permitting any of its members to leave the commune. Every conceivable obstacle was placed in the way of a peasant who proposed to seek permanent employment elsewhere. Seasonal work in the factory might bring advantage to the community as a whole, but permanent wage-work

[1] In something like a quarter of the number of peasant communes at the beginning of the reign land was held in hereditary tenure.

in the town was a different matter. In order to leave the commune, a junior member of the household required first of all permission of the head of the household. That granted, he might possibly receive the consent of the elders by a promise to continue payment of his share of the collective dues or by persuading another peasant to assume his obligations.

The bonds of the commune were fatally restrictive in the circumstances of the rapid increase in peasant numbers. For a century before the act of emancipation serfdom had been the one burning question in Russian society; for a half-century afterwards the crucial problem for society and government alike was the growing impoverishment of the Russian village. Every new development appeared to make it more intractable. Even under serfdom the peasant's allotment had seldom been large enough to keep him occupied for more than three days in the week. With the growth of population the original halving of the amount of land he had formerly cultivated was disastrous. In the years immediately after 1861 the holdings worked by peasant households in European Russia probably averaged between thirty and thirty-five acres; for the adult male in each household the corresponding figure was about eight acres. The size of this original holding was desperately uneconomic because Russian peasant agriculture, still based on the strip system, was as primitive as it had been a couple of centuries earlier, and because the peasant had neither capital nor knowledge. On top of all this the periodical redistribution of the land stifled initiative; the commonest incentives were lacking; the pace set for the village was as often as not the pace of the slowest. And still peasant numbers increased. When to low productivity was thus added a constant shrinking in the size of peasant allotments the ever deepening poverty of the village indeed seemed to be beyond remedy. Perhaps the cruellest period of peasant want came during the fifteen or sixteen years before the accession of Nicholas II, when with the harvesting of the great wheat prairies of the western hemisphere the world—and Russian —price of grain fell sharply.

True, a class of relatively prosperous peasants was in the making. The law permitted not only the communal lease of further land but also the purchase of land by an individual peasant in complete independence of the commune and in full ownership, and in most parts of the country there were peasants who had availed themselves of the opportunity. But the reverse side of this picture of a rising *kulak* class[1] showed the growth of a landless or almost landless rural proletariat. The expansion of industry, striking though it was, was still too small to absorb surplus labour in the village.

Thus for perhaps the majority of the peasantry the end of the settlement effected in 1861 was in some ways worse than the beginning. The climate of freedom was less harsh than the climate of serfdom, yet perhaps it was not radically different. A generation after the emancipation much of the old system of peasant-landlord relations survived. The peasants' fields were almost always mixed up with what remained of the landowner's estate, and there was constant friction over peasant access to pasture, woodland or water, which the landowner had generally retained in his own hands. More significantly, the old feudal relationship, so reminiscent of four-teenth-century England and eighteenth-century France, survived in the peasant's need to hire himself out as a day labourer to his former master or, worse still, to rent a piece of ground from him on a cash or crop basis or in return for cultivating another part of the landlord's estate with his own horses and implements. Burdensome though the conditions of tenure were, however close to serfdom, the peasant had no choice but to acquire more land.

In the availability of more land for peasant cultivation—land still in the possession of the former serfowners—lay the crux of the situation for the larger part of Russia's peasant population right up to 1917. How should there not be more land, the peasant argued, when what had been allotted to him at the emancipation was only half or less of the amount of land he had held as a serf? The argument appeared the more self-evident to him because of his conviction that the portions of land of which he had then been deprived—the *otrezki*, or 'cuttings-off'—had always been, and still were, legally his own. Yet though the logic in favour of 'a second emancipation' seemed straightforward enough, the assumptions behind it, as will be indicated, were being eroded by changes in land ownership.

The everyday commonplaces of the peasants' way of life in the years before the accession of Nicholas II need to be clearly borne in mind, since more than all it was the tension of peasant discontents

[1] Endless controversy has raged on whether and to what extent the dif-ferentiation between rich and poor peasants increased during the last decades of the nineteenth century.

which was released in the upheaval of February 1917. Within our own lifetime the 'condition of the people' problem in the western world has changed out of all recognition, and for that reason it is easy, perhaps, to present too sombre a picture of the realities of the Russian countryside in, say, the 1880s. Rural Russia was not in any sense perpetually joyless. The virtues of simplicity and shrewdness, of vitality and humour, which belong to peasant character in most lands, were always apparent in Russia. But against these things must be set the extreme of rural poverty.

It was not uniform. Even before 1861 there were some peasants rich enough to employ hired labour. In some fortunate areas the standard of living was no lower than that of central Europe, while here and there oases of rural contentment were to be found. Inequalities were most marked, on the whole, in those western and south-western provinces where peasant tenure was for the most part hereditary. West of the Urals, however, a bleak and degrading wretchedness marked the lives of the great majority of the peasant population. A much travelled English member of Parliament on a visit to Russia in 1891 wrote: 'In no other great country in the world is poverty to so great an extent the national characteristic of the people'. The poverty, and all that went with it, are illustrated in the novels of Gleb Uspensky and in the haunting picture drawn by Chekhov, for instance, in a story like *The Peasants*.

Tens of thousands of villages presented an almost identical scene. Imagine a rough track as wide as a field, thick with summer dust or heavy with mud or snow, and skirting it anything from a few dozen to a few hundred earthen or wooden huts and a church set in their midst. In each hut, complete with brick stove and lamp-lit icon on the wall, three generations commonly lived together under the patriarchal rule of the head of the household. There was, as a rule, no ventilation; there were no beds; the hut was almost certainly verminous. The family's diet consisted largely of grain. The rude health of the peasantry was, in part, myth. The infant mortality rate was high; diphtheria, typhus and malaria came in recurring epidemics; syphilis was possibly more widespread than anywhere else in the world. All this entered into what Lenin was later to call 'the idiocy of village life', for with brutalizing poverty, squalor and drunkenness went the 'darkness' of the masses, the vast ignorance compounded of illiteracy and superstition. In 1897 less than one person out of every five in rural Russia could read. Between the *muzhik* and the rest of society there existed an impassable barrier of custom, speech, dress and habit.

The continued backwardness of peasant farming bred continued inertia. Allotments consisted of twenty or thirty strips, even more, usually at some considerable distance from the village and often so narrow as to be scarcely workable. The plough in use was mostly the light wooden plough called the *sokha*, a reasonably efficient implement for black-earth land but one which elsewhere scratched the earth rather than dug into it. Productivity was so low that grain in the household seldom lasted from harvest to seed-time, while drought in the most fertile black-earth provinces brought the constant menace of famine.

In the reign of Nicholas II's predecessor, Alexander III, all but one of the measures taken to alleviate these rigours of peasant existence touched only the fringes of the problem. In 1881, and again in 1884, redemption payments, which showed an enormous accumulation of arrears, were scaled down. Simultaneously a State Peasants' Bank was founded to assist peasants to buy land on credit. For several years more, however, most peasant purchases of land were made by other means, and even after the original funds at the bank's disposal had been enlarged those in greatest need remained unassisted because the terms of repayment were beyond the means of all but the richer peasants. In 1886 the poll-tax, which with the growth of the volume of indirect taxation had formed a diminishing part of the state revenue, was abolished. None of these measures went far in achieving what in contemporary England was called betterment. The only hopeful step was taken in 1889, when migration to the empty lands of Siberia was formally encouraged. Until then it had been obstructed in every possible way by local authorities bent upon ensuring a supply of cheap labour for the private estates and by the commune itself. A year before his death Alexander III had even tightened the bonds of the commune; where formerly a peasant who had been able to pay off the whole of his redemption debt was free to depart, by law he now required the consent of two-thirds of the village assembly. But in that same year 1893, two years after the construction of the Trans-Siberian railway had been begun, a government railway committee put in hand the first tentative steps to organize peasant colonization of Siberia, until then a perilous venture. The colonists, preceded by scouting parties, migrated in groups; entire villages uprooted themselves from the over-populated central provinces and went east.

One further development touching land ownership during this

period remains to be noted. In 1885, a year or more after the Peasants' Bank began operations, a State Bank for the Nobility also came into existence. Its purpose was to provide mortgages for those harassed or improvident nobles who sought to retain their estates for the benefit of generations of nobility yet unborn. For the depression in agriculture continued and in increasing measure a spendthrift gentry were being obliged to part with their land—not so much to peasant communes as to members of the class known as 'merchants and honorary citizens' and to the richer townsfolk generally. Such sales, which had been common enough before the emancipation, became more frequent in the decades after 1861. Since the maintenance of the landed gentry as a ruling class was held to be a stabilizing factor, the terms offered by the Bank for the Nobility were appreciably more favourable than those granted by the Peasants' Bank. Even so, the transfer of private estates to non-noble hands continued on an increasing scale.

Although it had left intact the basic pattern of the state, the emancipation of the serfs had shattered a structure of local administration built on semi-feudal law and custom. Into the new order in peasant affairs, therefore, stepped the elected council called the *zemstvo*. Next to the emancipation itself, this was the greatest landmark of the so-called 'era of great reforms'.

The introduction of the zemstvos in 1864 represented a genuine if unhappily frustrated effort to establish local self-government in Russia. For that reason alone they have a distinctive place in the history of the decline of tsarist absolutism. But the zemstvos were also the seed-bed of liberalism as a political movement in Russia, and their original character and ideals may perhaps still throw light on the failure of Russian liberalism in competition with more extreme forces.

The zemstvos were elected councils for the province and for the county (*uezd*), a sub-division of the province, functioning side by side with local organs of the central authority and charged with the supply and maintenance of local services for which the government made no provision. Empowered to levy a small rate on property for these purposes, they confined their energies, to begin with, to such matters as the repair of roads and bridges, hitherto a recognized part of serf obligations, and to poor relief. To these activities were soon added the provision of elementary schools and of public health and agricultural advisory services.

In some official quarters the original scheme devised for the zemstvos, like the original scheme of emancipation, had been both bold and constructive. Like emancipation, the reform had been severely whittled down in deference to the interest of the landed nobility. The plan of giving equal rights of representation to peasants, townspeople and the peasants' former masters was scrapped in favour of a system of indirect voting in separate classes or estates which ensured the heavy predominance on the councils of the gentry. As for the zemstvo revenue, the average rate on peasant land was twice the rate on the private estates.

The zemstvos were set up only in the strictly Russian parts of the empire, first in twenty-seven provinces, then in seven more, and were not extended to the wholly or largely non-Russian border areas or to Siberia. A zemstvo assembly was elected for three years and chose from among its members a permanent governing board. Over each assembly in province or county presided the local marshal of the nobility (the titular head of the statutory local assemblies of the hereditary nobility), who exercised a right of veto over its deliberations. Although as a class the nobility were supremely indifferent to the work of the zemstvo boards, as individuals many of them soon brought to it sincere enthusiasm. From the start there were active as well as indolent zemstvos, liberal together with less liberal representatives; some of the most liberal were those elected by peasant votes. Almost from the start, too, there were zemstvo leaders who saw in even this small degree of local self-government the prospect of larger reform and the hope of more fundamental political change.

The work of the zemstvos was often cramped by the influence of the marshal of the nobility, still more often obstructed by the governor of the province and always hedged in by the fears and apprehensions of the Ministry of the Interior, which from first to last was concerned to scotch any form of public initiative. It was restricted, too, by their narrowly circumscribed powers of taxation, and in the earlier period of their existence the sum total of their achievement was trifling. Yet the more enterprising councils slowly went ahead with the building of primary schools, the provision of hospital and first-aid services, the organization of technical aid and instruction in peasant farming. One of the most conspicuously successful of all zemstvo activities was road-building; in a land of immense distances, in which spring floods or autumn rains made existing tracks impassable and snowstorms might isolate a village for weeks on end, the provision of rough country roads did almost as much as anything for economic progress. Basic statistical studies in agriculture did only a little less Gradually a new body of salaried zemstvo employees came into being— teachers, doctors, midwives, farming and veterinary experts—who in time became known as the 'third element'.[1] Though the effect of what even the most active zemstvos could achieve was only to scratch the surface of peasant want and ignorance, the achievement was a notable one in the bureaucratic environment of the period. It demonstrated, among other things, that a technique of local self-government was indeed being learned.

Yet this was not the most fruitful outcome of zemstvo activities. More significant, in the era of reforms of the sixties, had been the temper of political opposition evoked by the spectacle of the needs of the masses and the indifference of St Petersburg. It had little in common with the nascent revolutionary sentiment of the decade. But it went deeper than the parallel demand among various assemblies of the nobility for an elected national assembly. The voices raised in this somewhat romantic longing for a revival of the seventeenth-century *zemsky sobor*, or assembly of the land, were for the most part those of an impoverished and conservative section of the nobility, whose purpose was not so much reform as the restoration of their lost powers and privileges. The more active reformers went closer to the root of the matter, founding their hopes in the first place upon the rule of law in government and administration. For the rest, there remained the vision of political liberty. The zemstvos were elected: when, in the familiar phrase of the period, 'would the building be crowned?' For the radicals among the zemstvo workers local self-government marked no more than a preliminary stage on the road to constitutional government. Until revolt against the scheme of autocracy stirred underground in the next decade and the tide of reform ebbed, the assembly of the land which the boldest of them had in mind was a representative legislative assembly.

In the eighties, after the revolutionary terrorists had achieved their end in the murder of Alexander II, political agitation was silenced. In the prevailing climate of repression, which was fortified by a stringent censorship, it could not seek expression even in

[1]The other two elements in local government consisted of officials and elected representatives. The title of 'third element' did not come into use until 1899.

the veiled or 'aesopian' style of language which had been adopted in an earlier period. Only at the beginning of the nineties, during the last years of the reign of Alexander III, did the liberal dream revive. But by that time one thing had become plain. As a political movement, which had sprung from the promptings of conscience and good sense and in its reforming endeavours had urged the claims of civil liberty, the liberal zemstvo movement was a head without a body. With the masses beyond their reach, its leaders could appeal only to the enlightened gentry and to a section of opinion among the professional and educated part of society who were slowly assuming the likeness of a middle class in Russia. And this was as yet a negligibly small middle class. It included few even of the intelligentsia, that strangely Russian phenomenon, whose members, drawn from people of all ranks and more particularly from the *déclassés*, were united only by a certain intellectual extremism in their mode of life. In the appeal to a tiny middle-class minority in the name of political liberty lay the confusion and instability of zemstvo liberalism. For this was in every sense an appeal above the heads of the peasant masses, who, since zemstvo dues were collected by the police, continued to look on the zemstvos as fiscal agencies of the landowning nobility. For the peasant all the constitutional government in the world mattered less than an acre of land. The idea of the state was beyond his horizon.

The political history of Russia is essentially a history of ideas. The same basic institutions, modified in outward form only, have been perpetuated by different myths. Constitutionalism, the hope of a rising middle class, was one such myth. Amid the repression of the eighties, not even the bravest 'public men' (*obshchestvennie deyateli*), as the zemstvo representatives and their kind were called, could voice their hopes of a constitution; the very use of the word was forbidden. They were absorbed, as in later years they wrote in their memoirs, in defending the great reforms against reaction. The policy of Alexander III, after the assassination of his father, was bleak and uncompromising. Since reform had ended in treason, it was necessary at all costs to undo reform, to return in spirit to the inflexible and salutary conservatism of the past.

The act of regicide had behind it a half-century of intellectual revolt against the scheme of Russian autocracy. Revolt had stirred in the 1830s in the overtones of the philosophic debate between westerners and slavophils: must backward Russia follow where

Europe led or had she a separate path of destiny of her own? A generation later, after the humiliation of the Crimean War and the soul-searching which had fostered reform, the old controversy had been revived in a new guise. What, for Russia, was progress? Since the 1860s the Narodnik (Populist) movement, that generous and sentimental tide of sympathy for the cause of the *narod*, the people, had quickened every untutored impulse of idealism in Russian society. In pursuing a vision of peasant socialism the Narodniks had preached the necessity for a violent upheaval if freedom and justice were to reign in Russia. Faith in what Herzen had called 'the instinctive socialism' of the peasant masses, faith in the village commune (and in similar co-operative and self-govern-ing associations of producers in manufacture) as the foundation of an egalitarian order of society, faith in Russia's unique destiny and her mission to escape the horrors of capitalist development—all this had possessed the mind and heart of many of the younger generation of the sixties and seventies. It had lighted the way in 1874 for an astonishing procession of intellectuals, students and young women in their naïve and exalted crusade 'to the people'. It had bred finally the underground movement of Land and Liberty and the terrorist organization of The People's Will, the assassins of Alexander II.

In the reign of Alexander III the Narodnik hope was in eclipse. The small group of conspirators of the People's Will, the object of the devoutest sympathy of Victorian liberals, had been wiped out. Its leaders had perished on the scaffold, their accomplices were immured in solitary confinement in the fortress prison of Schlüssel-burg or were in exile in Siberia or abroad. Within Russia sedition had been crushed. On 14 August 1881, five months after Alexander III's accession, special powers had been conferred upon the government to proclaim a state of emergency in any part of the empire in the interests of 'order and social tranquillity'. This enabled the governor of an affected province to take progressively severe measures of 'reinforced security' or 'extreme security'—the further right of resort to martial law still remained—and invested him and the local agencies of the Ministry of the Interior with sweeping extra-judicial powers of search, arrest, imprisonment and deporta-tion.[1] Other measures of repression in succeeding years had been

[1]Designed as a provisional measure, this emergency legislation was in fact retained throughout the reign of both Alexander III and his successor. During the entire period there was scarcely an interval of weeks when conditions of special security were not being enforced over large parts of the country.

specially directed against the intellectual life of the country. In 1882 the press had been subjected to new censorship regulations; the preliminary censorship of newspapers was abandoned, but both newspapers and periodicals were gagged by a system of ministerial warnings, by restrictions on sale in the street, restrictions on advertisements, a ban on the employment of the politically suspect, while a special inter-departmental committee was given the right of suspending any newspaper or newspaper editor. In 1884 the last vestiges of university autonomy were abolished and the appointment of rectors and the holders of the principal university chairs now passed directly into the hands of the Minister of Education. Three years later a notorious ministry circular was issued which aimed at excluding from the *gymnasia* (the grammar schools), and hence from the universities, the children of 'coachmen, cooks, laundresses, small shopkeepers and such people'—that is, of the non-noble or non-official classes.

For the government of Russia all this was still inadequate insurance against a renewal of agitation or disorder, particularly in the countryside. Continued peasant disturbances bore witness to the need for stricter discipline. Though the emancipation itself could not now be undone, its menace to social tranquillity could at least be countered. Thus in 1889 there was established in every canton (a grouping of villages) the office of land captain (*zemsky nachalnik*) with overriding authority in all that concerned the organs of peasant self-government. Appointed by the Ministry of the Interior, from which he took his instructions, and chosen as a rule from among the minor nobility of the neighbourhood, the land captain was enthroned in the village as sovereign arbiter of peasant affairs. All decisions of the village or cantonal assemblies were now subject to his approval. In violation of earlier statutes, he exercised both administrative and judicial functions. The peasantry had elected their own officers to the cantonal lower courts, while in remote rural areas the law was administered by justices of the peace elected by the county zemstvo assembly. The rural justices of the peace were now done away with and the cantonal courts brought under the immediate control of the land captain. Peasant elections to the courts were replaced, in effect, by his right of nomination. Decisions by the courts could be set aside at his will. The land captain had the right to disallow the election of any peasant official or to suspend him from duty and the right to impose fines and punishments without trial. His task, in short, was to secure the compliance of the peasantry in his own arbitrary rule over them.

No single act of government in the reign of Alexander III stirred the Russian peasant to more bitter resentment. For all practical purposes this was the restoration of the despotic power over the life and affairs of the peasantry which had been exercised by the landowner under serfdom. It brought back, in truth, the breath and being of serf law.

A further blow struck for the rights of the gentry was delivered in the following year, when the law governing the composition and competence of the zemstvos was drastically amended. Class or 'estate' representation in the assemblies, already flagrantly inequitable, was further modified in the interest of the gentry by a change in peasant voting procedure. The peasants did not now elect their representative but only chose a number of candidates, from whom the governor made his own selection. It was not difficult by such means to ensure the complete ascendancy of the gentry throughout the zemstvo structure. For the rest, even more rigid control of every branch of zemstvo activity was secured by the powers of supervision of the governor of the province.

The new law reflected the government's ever deepening distrust of all forms of public initiative. Almost at once it was put to the severest test, and in the result both the reputation of the Russian government in the eyes of the world and the lives of millions of Russian people were barely saved by public initiative. The famine of 1891 in some twenty of the most fertile provinces of European Russia was the worst for a generation. In its wake came an epidemic of cholera. Tens of thousands of people died of hunger or disease. The government itself was totally incapable of organizing swift measures of relief on an appropriate scale, and yet, having begun by denying the existence of famine and prohibiting the very mention of the word, it went on to ban all organized voluntary aid in the stricken provinces. Only after a great outcry of protest had gone up from every responsible section of society did the government rescind the ban.

It was now, in the work of hundreds of improvised relief and welfare committees, that the barrier between the classes and the masses was temporarily thrown down and large numbers of educated men and women were faced for the first time with the realities of peasant existence. The conscience of society once more came to life. Narodnik sentiment, never wholly extinguished among the intelligentsia, began to revive in a modified and more realistic form.

The zemstvo liberals grew bolder and put at the immediate head of their programme the need for a central zemstvo organization. The radicalism of the 'third element' became increasingly articulate. From the famine year 1891—there was famine again in the following year—dates the rebirth of a vision of representative government in Russia.

If for the peasants in the villages the brute reality of existence in the last decade of the nineteenth century was an extreme of abject poverty, a scarcely distinguishable poverty likewise characterized the lives of the factory workers in the towns. Unlike the peasants, however, the factory workers had an elementary sense of politics.

Industrial capitalism came suddenly to Russia as well as late. Mines and factories had been in operation a century or more before Peter the Great set to work to equip his armies with the products of native industry, but the labour employed was then serf labour. The existence after 1861 of so vast a free labour market gave capitalist enterprise its opportunity. In the middle of the nineteenth century the urban population of Russia was about three and a half million. In 1897, according to the census figures, it had risen to nearly sixteen and a half million, representing some thirteen per cent of the total population.

In origins and development capitalist industry in Russia differed from the western variety in several significant ways. It emerged new-born with an advanced technique and equipment—a phenomenon which in our time has become increasingly familiar. From the beginning it was highly concentrated; production was centred in some half-dozen main industrial regions. From the beginning, too, Russian industry was heavily state-aided and found in the state its chief patron and purchaser. And the close participation at every stage of its growth of foreign capital and of foreign organizers and engineers gave it a semi-colonial character. Nothing illustrates so graphically the juxtaposition of a nascent modernity and an agelong backwardness in imperial Russia at the turn of the century as the advanced condition of industry in a primitive peasant economy.

The expansion of industry held a central place in government policy under Alexander III. Direct state investment during the reign was supplemented by a programme of loans and subsidies, of concessions and privileges to foreign capital. A mounting tariff afforded protection to almost every branch of industry, with the

The Russian Empire: Communications and principal tow

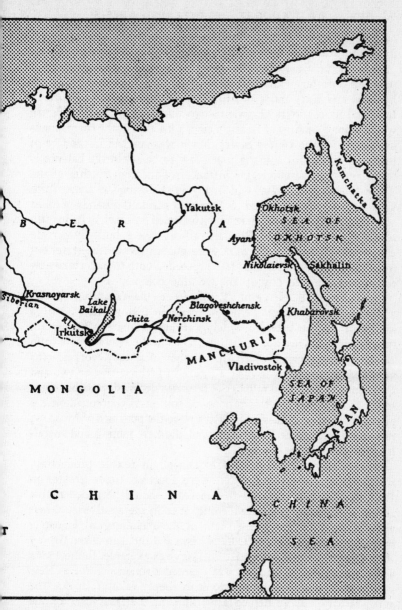

industrial centres in the early years of the twentieth century.

notable exception of heavy machinery, which Russia was as yet unable to produce.

Railway construction, in Russia as elsewhere, is a rough index of nineteenth-century industrial development. In 1855 there were six hundred and sixty miles of railway in Russia; in 1881, fourteen thousand miles; in 1895, twenty-two thousand miles. The figure was low for a country of Russia's size, a fraction of the corresponding figure for the United States, but it was reached in the face of immense difficulties. Among much else to be set in the balance is the daring and resource, for instance, of the construction of the Trans-Siberian railway, which involved laying a track from Cheliabinsk (already linked to Moscow) across thousands of miles of wilderness, the subsoil permanently frozen for much of its length, to the Pacific. The first Russian railways were built by private enterprise, though their profits were guaranteed by the state, but from the 1880s onwards the state proceeded both to undertake new construction and to buy up the existing companies.

Russian statistics have at all times been flagrantly unreliable, and on not a few major themes of economic history the student is invited to choose between widely varying estimates. But certain broad tendencies are not in dispute. Thus in the twelve years from 1881 to 1893, during which the number of factory workers was very nearly doubled, reaching a figure of perhaps two or two and a half million, the total number of factories declined, possibly by as much as a quarter. In this process of continued concentration the principal centres of Russian industry were the province of Moscow, the capital city of St Petersburg and the new mining and metallurgical areas in the south.

As evidence of the rate of expansion in textile production, Russian imports of raw cotton were fourteen times greater in 1894 than in 1863, and to this increase should be added native cotton cultivation over a widening area in the south-east. Most significant of all was the growth of the metallurgical industry, based upon the coal of the Donets basin and the iron of the Krivoy Rog. One celebrated enterprise will serve as example. In the 1880s a Welshman named Hughes was granted a concession for a 'New Russia Company' which undertook to supply rails. Yuzovka, the small factory village named after him, in the last years of the century had become a town of thirty thousand inhabitants with one of the largest steel plants in Europe. (It was later to become known as Stalino.) Although at the close of the tsarist period, indeed,

Russian heavy industry still trailed far in the rear of the leading countries of the west, the rate of increase in the output of coal and iron during the previous decades had been much higher than that in Britain or Germany, higher even than that in the United States. As for the oil industry in the Caucasus, centred in Baku, while in 1875 the total output of crude oil was eighty thousand tons, twenty years later it had risen to nearly six million tons and Russian production was half of the world's total.

In the still slightly fearsome categories of Marxist analysis, Russia was, as Lenin said, 'a semi-colonial appendage of western European finance-capital'. The precise extent of foreign capital investment is, once more, difficult to determine with accuracy; it was heaviest in mining and metallurgy, where it may well have represented nearly a half. The tempo of investment, which was largely governed by Russia's foreign relations, is more readily apparent. Of the two hundred and sixty-nine foreign companies in Russia in 1900 all but eighteen had been formed since 1888; clearly a peak in the scale of foreign investment was reached in the early years of the reign of Nicholas II. The largest share was French; next came Belgian, German and British investment. Britain held first place in Russia's foreign trade until the 1880s, when she began to give way to Germany. In the closing years of the century the latter country took about a third of Russia's exports and supplied rather less than a third of her imports. The principal Russian export was, of course, grain, which was shipped mainly from Odessa and other Black Sea ports. In the eighties it represented about half of the total value of Russian exports and some fifteen per cent of the total Russian production of grain; in subsequent years this latter proportion was sometimes exceeded. The sale of so large a volume of bread grains, whatever the extent of hunger at home, was obligatory for the discharge of Russia's foreign indebtedness and the maintenance of her international credit. It was a factor of growing significance in the psychology of the industrial worker in Russia.

The rapid advance of industry bore directly upon economic conditions in the village. Peasant handicrafts, which in a great many households and even in whole rural districts provided an important supplementary source of earnings, declined sharply in the last decade of the century in competition with factory manufacture. Of more lasting consequence was the gradual rupture of ties between the peasants employed in the town and the peasants in the village. In the earlier phase of recruitment by industry of free peasant labour the factory worker was still an urbanized peasant, who almost always maintained the link with his native village. Sentiment and self-interest alike were involved; if in a period of slump or through illness he lost his employment in the town, an allotment of some sort, which was the only thing that stood between him and complete destitution, awaited him in the village. Yet increasingly the connexion was being broken. An industrial proletariat was beginning to emerge as a separate and coherent body in society with an outlook on life quite distinct from that of the peasantry and even in some respects alien to it.

Of immediate moment was the effect on conditions of industrial employment of the surplus population in the village. The desperate competition for work in the factories kept the level of wages at a minimum level and played its part in reproducing in Russia's dark, satanic mills all those evils of an industrial revolution which western Europe had by this time largely outgrown. The wages that barely sufficed for bread were sometimes paid twice a year only, a system of truck was widespread, fines were levied on the worker on every possible pretext, general labour conditions were often recklessly insanitary and an all but total absence of living accommodation for factory workers often obliged them to sleep beside their machines. Worst of all, as in the west at an earlier period, were the conditions of employment for women and young children, more especially in the textile factories.

Half-hearted attempts were made in the reign of Alexander III to remedy the worst abuses. In 1882 the government appointed a small number of factory inspectors and prohibited the employment of children under the age of twelve. Three years later a ban was imposed upon night work in textile mills for women and young persons, and the ban was afterwards extended to other industries. In the following year it was laid down that wages should be paid at least once a month and payments in kind were prohibited. But the regulations were little observed, the factory inspectors lacked real powers of enforcement, the Minister of Finance responsible for these beginnings in factory legislation was dismissed on suspicion of 'socialist leanings', and even the new conditions governing the employment of women and children were formally amended in the employers' favour. Not until the next reign was a maximum working day of eleven and a half hours for adult males established.

The industrial workers could look for little aid or favour from the city authorities. The chief function of the town commandant, who in the large cities exercised supreme local authority and who held equal rank with the governor of a province, was that of a police auxiliary of the Minister of the Interior. As for the town duma, or municipality, originally set up by Catherine the Great and reorganized on an elective basis in 1870, it was essentially a corporation of the largest property-owners and was as consistently conservative as the best of the zemstvos were liberal. Election to the town duma, like election to the zemstvo, was by a heavily weighted system of separate voting groups; the balance was held by the rich merchant community, the industrial workers as a whole were rigorously excluded, and even a considerable part of the professional class, lacking the required qualification in respect of house property or the payment of a trade tax, were disfranchised. Flagrantly unrepresentative in character, the town duma was at best perfunctory in promoting education and public health,[1] all the more so because it was virtually denied the right of levying a rate and relied largely for such services as it provided on voluntary contributions. It became still more unrepresentative when in 1892 legislation was introduced, parallel with the institution of land captains and the manipulation of the zemstvos, which disfranchised the great majority of the urban population and gave the commandant or provincial governor a right of veto over all decisions of the town duma. The factory workers, in truth, had nothing to hope for from city government.

It was in these circumstances that their minds turned towards politics. Or, rather, it was to politics that their minds were directed by a new breed of Russian intelligentsia. Though strikes, like all forms of labour organization, were illegal, there had in fact been sporadic strikes of textile and other workers since the seventies. These were strikes for economic ends, designed to win a farthing or two more an hour or a shorter day, or to protest against an arbitrary labour discipline. But in the last years of Alexander III's reign other motives were beginning to work obscurely in the minds of at any rate a minority of workers. The stimulus of propaganda came not from the zemstvo liberals and their kind, not even in the first place from Russia, but from thinkers or agitators in exile. Marxism was establishing a footing in the factory.

[1]The outstanding exception was the Moscow city duma. But there were other dumas of fairly large cities which had not set up a single primary school even at the close of the century.

Revolutionary conspiracy in Russia, it had seemed, was a thing of the past. It had returned for an instant in 1887, when a hesitant plot to murder Alexander III was discovered and five young university students, among them Alexander Ulianov, whose younger brother afterwards took the name of Lenin, paid for it with their lives. But silence had closed over their graves, or so it seemed. Yet in obscure circles outside Russia a noisy and curious debate on the theme of revolution, a debate at once exceedingly abstract and narrowly practical, was in progress. It had been precipitated at the start of Alexander III's reign by a small group of Russian intellectuals, former Narodniks, now in exile in Switzerland. From having questioned the Narodnik philosophy and Narodnik tactics they had returned to first principles. Socialism, they agreed, implied revolution. But was not the vision of a socialist society in Russia based upon the peasant commune a fantasy? Did not all the evidence prove that Russia was following in the tracks of the west and had still to pass through an advanced stage of capitalism? If that was so, not the peasants but the industrial proletariat must be the mainspring of a social revolution. The argument, in brief, was that the future lay not with Narodnik sentiment but with the scientific socialism of Karl Marx.

The distinguishing feature of Russian social and political thought has always been a remorseless habit of abstract reasoning, an addiction to the extremes of logic, an incapacity for intellectual compromise. It is not difficult, perhaps, to understand why. In a society at once so undeveloped and so rigidly controlled, a society which provided its most thoughtful elements with so little opportunity to share in the conduct of public affairs and the problems of government, only speculation on social and political subjects was free. In this freedom it suffered none of the disabilities imposed by experience. Impotent in practice, the intelligentsia, like the intellectuals of France before 1789, compensated itself by an abundance of theory; in face of extreme reaction, it constructed philosophies of good government and the good life which were no less extreme. Or, more accurately, since there was no native tradition of philosophic thought, it borrowed political doctrines from abroad and carried them to Russian extremes. Hyperbole and extravagance have at all times stamped the Russian revolutionary ethos, and Russian revolutionaries have almost always inhabited a world of phantoms. It was thus that Bakunin, for instance, in exile in the 1860s had derived from a hotch-potch of foreign sources his essentially Russian doctrine of the liberating ideal of universal destruction. Two decades later, while the echoes of Bakunin's quarrel with Marx still rang in the west, the newest current of speculation within Russia flowed from German materialist philosophy. Marx's *Capital* was translated into Russian in 1872, and eleven years later the first Russian Marxist group came into existence abroad.

Its founder, and the founding father of the Russian Marxist movement, was George Valentinovich Plekhanov. Born in 1857 of a family of nobility and intended for a military career, he had enrolled as a student in the ranks of Land and Liberty in the mood of abnegation of the 'conscience-stricken gentry' of the seventies. It was he who had led the retreat of a section of the Narodnik movement from the policy of terror. Cultivated, fastidious, of great intellectual gifts, somewhat vain and a little lacking in generosity of spirit, Plekhanov's powers of leadership were those of a thinker. As a Russian Marxist his supreme distinction is that, unlike his chief disciples, he did not invariably push theory to the farthest limits of abstract logic. Unlike them, too, he preserved a ruling sense of moral values. His influence in the small Russian colony in Switzerland was decisive when in 1883 he founded a group known as *Osvobozhdenie Truda*, or Liberation of Labour—liberation, that is, from the yoke of capitalism. Next year, in an essay entitled 'Our Differences' which was directed against the old Narodnik standpoint, he published the earliest positive statement of the Russian Marxist creed. The advance of capitalism in Russia, he declared, was a portent of progress, but the contradictions of capitalism there as elsewhere laid upon the industrial proletariat the historic obligation of leading the masses towards the goal of a classless socialist society. In urging the supreme need of educating the proletariat in the class struggle, Plekhanov rejected the notion of a revolution imposed by force as a betrayal of socialist ideals. Russian Marxism before Lenin was essentially democratic.

During the next dozen years and more the controversy between Marxists and Narodniks in exile swelled into what has been fairly styled a paroxysm of ideological warfare. This, in turn, was succeeded by a more complex and still more envenomed debate between Marxists of one sort and Marxists of several successively different sorts. These need not concern us here: the material fact is that from Switzerland Marxist doctrine percolated into Russia, where Marxist study groups sprang up among the intelligentsia.

In the eighties they had as yet little or no contact with the industrial workers; Marxism was a literary, a scholastic movement. But it claimed a growing interest among university students. The university statute of 1884, though it had chiefly affected the intellectual freedom of the academic staff, also prohibited all forms of corporate student activity. Only the 'fraternities' (*zemliachestva*) of students from the same town or the same part of the country were tolerated by the guardians of law. But within the walls of the university they provided no outlet for the ideals of youth. It was thus partly by way of a handful of university students that Marxist agitation spread to the factories. From the beginning of the nineties simplified forms of the doctrine of the class struggle began to capture the mind of small groups of industrial workers.

Beyond these visions of constitutional government entertained by an enlightened section of the gentry and a nascent middle class, these stirrings of revolutionary sentiment in the intelligentsia and among the industrial workers, what light and leading were given to Russian society in the years before the accession of Nicholas II? The truth is scarcely strained by replying none at all. For the dogmas of autocracy, it seemed, now excluded all other inspiration. Little light came from literature. The great age of the Russian novel was over. Leo Tolstoy was a revered name and a moral force, but his teaching stopped short at a primitive Christianity and no other voice spoke with a syllable of his authority. And from the Church came only a soulless instruction.

The thirteen years of Alexander III's rule had resurrected the classic formula of an earlier age, Orthodoxy, Autocracy, Nationality. More firmly than before, indeed, the supremacy of the Orthodox faith and the predominance of Great Russian nationalism buttressed the system of monarchical absolutism. The Church was subject in every particular to the civil power. Governed by a Holy Synod which for all essential purposes was a department of state, over which presided as chief procurator during these years the chilling figure of Constantine Pobedonostsev, it was steeped in a rigid formalism. It contributed not much more than the trappings of faith to the spiritual life of the Russian people. The intelligentsia, remembering the Church's eloquent defence of serf law as a divine institution, had long been alienated from it. With few exceptions, its princes were set high above both the people and the body of the priesthood. The latter all too often functioned as minor government officials, lamentably ill-paid, ignorant, scarcely to be distinguished from the peasants by whose side many of them laboured in the fields. Here and there, perhaps, some were touched by the spirit of radicalism, but in general the village priest was much more nearly the creature of the civil authorities than the spiritual guide of his flock; he was not chosen by the peasants he served, nor did they for their part necessarily respond to his ministrations. No view of Holy Russia is so extravagant as that which endowed the Orthodox peasantry with the sublimities of religious emotion. The ritual of the Orthodox Church has never lacked pomp or power, nor has the humility of worship of the illiterate ever failed to excite wonder, but the exalted piety which foreign travellers discovered in the Russian peasant makes sense only on the medieval assumption that poverty, dirt, ignorance and disease are emanations of the spirit. In point of fact, almost all that was of spiritual substance in Russian religious thought in these years came from half-heretical laymen like Tolstoy on the one hand and Vladimir Soloviev on the other, and almost everything that expressed a genuine spiritual need among the masses was contributed (as in eighteenth-century England) by the dissenters and sectarians.

It was, not unexpectedly, upon dissenters and sectarians that the chief weight of religious persecution fell. Some small degree of favour was shown to the enormous body of Old Believers, the oldest and most formidable of the dissenting sects, who were much more numerous than the Church authorities were willing to concede,[1] and who included a rich and pious merchant community. In 1883 a number of disabilities from which they had suffered for a couple of centuries were lifted from them, though many remained. But by the same law the lot of all the other dissenting bodies was made intolerably harsh and burdensome. Taxed, fined and imprisoned, often denied the right to open houses of prayer or to appoint pastors, excluded from particular localities and occupations, their marriages not recognized as legal, in some instances deprived even of their children, they were pursued by the civil authorities as enemies of order. The severest penalties fell upon the small following of exotic and fanatical sects like the Skoptsy, who in the conviction of the imminent end of the world practised castration, or the Khlysty, who in eastern fashion apparently whirled themselves into ecstasy as a prelude to orgiastic rites. But the chief

[1] At the turn of the century the Old Believers may have numbered anything between fifteen and twenty million.

sufferers were the sober evangelical sects, the Molokane (milk-drinkers), the semi-Tolstoyan Dukhobors (fighters of the spirit), who refused military service, and above all the Stundists, who had much in common with the Baptists. Religious discrimination in so punitive a form played no little part in the ultimate disintegration of the empire and made it all the more certain that the Orthodox Church would share the fate of the monarchy.

The assault upon the national minorities contributed even more to the process of disintegration. Religious persecution and nationalist intolerance were closely joined in the border areas of the empire, inhabited as they were largely by non-Russian and non-Orthodox peoples. The Roman Catholics in Poland, the Lutherans in the Baltic provinces, the Moslems in Transcaucasia were sub-jected to rigorous penalties. To further the suppression of Polish culture—the official designation of Russian Poland was the 'Vistula provinces'—teaching even in the primary schools was conducted largely in Russian. From Poland the russifying mission was extended to the historic enclaves of Polish sentiment in the Ukraine and to the Ukrainians themselves. In Finland only the first steps were taken to reduce the autonomous institutions of the duchy, but the sequel came with shattering effect in the next reign.

The harshest persecution of all was aimed at the Jews. Both Alexander III and his principal advisers were rabidly anti-semitic. The raw nationalist element in anti-semitism was reinforced by the presence of Jews in the ranks of the revolutionary terrorists. The murder of Alexander II had evoked instantaneous Jewish pogroms in Kiev, Odessa and elsewhere, not seldom with police connivance, and a spate of anti-Jewish decrees followed. The Jewish pale of settlement—a legacy of the partitions of Poland—was still further restricted. Jews were forbidden henceforth to acquire rural property, which was interpreted by many communes as an instruction to expel all Jews from their midst. Quotas for Jews were introduced in all universities and secondary schools, even the secondary schools within the pale. Jews were excluded from the legal profession and from the lists of zemstvo and town duma electors. In 1891-2 the grand-duke Sergey Alexandrovich celebrated his appointment as governor-general of Moscow by the summary expulsion of some twenty thousand Jews from the city. In an even more candid gesture of persecution, the adoption by Jews of Christian first names, a normal proceeding in educated families, was declared a criminal offence.

Two significant consequences flowed from this anti-Jewish legislation. The 1880s marked the beginning of the mass migration of Jews in the western and southern provinces of Russia to the United States and, in lesser degree, to the countries of western Europe. And the special disabilities of the Jews who remained in Russia, more especially the restrictions upon educational opportunity, drove the most ardent in increasing numbers into the thick of the revolutionary movement.

Domestic policy, as might be expected, left its mark upon the course of foreign policy, but at the same time was often incongruously at odds with it. If imperial adventure in the Far East was closely attuned to nationalism at home, the progressive phases of the alliance with republican and democratic France were completely at variance with Russia's absolutist tradition.

The Balkans, central Asia, the Far East and western Europe constituted separate and largely distinct spheres of Russian diplomacy. In the Balkans Russian designs had suffered a disastrous setback at the Congress of Berlin in 1878. The corpse of Turkey in Europe had once more been revived by the western powers, and the Russian panslav idea, in which St Petersburg played the part of mentor and guardian of the Balkan Slavs, was in retreat. The cause of the Orthodox peoples of the Balkans still lay close to the heart of a substantial part of Russian society; access to the Mediterranean and the world's maritime routes was still an integral part of Russian strategy; and for Alexander III personally the possession of the Straits and Constantinople was still an obligatory Russian ambition. But for the time being, and in face of the rivalry of Austria, Russia had no choice but to be quiescent.

By contrast with the colonizing impulse of earlier ages of Russian expansion, the Russian advance in central Asia had been an operation of war conducted in the familiar guise of a civilizing mission. The advance continued in the nineties, when the Russian frontier touched the Pamirs. Relations with imperial Britain had been tense for a generation and more, and Russian pressure on Afghanistan once more brought the prospect of war very near. But the restraint of the British Cabinet, together with the little that could be done by the Foreign Minister in St Petersburg to discount the bravado of the Russian war lords in central Asia, tipped the balance, and the Anglo-Russian conflict remained a conflict of diplomacy only.

In the Far East Russia had pursued a policy of steady economic penetration since the 1860s. All the wealth of China appeared to beckon to her from across the Amur-Ussuri frontier. It was this prospect which inspired the construction of the Trans-Siberian railway.

The determining element in Russia's foreign policy throughout the reign of Alexander III, however, sprang from relations with Germany. A multiplicity of common interests—the absolute rights of monarchy, imperial family relationships, the preservation of a semi-feudal aristocracy, reciprocal trading advantages, the suppression of Polish nationalism, hostility to Britain—still seemed to operate to draw the two empires together. But Russian and German policies clashed at many points, above all in the Balkans. Russian resentment at Germany's part in the Congress of Berlin still lingered after the renewal in 1881 of the 'three emperors' league', by which Russia, Austria and Germany were pledged to co-operate in any further re-shaping of Balkan affairs. Six years later, when with tacit German and Austrian support the Bulgarian nationalists threw off Russian tutelage, the league was dead and Russia's international relations took on an anti-German orientation. The secret 're-insurance treaty' of 1887 between Germany and Russia represented Bismarck's final attempt at maintaining a firm diplomatic accord with St Petersburg. The price he was apparently prepared to pay for it, in return for Russian neutrality in the event of war between Germany and France, was not only disinterestedness in the Balkans but some measure of support for Russian policy on the question of the Straits. Yet the treaty was rendered almost invalid from the beginning, economically by the tariff war between the two countries, strategically by the renewal of the Triple Alliance of Germany, Austria and Italy. Designed to remain in force for three years, it had all but foundered even before the fall of Bismarck in 1890, after which it was permitted to lapse.

The road to the Franco-Russian alliance, a short cut to the cross-roads of history but a logical enough development in the manoeuvres of the Great Powers, was paved with French loans. A French republican government might be the complete antithesis of tsarist autocracy, but its scruples were overcome in the last resort by the French *rentier*. French purchases of Russian securities from 1887 onwards prepared the way for Russian conversion loans on the Paris money market. With the further renewal in 1891 of the Triple Alliance, France and Russia entered into immediate negotiations for a counter-alliance. In July of that year a French squadron visited Kronstadt and Alexander III stood most remarkably to attention at the playing of the *Marseillaise*. An exchange of notes on 14/27 August was consummated in the secret military convention of 4/17 August 1892. The convention was ratified at the end of the year, but the military obligations assumed on either side, based upon the pledge to decree simultaneous mobilization if Germany mobilized, were still a secret when war came in 1914. They were made known only after the Bolsheviks had seized power.

Alexander III, wrote the French historian of Russia, Leroy-Beaulieu, was less a contemporary of Queen Victoria than of Isabella of Castile. In the closing decade of the nineteenth century Russia still lived, in truth, in the shadow of the fifteenth. Her backwardness was to be measured in the brutalizing poverty of the vast majority of the population of the empire, her distance from western Europe in the total rejection of a constitutional order of government. The one owed more than all else to geography and climate, the other derived largely from centuries of empire-building. Serfdom and autocracy alike in Russia had served what in the Marxist vocabulary is styled historic necessity. Yet in the climate of the fifteenth century her people nevertheless stood on the brink of the twentieth. At the accession of Nicholas II modern capitalist industry had broken the primitive mould of Russia's economy and western ideas had transformed the horizons of the thinking part of the population. Once again, as in the years before the emancipation of the serfs, the prospect of fundamental reform offered the sole alternative to revolution.

Even among the higher bureaucracy there were those who read the portents of the times. Their advice was seldom sought. A despot by temperament as well as by vocation, Alexander III chose to reject reform. In this decision he was sustained by Pobedonostsev, the grey eminence of the reign and of the reign following, and by those purblind influences near the throne which are so often the curse of imperial and other dynasties.

2. The Heritage and the Heir

Alexander III died at Livadia, a favourite imperial resort in the Crimea, on 20 October 1894, in his fiftieth year. The burden which he had borne and which had exhausted him fell upon a son and heir who in what must always seem the continuing tragedy of Russian history was totally unfitted to bear it.

As a human being Nicholas II is not specially interesting. A negative character, commonplace in mind, weak of will and fatalistic in temperament, he was thrust into the blinding light of great events and is saved from complete insignificance only by the macabre pathos of his end. But as tsar and autocrat he remains a key figure in the events of his reign. He presents, indeed, a strange study in that fortuitous interaction of persons and events which perhaps alone gives history a lasting interest. Certainly Nicholas's conception of his role as autocrat is a principal thread in the pattern of revolution unfolded in 1917.

His portrait has been drawn often enough, seldom with any striking variation of judgment, but a brief sketch can scarcely be omitted as frontispiece here. Born on 6 May 1868, he was educated in the eclectic fashion normally prescribed for the heir to the Russian throne and in rigorous obedience to a father whom he always feared and who at all times thought him childish and undeveloped. Neither stupid nor intelligent, he applied himself only indifferently to his studies under private tutors and acquired little more than a fluent command of German, French and English. Like every other nineteenth-century Russian monarch, he took kindly in youth to the atmosphere of the parade ground and to military reviews and manoeuvres and was very much at home in the officers' mess of the regiments of the Guards in which he was formally commissioned. As heir apparent he showed no marked inclination for anything more than that. In 1890-1 he was sent on a long tour of the Far East, visiting India and Japan and laying the foundation-stone of the Trans-Siberian railway terminus at Vladivostok. His father, with rough but good-natured contempt, made no attempt to school him in affairs of state. Nicholas was permitted to attend occasional meetings of the committee of ministers and of the State Council, but little else in this respect was required of him.

An element of the childish and trivial was indeed conspicuous in the new emperor, and persisted in him until the end. Those near the throne had viewed his accession with some anxiety, as well they might. Every student of the most portentous period in Russian history must marvel at the all but unrelieved triviality of the personal diary which Nicholas kept regularly before and during his reign. It is the diary, one is tempted to say—the unamusing diary—of a nobody, of a man transparently immature and of patently insignificant interests. Two lines on this official audience, three lines on that, the bare mention of a shattering disaster like the destruction of the Russian fleet at Tsushima, but otherwise triviality piled on triviality. The entries stretch out into a succession of daily observations of the weather, linked by a record of outdoor occupations, from taking the dogs for a walk or gathering mushrooms to shooting, cycling, skating or rowing, and of the smallest incidents of domestic life. Resounding events or the dominant issues of the day are noted with brief unconcern or are not noted at all.

If Nicholas had merely indulged the modest tastes of a Russian country gentleman and the fond habits of an exemplary husband and father, there would be nothing to add to the bleak evidence of his diary. But no Russian emperor was more completely possessed by his prerogative as autocrat. In that strange region of the mind where men believe they are anointed of God, Nicholas staked faith, duty and all else upon the dogma of autocracy. In the dutiful and cloudy phrases of its apologists, it was the divine principle of the nation's destiny, an emblem of the sacred union of crown and people, the very breath of eternal Russia. Nicholas himself was resolved it should continue to be these things. More practically, he looked upon the absolute power he had inherited from his father as an inviolable trust, to be transmitted whole and unimpaired to his successor. Through every mischance and portent of crisis in his reign his first rule of conduct was to seek to preserve it.

The notorious irony of this devotion to his father's memory lay in the son's weakness of character. Where Alexander III had been all strength of purpose his son was all weakness. Nicholas was incapable, except in the obstinacy of the weak, of a mind of his own. It is significant, perhaps, that he had nothing of his father's giant physique; like Charles I, whom in many ways he so much re-sembled, he was very short, and had been advised to appear in public whenever possible on horseback. He had less than nothing of Alexander's brutal power of decision. Yet since all decisions were ultimately his, the thing above all others that Nicholas would not tolerate from those about him was argument or persuasion. He was, in fact, easily influenced—none more so; his entire reign bears the stamp of the various personal influences which at different times were exerted upon him. But these, at least after the first few years of inexperience, were exerted insidiously and with due flattery. There was nothing the emperor resisted more jealously, or with more calamitous consequences, than advice tendered in all candour. In defence of his sovereign rights he refused the aid of a private secretary and himself sealed the envelopes upon official documents bearing his decision.

The fruits of this conception of sovereignty were apparent in the powers of dissimulation which Nicholas shared with every other nineteenth-century Russian monarch except his father, in an exceptional degree of self-control in public, and in a fair share of the famous Romanov charm. The charm was something that even those he used worst always remembered, however bitterly. To his ministers and officials, as to grooms and footmen, Nicholas was invariably courteous, even more than courteous; his regard for them had every appearance of warmth. But sooner or later they all learned, as one of them put it, that 'you could not rely on him'. Again and again his courtesy was only a deceiving prelude to the mark of his disfavour. The decision to which he gave explicit approval in audience was countermanded by imperial instruction a few hours later; the minister who had been received with a flatter-ing show of kindness learned from an imperial note sent by courier next morning that he had been dismissed—or, worse still, dis-covered from the morning's newspaper that he had tendered his resignation. These sudden dismissals and reversals of policy frequently sprang from the last private word in the emperor's ear. Like the marks of favour, they had little to do with personal feel-ing on his part; all were his servants and no question of feeling, other than the need to spare himself embarrassment, arose between him and them. As one of his officials wrote, the emperor 'lacked the capacity for becoming attached to those who surrounded him, and parted from them without sorrow'.

It was this indifference to those who served him which blunted the edge of Nicholas's good intentions. Charles I and Louis XVI, both monarchs by similarly divine right, meant equally well. In his pathetic ineffectualness Nicholas recalls Louis; in his duplicity and obstinacy, as in the ingratitude with which he cast off those who might have saved him and set himself to digging his own grave, the likeness with Charles is unmistakable.

It is apparent also in his self-chosen isolation. Outside the narrow circle of his personal entourage Nicholas saw scarcely anyone. Few even of the members of the grand-ducal clan—there were twenty-nine of them at the beginning of the reign—had access to him except on formal occasions two or three times in the year. Nicholas made an exception of three of his uncles; the right which he conceded to them of proffering counsel almost marked a return, as Witte says in his memoirs, to the appanage system[1] of ancient Russia. And for the first few years of the reign, when the emperor was conscious of his own inexperience, there was the influence of his mother, the dowager empress, a sister of Queen Alexandra. But Nicholas's sense of inexperience soon passed and, while submitting himself to those of stronger will and subtler mind, he grew convinced that he understood better than anyone else, as he desired better than anyone else, the true advantage and greater glory of the empire he ruled.

One of his most maleficent advisers after the first few years was Prince Vladimir Meshchersky, a grandson of the historian Karamzin. Cynical, corrupt and of unsavoury reputation, the editor of a weekly journal of viciously reactionary temper, *Grazhdanin* (*The Citizen*), which at Nicholas's instructions was subsidized out of state funds, Meshchersky had mastered the most brazen arts of flattery. His letters to Nicholas, so honeyed and so loyal that the emperor's replies were couched in the intimate second-person singular, are a sinister glorification of the rights of autocracy. Not law, Meshchersky ventured in humble duty, but the authority at every level of the Russian administration to imprison and to flog was the sovereign remedy for Russian evils. The most affectionate of husbands and fathers Nicholas might be, but this was apparently doctrine after his heart.

The dominant and most baleful influence of the reign, however, was Constantine Pobedonostsev. Tutor to Nicholas, as he had been tutor to Nicholas's father, he was the philosopher behind the

[1]The system of hereditary sovereign princes within the dynastic order of a suzerain grand-prince.

throne who in effect did almost as much as any man to demolish it.

Emaciated, the face coldly ascetic, the eyes hard and casuistical behind large horn-rimmed glasses, he is a forbidding figure. Born in 1827, a jurist and scholar with a translation of Thomas à Kempis to his credit, he had graduated from a chair of civil law at Moscow university to membership of the Senate, then of the State Council, and in 1880 had been appointed chief procurator of the Holy Synod. From the beginning he had won the unreserved confidence of Alexander III. It was Pobedonostsev who had composed the principal decrees and manifestos issued in the name of his sovereign.

His was a strange mind, brilliantly gifted in some respects but steeped in bigotry and perverted by a cold pessimism and misanthropy. What it possessed of integrity was subtly qualified by a vein of studied flunkeyism; Pobedonostsev could be as fulsome as any courtier in protestations of devotion to the throne. But his slavophil faith in the destiny of Russia was beyond all doubt sincere. From the west, he maintained, came only disruptive influences—doctrines of rationalism, of progress, of liberalism. He rejected all liberal ideas and institutions, condemned all parliaments and civil liberties. Parliamentary government was 'the great falsehood of our time', a constitution was 'that fundamental evil', a free press the instrument of universal corruption. Against all the seductions of the west he set the divine principle of Russian autocracy and the boundless loyalty of the Russian Orthodox peasantry to the person of the autocrat.

From the chief procurator of the Holy Synod more than from anyone else Nicholas drew support and counsel during the first eleven years of his reign. Only afterwards did he yield to a more potent and still more destructive influence. The empress, always the person closest to his thoughts, began to gain complete ascendancy over him in the year of revolution 1905. The parallel she presents with both Henrietta Maria and Marie-Antoinette is pronounced, though hers is a heavier personal responsibility for disaster. Born Princess Alice of Hesse-Darmstadt, daughter of Princess Alice of England, and brought up at Kensington Palace by Queen Victoria, she belonged in taste and domestic habit to Victorian England while possessing all the characteristics of a German princess of some petty court. Nicholas had married her three weeks after his accession. Except for the celebrated ballerina Kshesinskaya, with whom he had had a brief affair a few years before the marriage, Alexandra Fedorovna, as the empress was styled, was the only woman in his life. It was a singularly happy union. Four children were born of the marriage, all girls, and then, in the summer of 1904, amid much joy and thanksgiving on the part of the imperial pair, a son and heir to the throne. Nicholas's devotion to his wife and children was heightened by the empress's worsening health and by the haemophilia that always threatened the life of the tsarevich.

Together with the style of Alexandra Fedorovna the empress had adopted, as was obligatory, the Orthodox faith. Devoutly Protestant, she had long hesitated over the need to do so, but in the result had discovered in the Orthodox Church a never failing source of emotional satisfaction. Shy, awkward, highly-strung, something of reserve or arrogance in her so exaggerated by the atmosphere of the Russian court that she was never to become in the least popular, her mind seized avidly on the principle of autocracy to which the Church bore witness. The sacred union of crown and people became, for her, a mystical prop and solace in difficulty; her religion and her power to fortify her husband's absolute prerogative were all but identical. The saying of Péguy, 'Everything begins in mysticism and ends in politics', has a strange and apocalyptic relevance to her case. The empress did not expressly interfere in the politics of the empire until the course was already set towards catastrophe, but nothing prompted her fateful interference so much as a growing hysterical religiosity.

At the outset of the reign Nicholas was content to retain most of the ministers and senior bureaucrats who had served his father. Other than Pobedonostsev, the most important figure in the government was the Minister of Finance, Sergius Witte. A new Foreign Minister was appointed after the death of the elderly and failing Giers early in 1895 and in April there were several minor changes. They included, on the recommendation of Pobedonostsev, the appointment of Ivan Logginovich Goremykin, assistant Minister of Justice, as assistant Minister of the Interior. That living emblem of the vices of the Russian bureaucracy, who towards the end of the year became head of the ministry, was destined to appear in the foreground of events at two major crises in the reign.

As always at the opening of a new reign in Russia, there were stirrings of hope in society, subdued but anxious longings for a fresh start. They were the more keenly felt after the depression of

spirit bred by the previous reign. All too little was known of the
new emperor among the educated classes, but his youth seemed to
speak in his favour. Nowhere was hope more ardent than in the
zemstvo assemblies. As yet they asked for nothing more than
acknowledgment of their aspirations towards a representative
system of government. With all deference and loyalty these were
introduced, in careful phrases, into some of the customary con-
gratulatory addresses to the throne. The imperial response was not
long delayed. On 17 January 1895, Nicholas received a group of
representatives of the zemstvos and the nobility in order to
acknowledge their courtesies. Reading from a sheet of manuscript,
he delivered himself of the famous and echoing phrase, 'senseless
dreams' (*bezmyslennie mechtaniya*). 'It is known to me', the
emperor said, 'that voices have been heard of late in some zemstvo
assemblies of persons carried away by senseless dreams of the
participation of zemstvo representatives in the affairs of internal
government. Let all know that, in devoting all my strength to the
people's wellbeing, I shall preserve the principle of autocracy as
firmly and as undeviatingly as did my . . . father.'

The words—which were almost certainly dictated by Pobedonostsev—could be interpreted only as an open declaration of war.
The implications were indeed ominous, and there were some even
then who recognized them for what they were. Two distinguished
liberals of the reign, Miliukov and Kizevetter, both tell us that a
day or two after Nicholas's use of the phrase 'senseless dreams',
the great historian Kliuchevsky, conservative though he was,
delivered in private his prophetic judgment: 'The Romanov
dynasty will end with Nicholas II. If he has a son, the son will
not reign.'

A host of small mishaps attended the magnificent coronation
ceremony on 14 May 1896 in the Uspensky cathedral in the Moscow
Kremlin. But the coronation festivities in Moscow four days later
were attended by disaster—disaster strangely reminiscent of that
which had marked the wedding festivities in Paris of Louis XVI
and Marie-Antoinette, though it was on an even larger scale.
A crowd of half a million people had gathered overnight on
Khodynka field, on the site of what is now Moscow's airport, in
readiness for the usual coronation distribution of small gifts.
Through the incompetence of those in charge the crowd stampeded.
Nearly thirteen hundred were killed and hundreds more were
severely injured. There was a great outcry, which was followed by

an investigation, and in the upshot, it appears, a single police official was dismissed. Nicholas and the empress were insensitive enough to keep their engagement that same evening to attend a ball at the French embassy, a piece of unwisdom not easily forgotten.

There were prolonged echoes of the Khodynka catastrophe. Even the zemstvo representatives contributed to the political agitation which it aroused. Already they were split into a moderate and a radical wing. The moderates were led by D. N. Shipov, chairman of the executive board of the Moscow provincial zemstvo, a man of practical mind and high integrity who was profoundly respected in the movement as a whole. They still looked for a conciliatory gesture from the throne in the Russian tradition of reform 'from above' and went no further in their hopes of representative government than a consultative legislative assembly. The radicals, on the other hand, among whom perhaps the most honoured figure at this time was a country squire of militant temper, Ivan Petrunkevich, had already reached the point of seeking fundamental political change through a constituent assembly. In this ardent but ill-defined aim they were all but prepared to claim the support of the revolutionary intelligentsia. Though not yet willing to play with fire, they were agreeably warmed by it.

Both wings were united in the immediate desire to extend the field of zemstvo activities. To this end they could count upon the faith and energy of the small but growing numbers of the third element. The latter had vainly sought the right to form professional unions for the discussion of common problems (a right simultaneously claimed by doctors, teachers and others outside the zemstvo movement), and had fallen back whenever possible upon local conferences. The authorities often intervened with a ban on such meetings, or, in permitting them, subjected them to police supervision. In the absence of such restraints, the conferences were held in an atmosphere in which political issues of set purpose came up for discussion. At this the government took fright. A crop of arrests and dismissals of zemstvo employees as subversive agitators followed.

From arrests and dismissals of agitators in the zemstvo service the government passed to other and more damaging reprisals. In several provinces the governor refused to endorse the election of zemstvo representatives, even those of moderate opinion. Decisions of the executive boards were summarily set aside. It was now, too, that the government chose to renew the threat, made on several previous occasions and dropped only out of reluctance to shoulder the cost, to take over the zemstvo schools, which were the apple of many an assembly's eye. And then there was the ban on Shipov's scheme of joint zemstvo consultation. In the hope of furthering the prospects of a central zemstvo organization he had secured the consent of Goremykin to the holding of annual conferences of zemstvo chairmen. At the first, held in Nizhny-Novgorod in August 1896, among the subjects that had been debated were the ills of peasant agriculture and the need to extend primary education. This unlicensed discussion of public questions was held to be incompatible with 'the existing order' and the conference arranged to take place in St Petersburg in the following year was forbidden. The government, it appeared to many zemstvo representatives, was bent upon alienating in every possible way precisely those elements in educated society on which in its own interest it should have relied most.

In 1898 it was proposed by Goremykin, who at this time still retained something of the reputation of a liberal, to introduce in the western border provinces a restricted form of zemstvo organization. The proposal met with curt opposition from Pobedonostsev and with various objections from other ministers, including Witte. In a famous memorandum, 'Autocracy and the Zemstvos', addressed to Goremykin, Witte argued that local self-government, however desirable elsewhere in the world, was incompatible with autocracy. This stated, he went on to advance a case that might appear either to favour the general principles of the zemstvo or to condemn them. 'You cannot create liberal forms', he observed, 'and leave them empty of liberal content.' Inevitably the zemstvos would wish to enlarge their functions and would reach out towards a wider system of popular representation. In so doing, Witte observed, they must sooner or later come into open conflict with the autocratic system of government. What, in any case, he asked, was the Ministry of the Interior itself doing except to suppress all forms of public initiative?

Witte was less ambiguous, as will be apparent later, than he seemed, or was ambiguous only because as always the Ministry of Finance and the Ministry of the Interior were at odds and he was not unwilling to do what he could to injure Goremykin. In the event, after the usual doubts and hesitations on his part, Nicholas rejected the proposal. On 20 October 1899, Goremykin was dismissed. His place was taken by another bureaucrat, D. S. Sipiagin, a man of less indolent but of cruder and coarser temperament. Not merely the place of the zemstvos in the national life was now at stake.

Together with much else, Nicholas had inherited from his father the secret agreement with France. He learned of it from the dying Giers only a few days after his accession. From that time onwards, although there were spells of low temperature in the alliance of the two countries, the agreement was the shaping factor in Russia's foreign relations. For a dozen years or more Germany continued in her attempt to attach Russia to her own designs in Europe. The ruinous tariff war between the two countries had been ended by a commercial agreement on most-favoured-nation lines even before Nicholas came to the throne, and the susceptible Nicholas himself came under the constant pressure of the German emperor's false confidences and falser flatteries. In spite of this, and although there were always convinced supporters at the Russian court and among ministers of a policy of intimate Russo-German collaboration, the military tie with France held.

How much its maintenance owed to Nicholas personally it is hard to say. Probably not a great deal. In the Russian imperial tradition he liked to think of himself as his own Foreign Minister and the official tenant of the ministry, whoever he might be, as the clerkly instrument of his wishes. In the role of a man of honour Nicholas may have been resolved to observe the agreement. Yet he had, in point of fact, as little conscience in foreign as in domestic politics; in diplomacy, since he could never make up his mind, he was often driven to deceit. It was his impulsive dabbling in the conduct of affairs, indeed, which at crucial moments lent Russian international relations a more than ordinary ambiguity.

In support of the French alliance he paid a visit to France in September 1896. This formed the climax of a European tour during which the empress and he spent a fortnight with Queen Victoria at Balmoral. In Paris, where he laid the foundation-stone of the splendid Alexander III bridge across the Seine, there were solemn and triumphant festivities to celebrate the alliance. Incongruously, the *Marseillaise* was played or sung almost without pause in the presence of the autocrat of all the Russias. In the following summer the German emperor paid a visit to St Petersburg, and from now onwards William addressed himself to the task of convincing Nicholas of Russia's manifest destiny in the Far East.

It is perhaps appropriate to record the Russian part in The Hague peace conference of 1899. Was Nicholas's startling appeal to the nations of the world to inaugurate an era of perpetual peace a throw-back to his great-grandfather's original ideals for the Holy Alliance? Or was the accompanying plea for a reduction in the general level of armaments to be attributed to the anxiety aroused in Russia by the threatened re-equipment of Austria's artillery? However that may be, a world undoubtedly excited for a moment by Nicholas's appeal soon recovered, and the delegates of the twenty-six nations who met at The Hague in May rejected his disarmament proposals but adopted the convention for the peaceful settlement of international disputes which was afterwards embodied in the permanent court of arbitration.

3. The Hungry Village

The 'peasant question', with all that it implied in rural impoverishment, land hunger and the menace of agrarian revolt, hung like a millstone round the neck of the government in St Petersburg during the first twelve years of the reign. In none of its superficially changing forms was the government a humane government and seldom if ever was it an enterprising one, but if it failed to address itself realistically to the question the reason was not that the issues at stake seemed at any time unimportant. On the contrary, their importance was plain at a glance. And indeed the adoption of fresh palliatives of one kind or another, together with reports on this or that aspect of Russian agriculture by one conference or special commission of enquiry after another, attested a serious enough official concern. The government's failure of realism sprang rather from the intimidating dimensions of the agrarian problem as a whole and from the need, in the prevailing climate of repression, to give first thoughts to the interests of the landed gentry. To these obstacles were added the indirect consequences to Russia's peasant economy of policy in other fields. The government had chosen to sacrifice peasant interests, and even private landowning interests with them, to financial and industrial policy.

Here the chief responsibility lay with the minister who for most of the period directed the economic affairs of the empire, Sergius Witte, the most considerable political figure of the reign. In pursuing innovation in any form the hostility that Witte had always to meet from both the landowning class and the higher bureaucracy, and most of all from the Ministry of the Interior, undoubtedly hampered him greatly. Belatedly, perhaps, he came to recognize the significance of Russian peasant agriculture in the political life of the country and was realist enough to perceive something at least of what should be done to give it a new lease of life. But he refused to stake his career upon agrarian reform.

He remains, after everything has been said about him, a curiously unfinished and puzzling character. A statesman of exceptional vigour and resource, vulgar in spirit but with more vision than any

of his contemporaries, Witte was inconsistent even in the exercise
of his least attractive qualities. Big, burly, unhandsome, commonplace in feature but penetrating in expression, he was visibly ridden
by ambition and was unscrupulous in pursuing it. Yet smaller men
constantly defeated him. For all his astuteness he could fail
lamentably in calculation; his energy and drive notwithstanding,
he was all too often evasive. Perhaps, after all, these are the normal
marks of the opportunist in politics, however gifted; or perhaps in
the last resort it was merely the arbitrary workings of the Russian
scheme of autocracy that put Witte at a disadvantage. In his desire
to get things done he was impatient of Byzantine ceremony, in-
tolerant of human nature in politics. He has been described by a
conservative contemporary as 'a first-rate administrator but no
politician'. There is something in the criticism, though in point of
fact Witte was a master in the arts of political intrigue, as a
minister who maintained his place under Nicholas II for so many
years could scarcely fail to be. Too self-seeking to make friends,
he leaves an impression of coarse, often unprincipled but not always
unkindly cynicism. His reminiscences, written in secret after his
fall from power, are among the most valuable and illuminating
documents of the period, though they need to be handled with
more than ordinary care. The reign of Nicholas II produced a
prodigious and infinitely depressing crop of historical memoirs,
almost all of them consisting of recrimination, rancour and a passion
of self-extenuation. Witte's recollections are seldom free from
these or from crude boastfulness. Yet in spite of the personal failings to which they bear witness, they also suggest that nobody was
shrewder in analysis of the practical course of Russian events
during the years 1894–1906.

Born in Tiflis in 1849 of a family ennobled in state service—
his father was of Dutch extraction—Witte, by training a mathe-
matician, rose rapidly in the railway administration and had become
the directing figure in railway construction in the 1880s even
before he was appointed to the post of Minister of Communications. Under Alexander III he found wide scope for his administrative abilities. In 1892 he took over the Ministry of Finance, and
in this capacity was retained by Nicholas II until 1903. During
those eleven years he presided over an intensive phase of the
industrialization of Russia.

Witte put his faith in Russia's industrial future. He was himself
originally influenced by the celebrated chemist Mendeleyev, who

had been captured by the prospects of large-scale exploitation of Russia's natural resources. To Witte's two immediate predecessors at the Ministry of Finance it had been plain that the chief hindrance to Russian foreign trade and a more rapid growth of industry was the instability of the paper rouble. In pursuing a remedy they had amassed a large quantity of gold by a policy of stimulating grain exports while raising formidable tariff barriers against foreign manufactures. Witte, seeking to attract investment capital from abroad on a bigger scale, continued the process even more drastically during 1893-6. He was helped by four good harvests. His technical measures to combat the fluctuations of the paper rouble, which included an ingenious manipulation of its gold value, met with formidable opposition; the landed nobility, in particular, were apprehensive of a reduced return on grain exports. But as Minister of Finance Witte persisted in the face of every hostile argument and in January 1897, almost without publicity, achieved full convertibility into gold.

The establishment of the gold standard promptly accelerated the rate of expansion of Russian industry. But it was effected at a heavy price and brought in its train severe burdens. Russia was financially too weak to maintain the service on an increasing flow of foreign capital[1] without further aid, and the effect of continued loans from abroad was to aggravate the strain. This could be eased only by creating at all costs a favourable balance of trade. It was therefore essential to reduce the volume of imports by resort to still higher protective duties and, more significantly, to swell exports of grain. The price of the barest necessities in manufactured goods was thus raised to a level which put them beyond the reach of the vast majority of the peasant population, who were already penalized by the heavy indirect taxes on such things as sugar, tea, tobacco, vodka, paraffin and matches, and more grain was shipped abroad even though Russians starved.

Though he recognized the nature of the agrarian problem, it is doubtful whether Witte had any intimate grasp of the daily exigencies of Russian agriculture. Yet he could scarcely ignore the spectacle of the hungry village. A year after he had been appointed Minister of Finance a Ministry of Agriculture was formed out of the former Ministry of State Lands. Its officials, confronted by the

[1]Towards the end of the century the interest paid on foreign loans was at the rate of 150 million gold roubles a year. About half as much represented further expenditure by Russians living or travelling abroad.

statistical evidence of mounting arrears in redemption payments and peasant taxes, especially in the fertile black-earth provinces of central Russia, could not doubt that peasant conditions were steadily deteriorating. But not the peasants only were involved. Of equal importance to the ministry and of greater concern to the government as a whole was the impoverishment of a large part of the landed gentry. In order to ensure a continued supply of cheap labour for industrial development Witte's policy was to keep the price of bread at the lowest possible level. This, of course, necessitated a low price for grain in the domestic market. The largest landowners, whose resources enabled them as a rule to adopt more scientific methods of farming and to increase yields, could survive low prices, but even in years of good harvest the position of many owners of small or medium-sized estates was desperate. It should not be thought that all the landed gentry in Russia were spend-thrift in habit, without enterprise and without conscience. On the contrary, there were model farmers and model landlords among them. But the enterprising and the inert alike were often in diffi-culty, and many were losing their estates to the new urban bourgeoisie and the richer peasantry. After a year of bad harvest, as was 1897, for instance, sales of the gentry's land rose spectacu-larly. Witte himself had little tenderness for the gentry. But it was the government's declared purpose to give them as a class every assistance, and in that year a special commission was set up to report on their needs.

The commission continued in being for five years, during which the failure of crops in 1897 was repeated in the following year and again in 1901. There was alarm in many quarters at the continued worsening of peasant conditions, and a round of minor agrarian disturbances aroused widespread sympathy. The burden of redemp-tion payments[1] was once more examined in the light of accumulated arrears. Early in 1894 provision had been made for the repayment of arrears at the end of the original term of forty-nine years pre-scribed for the purchase of peasant allotments. In May 1896 this concession was elaborated with an even more conspicuous want of realism: payment of the outstanding redemption debt, together with arrears, was now spread over an extended period that in some

[1] It has been argued that this was not in fact a heavy burden, since during the period 1894–1903 redemption payments averaged no more than 92 or 93 million roubles in a state budget which simultaneously rose from 1,145 million to 2,032 million roubles. But this is to lose sight of the precariously narrow margins of peasant existence.

instances stretched into the 1950s. It was scarcely an occasion for surprise when arrears were cancelled three years later.

Among the various small measures designed to assist the transfer of land to the peasantry was a reduction in 1894 of the rate of interest on loans advanced by the Peasants' Bank. Two years later the Peasants' Bank and the Bank of the Nobility were combined in a single administration, and two years later still an equalized rate of interest on loans was further reduced to four per cent. Of greater consequence was the decision to permit the Peasants' Bank to acquire land in its own name for sale to peasants. The full promise of this measure was not realized for another dozen years, but in the meantime an enormous area of state, appanage and privately owned land was transferred into the bank's keeping. Much of it eventually passed into peasant ownership.

For the time being, however, the size of peasant allotments continued to shrink. It is estimated than an average household allotment of thirty-five acres in European Russia in 1877 had shrunk in 1905 to twenty-eight acres. In such circumstances the most hopeful development during these years was the official encouragement given to peasant resettlement in Siberia. In 1896 a special 'resettlement bureau' was set up in the Ministry of the Interior to facilitate migration from the over-populated provinces to suitable agricultural areas east of the Urals. The legal impediments which until now had hindered the movement of the land-hungry peasantry were largely removed, though local authorities were still able to enforce their own methods of prohibition. The chosen areas of resettlement were for the most part close to the Trans-Siberian railway line, which by this time already ran uninterruptedly as far as Irkutsk. The main effort to open up Siberia to peasant agriculture waited upon the dissolution of the village commune and did not begin until 1906; but from 1896 onwards increasing sums of money were spent on assistance to migrating peasant groups, and during the next four years nearly three-quarters of a million people moved into Siberia. The movement was badly organized, the promised land sometimes proved unfit for cultivation, and not all the settlers stayed. But the progress that was made is illustrated by the imperial decree of 12 June 1900, by which the courts were forbidden to impose settlement in Siberia as a legal penalty. Although penal institutions there were left intact, Siberia, by the emperor's pleasure, was no longer a land for bad characters.

The commission on the needs of the landowning gentry sat

until 1902. Long before the end it was plain that little or nothing could be achieved. In the spring of 1899, at the end of the second year, its deliberations slipped into the background of the work of a new and smaller commission, set up on the initiative of V. I. Kovalevsky, Witte's assistant at the Ministry of Finance, on the impoverishment of the central black-earth regions. It was now, almost for the first time, that the traditional conception of the peasant commune came seriously into question. The commune had been built into the foundations of state and society. For the government it had been the alpha and omega of a stable order in the countryside; while every movement of opposition to the government, whether radical or conservative, had sought to preserve it as an instrument of a better Russian future. The peasantry themselves were for the most part conditioned in mind and habit by the collective organization of village society; an essential part of peasant character was reflected in the commune. Yet one of the principal conclusions reached by the Kovalevsky commission during its two years' work was that the commune was a main cause of impoverishment in the central black-earth regions, since both the diminishing size of peasant allotments and the inertia of peasant farming sprang from the communal system of repartitioning the land. The commission looked upon this state of affairs as an unavoidable evil in the circumstances of the growth of population. But elsewhere the suspicion grew that a choice must be made between the commune and the progress of agriculture. In November 1901, after another catastrophic failure of crops, yet another commission was appointed, this time under the chairmanship of V. N. Kokovtsev, the newly appointed assistant Minister of Finance, to investigate conditions in the central black-earth provinces and in other parts of the empire. This, too, was overtaken subsequently by a more significant enquiry.

The apparent impotence of the government to check the growing crisis in peasant affairs played its part in aggravating the restlessness of educated society, more especially among the zemstvo representatives. But there were other and no less disturbing reasons for alarm and despondency among the liberal elements in the early years of the reign. The disappointment of their own hopes of a representative order of government apart, their conscience was profoundly stirred by the policies of russification which were now in full swing in the borderlands of the empire. These policies had been prepared, under the guidance of Pobedonostsev, in the previous reign, but only now were they being given full effect in an assault upon the civil and religious rights, the local institutions and national culture of the minorities. In Poland, in the Baltic provinces, in the Caucasus, the doctrine of Great Russian superiority was sedulously propagated by new legislation. Most drastic of all was the policy of russification in semi-independent Finland.

An autonomous grand duchy since its incorporation into the empire in 1808, by comparison with any other part of the empire Finland had remained ever since conspicuously tranquil. But in 1898 a new governor was appointed in the person of General Bobrikov, a Russian nationalist of fearsome repute even among his associates. Together with other schemes of russification, including the obligatory use of Russian in Finnish institutions, a project for extending to Finland the Russian law on military service had been debated by a special commission appointed by Alexander III. Legally, the project might seem valid, or very nearly so; as a major item in a programme of Russian domination it was something to be feared and distrusted by every Finn. In thus seeking, at any rate, to annul the existing constitutional restriction on the use of Finnish troops to Finland, St Petersburg had still to discover whether the Finnish Diet could be made to give its consent. One of Bobrikov's first steps was to propose an increase in the size of the Finnish army and in the length of service (which was to be reduced for recruits speaking Russian) as a prelude to absorbing Finnish troops into Russian units and making them available for use in any part of the empire. The protest in the Diet and in the country was instantaneous and impassioned, and showed no sign of dying down. Bobrikov awaited further instructions. On 3 February of the following year St Petersburg delivered its judgment: by imperial manifesto, all legislation on Finnish affairs that ran parallel to legislation elsewhere in the empire, or that involved the interests of the empire as a whole, now came within the competence of the imperial State Council. The function of the Finnish Diet in these matters was to be consultative only. Finland, that is, was being reduced to the virtual status of a province of the empire.

The blow delivered in this manner at the hitherto friendly if somewhat reserved relations of Finland to Russia was to have lasting consequences. In Finland the shock of anger healed every division between the Finnish and Swedish parts of the population.

Even the Finnish Senate, whose members were appointed by the tsar, resisted strongly; the publication of the manifesto in Helsingfors was secured only by the president's casting vote. From this point the pace of russification quickened. Until now the state secretary for Finland had always been a Finn. In August 1899 this tacit principle was ignored and the post was filled from St Petersburg by Viacheslav Plehve, police chief of the empire, who was soon to win even greater notoriety. In the same month, as part of the St Petersburg plan to control communications, the Finnish postal services were absorbed into the Russian system; in the following June the obligation was laid upon the Finnish Senate to maintain its records in Russian; and in June of the following year, 1901, the imperial system of conscription was formally introduced into Finland and the Finnish army disbanded. The most dramatic gesture of Finnish protest was still to come, but for two years liberal opinion in Russia observed the course of events with mounting anxiety. Its attention was distracted from Finland only by disturbances nearer home.

The restlessness of liberal society had communicated itself to Russia's university students and in the process had suffered a heady change. Not for nothing were the student body known as 'the barometer of society'. In the lull after the Narodnik storm the educated younger generation had been no less subdued than their elders. But in the mood of the nineties many had come under the spell of radical or revolutionary nostrums. Large numbers of students lived in squalid poverty, often hungry, often obliged to seek notoriously ill-paid forms of tutoring in order to complete their course of study. If the generous ardours of youth or the revolutionary sympathies of some of their teachers failed to work upon them, there was often the powerful incentive of their own insignificance to spur them on. Others, who in the ordinary way were untouched by extreme doctrines, were moved by a sense of student solidarity. In these circumstances the student fraternities in the closing years of Alexander III's reign were for the most part dominated by leaders who were in contact with the *podpolie*—the underground, or secret, opposition to the regime.[1]

[1] In his reminiscences V. A. Maklakov recalls the student orchestra and choir of Moscow University which was the only 'legal' society in the eighties. The decision—designed to give representation to the student body as a whole and to preserve its non-partisan character—to appoint at the head of the society an 'economic committee', of which half the members were drawn from

In the new reign, after long years of quiescence, dormant student passions woke noisily. In 1895 the united council of Moscow, representing forty-five fraternities in the university, staged a demonstration within the university precincts for the repeal of the 1884 statute and—among other things—the admission of women students. The police were summoned and the ringleaders were arrested and the council dissolved. In November of the following year a new council organized a further and more serious demonstration, this time in protest against those responsible for the Khodynka disaster. On this occasion there were skirmishes with the police and more than seven hundred students were arrested. The great majority were subsequently expelled from the university for a year or more.

An interval of quiet followed, and then all that had occurred before was dwarfed by the events of 1899. The disturbances began, once again, in St Petersburg, almost by chance, on 8 February, on the occasion of the annual university celebrations. Provoked by an official warning against rowdy behaviour, the student body abandoned all restraint. The brutality of the mounted police, who were called to the scene and who drove the students from the university buildings into the street, using their whips freely, provoked a fury of indignation in every university and almost every other higher educational institution in the land. That same evening the St Petersburg students declared a 'strike', by which was meant the refusal to attend lectures or examinations, and supported it by a campaign of 'obstructions', which signified the threat of violence against all potential strike-breakers. This was a new technique of student agitation. The strike—and the same tactic of obstructions—spread on 15 February to Moscow University, to Kiev and Kharkov two days later, and took in the universities of Riga and Warsaw on the way. In an attempt to check the contagion the government for a time prohibited mention of the strike in the press. But all to no purpose: within six weeks every university and almost every other institute of higher education had closed down.

They remained closed until the autumn, and in the meantime the authorities resorted to simultaneous appeasement and intimidation. A special commission, headed by the elderly and not wholly

---

the orchestra and choir and half from those outside, was strongly opposed by the radical students, among them the future Socialist-Revolutionary leader, Victor Chernov. They did indeed obtain political control of the orchestra and choir in the early nineties.

insensitive General Vannovsky, a former Minister of War, was appointed to investigate the causes of the disorders. It recommended the introduction of a system of student 'elders' to represent the various faculties and courses, proposed that students should be allowed to hold occasional meetings for purposes of study and hinted at the possibility of larger concessions in the future. The Ministry of Education jibbed even at this. It was prepared to accept, though in the vaguest terms, the formation of scientific and literary circles under the control of the teaching staff and inspectorate, and was willing to assist in setting up student hostels. But it condemned any scheme of student representation, even in the shape of faculty elders, as not merely superfluous but pernicious. At the end of July, it published another set of 'provisional rules' for the restoration of order. In addition to the continued ban on independent student activity, those students who had been expelled for a year or more were to be conscripted into the army for the period in question, even though they were otherwise exempt from military service. The government inspectors were charged with stricter powers of supervision. And the holders of various senior academic posts, more particularly in St Petersburg University, were dismissed on a charge of assisting the disturbances or of expressing sympathy with them.

The penalty of conscript service for taking part in student demonstrations was bitterly resented. Resentment had not died down when the universities opened again in the autumn. All through the following year there were small threatening incidents. Towards the end of 1900 passions flared up again in Kiev University, where a protest meeting was broken up by troops and police and some five hundred students were arrested. About half the number were drafted into the army. Immediately there were sympathetic student disorders in Kharkov, Moscow and St Petersburg.

The historic significance of these student disorders is that they were a potent leaven in the rise of the Socialist-Revolutionary Party, the most influential of the Russian revolutionary parties until the Bolshevik seizure of power in 1917 and the most popular for some little time after. More than any other party it was the party of youth. If at the turn of the century the majority of students in Russia, in spite of protests and demonstrations, were still politically uncommitted and only a small number had as yet been drawn into secret Marxist study groups, a sizable and growing minority were being enlisted into one or other of the various factions which had assumed the title of Socialist-Revolutionaries. Not until the summer of 1900 did these factions begin to coalesce into an organized underground party.

The party was in some sort a reincarnation, transformed in doctrine and strategy, of the old Narodnik movement. Still moved by faith in the 'natural socialism' of the Russian peasant, the new generation of Narodnik leaders had set themselves the task of evolving a policy which would demonstrably reconcile the interests of the peasantry with the cause of socialism. Their revolt was humanitarian rather than intellectual. Like their predecessors, they were not themselves peasants but members of the intelligentsia. They had before them the example of revered Narodnik figures of the older generation like Mark Natanson, one of the founders of Land and Liberty and an old friend of Plekhanov, and Catherine Breshko-Breshkovskaya, who was to become known as 'the grandmama of the Russian Revolution', both of whom had been permitted to return from exile in Siberia in the last two or three years of Alexander III's reign. Though the aims of the new and improved Narodnik party in the making were still not very precise, they took count of Marxist dogmas. Clearly, the leaders conceded, capitalism had arrived in Russia and the 'revolutionary process' therefore involved not the peasantry only. But if, as Chernov put it later, the industrial proletariat was the vanguard of revolution, the peasants—the *narod*—were still the main army. On them would fall the brunt of the battle. At the same time, it was argued, Russian capitalism was as yet so weak that the overthrow of autocracy would by itself create the immediate conditions for a socialist order of society throughout Russia. It was this simple vision of a millennial future founded upon peasant collectivism which kindled the imagination of perhaps the bravest of a rebellious younger generation. Revolutionary idealists, heroic legend notwithstanding, are not often men of exalted character, but among Socialist-Revolutionary personalities of coarser or indeed contemptible stamp were not a few students of genuine nobility of spirit.

The various Socialist-Revolutionary groups had obstinately refused to combine until the summer of 1900, when an assortment of delegates held a secret meeting in Kharkov at which questions of policy and organization and the future of the party's illegal journal, *Revolutionary Russia*, were thrashed out. The gist of the agrarian programme now adopted was that the land should become 'social property'. While only those who laboured on it, that is, would hold land, they would hold it on terms of use and not ownership; holdings would be equalized, and tenure in general would conform to the traditional usages of the commune. As for factories and workshops, what was envisaged was a system of producers' co-operatives on the lines of the existing co-operative craft association, the *artel*. The programme, naïve in the extreme from the vantage point of the present day but not quite so hollow at the time as may be supposed, nevertheless bristled with impracticalities and was in fact never worked out in detail. But its emphasis on the exclusive right of the peasants to the land soon echoed loudly in the village. For Socialist-Revolutionary tactics were not only to terrorize the forces of authority but also to win popular peasant support. Unlike the earlier Narodniks, that is, the party sought to combine terror against the government with propaganda in the village.

The 'fighting (*boevaya*) organization' of the party was set up in the following year. It was a small, secret, disciplined and dedicated group of zealots, whose task was assassination. Supported by a number of local groups in different parts of Russia, the fighting organization was composed of men and women of every rank in society, including the highest. Their record of murder over a period of six years bears witness to that nihilistic impulse which has always characterized the Russian revolutionary movement. At the same time it is darkened by the no less characteristic treachery of some of the revolutionary movement's principal agents. For the Socialist-Revolutionary and all other underground cells were inevitably penetrated by police spies and agents-provocateurs, and in the midst of sudden arrests and sentences of imprisonment or deportation it was seldom possible to distinguish terrorists from counter-terrorists. The first chief of the Socialist-Revolutionary terrorist group was a pharmacist and bacteriologist named Gregory Gershuni, gentle in temperament through all his murderous resolve and brilliantly audacious. In 1902 he and a fellow conspirator of different stamp, Yevno Azef, were the principal Socialist-Revolutionary emissaries from Russia to a conference in Switzerland attended by Victor Chernov and other like-minded Russian exiles. Only now was the structure and organization of the party fully elaborated.

By that time the campaign of political terror had borne spectacular fruit. On 1 February 1901, the Minister of Education,

N. P. Bogolepov, a former professor of Roman law, was mortally wounded by a revolver shot fired by the Socialist-Revolutionary Karpovich, a student who had twice been expelled from the university. The deed was openly applauded at student meetings in the capital. While Bogolepov lay dying the earliest of a historic succession of popular demonstrations in the square in front of the Kazan cathedral[1] was broken up by the mounted police. A crowd of several thousand which had gathered was scattered, some sixty persons were injured and nearly eight hundred were arrested. There were similar violent disturbances in Moscow a few days later. In the next month a young zemstvo worker, a statistician, fired several shots at close range at Pobedonostsev, who escaped unhurt. Tension in the capital and elsewhere rose swiftly. The government had no thought of concessions; its only response was to impose an even more stringent press censorship and to give the police department of the Ministry of the Interior a free hand. Yet in spite of arrests, expulsions, a ban on street assemblies and brutal methods of provocation, student demonstrations continued. Within and outside Russia, more especially in France, there were impassioned protests against the behaviour of the police by groups of men of letters.

The campaign of assassination went on. On 2 April of the following year the Minister of the Interior, D. S. Sipiagin, whose police regime had made him a marked man, was struck down in the Marinsky Palace, where a meeting of the State Council was in progress. The assassin was a twenty-year-old student named Balmashov, who calmly made his way into the palace in the uniform of an imperial aide-de-camp and fired at point-blank range. Plans had been made by the terrorists at the same time to ensure that Pobedonostsev and the military governor of St Petersburg, General Kleigels, would share Sipiagin's fate, but at the last moment the appointed assassins lost their nerve. Balmashov was tried by a military court, since a civil court could not pronounce sentence of death (Bogolepov's murderer had been sentenced by a civil court to penal servitude for life, but had promptly made his escape). He bore himself with impressive courage and composure, refused to plead for mercy and was hanged in Schlüsselburg on 3 May. It was the first but not the last capital sentence in the reign for 'political reasons'.

[1]This had been the principal scene of student demonstrations in St Petersburg since the 1870s.

In the countryside discontent took a narrower and more practical form than in the cities. Almost on the eve of the murder of Sipiagin peasant resentments suddenly blazed in the Ukrainian black-earth provinces of Poltava and Kharkov. Here, where peasant allotments had long been too small for subsistence and were still diminishing, the hatred for the landowner went deep. The rent paid for extra land leased from him came not so much out of the earnings of peasant agriculture as from the factory earnings of absent members of the commune. And in all too many cases such contributions were no longer being maintained. The disturbances in these provinces, though free from extremes of violence, were the most serious of their kind for some years. In the middle of March peasants from several districts presented themselves simultaneously at the local manor house and demanded grain and fodder for their cattle. Where these were granted the peasants returned with their spoils and in most instances left the landowner in peace afterwards. But elsewhere there was pillage in broad daylight, with peasants arriving in carts to remove grain, fodder, implements and whatever else they could lay hands on. No murder was done, though there was arson at night and some manor houses were completely burned down. Beyond satisfying immediate needs it was clear that the peasants' purpose, as so often, was to drive the landowners from their estates. Some sixty-four estates in the Poltava province were plundered in this way, twenty-seven in the province of Kharkov. Order was restored by punitive military expeditions. A number of peasants were killed in indiscriminate shooting, more than eleven hundred were arrested and brought to trial, there were mass floggings, and the injured landowners were enabled to impose fines by way of compensating themselves.

All these disorders reverberated in St Petersburg at a time when the government appeared at last to have taken alarm at the gravity of the agrarian problem. In January 1902, the emperor had returned to a proposal made by Witte four years earlier and had announced a special conference on 'the needs of the agricultural industry', with Witte as chairman. It was decided to conduct an enquiry throughout the country and to invite the views of interested bodies. But who, other than local officials and the landowners themselves, could safely be brought into consultation? Not the intelligentsia or those tainted by association with the intelligentsia, since they would certainly urge a political solution. Nor was the advice of the zemstvos in any way desirable. There, indeed, in the view of the Ministry of the Interior, was the crux of the matter.

For the past two years and more the ministry, as has been made plain, had been at war with the zemstvos. Besides all the veiled talk of constitutional principles (the use of the word 'constitution' in public was still forbidden), the assemblies had grown insistent on the need for universal primary education and the abolition of corporal punishment for peasants. In return, they had had their wings clipped by successive regulations. They had been deprived of the right to assist in organizing local food supplies—though this interdict had in fact been temporarily withdrawn after the failure of harvest in 1901; they had been forbidden to hold joint consultations with the municipalities or to make joint representations with them to the government; most serious of all, their power of raising revenue by a rate on property had been drastically restricted. And with all this their 'senseless dreams' had provoked, in support of the government, a sustained attack, led by the venal and sinister Prince Meshchersky, on the whole principle of local self-government. At the time of the murder of Sipiagin it was widely feared that the very existence of the zemstvos was at stake. With the appointment in succession to Sipiagin of the overbearing and ruthless Plehve, the former imperial police chief and the grave-digger of Finland's liberties, such fears were in no way allayed. It was certain at any rate that Plehve would desire even less than his predecessor to seek the aid of the zemstvos in the task of the conference.

In the protracted duel which was now fought between Plehve and Witte it was Witte who gained the first advantage. He saw in the conference an opportunity both to appease liberal opinion and to come to grips with the agrarian problem. After arrangements had been made for setting up some six hundred local committees, at Witte's persuasion it was left to the provincial governor or the county marshal of the nobility who presided over each committee to enlist the aid of such persons as he thought fit. Zemstvo chairmen were allotted a place in each provincial or county committee, but other zemstvo representatives who were invited to serve were present in a personal capacity only. In the result, the provincial committees assumed for the most part an 'official' character, while the county committees were more representative of 'society'. The work of compiling local reports was begun in the summer of 1902 and was completed early in the following year;

the full results of the conference were published soon afterwards in a report of no fewer than fifty-eight volumes.

It may be of advantage here to abandon strict chronology in order to describe the fruits of so considerable and significant a labour. Most of the local committees went far beyond the strict letter of 'the needs of the agricultural industry' and addressed themselves to almost every conceivable aspect of the life of rural Russia. Many were outspoken on such matters as abuses in the administration of justice. But the sharpest criticisms or the most urgent recommendations that had been made in committee were not always recorded. As the work had progressed so the Ministry of the Interior had asserted its powers. By means of the right of veto of the provincial governor or county marshal of the nobility, Plehve left his mark on the entire proceedings. The supervisory officials, indeed, interfered so flagrantly with the work of some committees, levelling menacing charges of 'anti-government activity' against the more radical members, that the latter frequently withdrew from further sittings. Often, too, the proceedings resolved themselves at the outset into an open conflict between the forces of government and society as a whole. Even so, however, there was, on the whole, a remarkable consensus of opinion on the practical reforms to be desired and few differences of opinion on the continued need for zemstvo activities. It was in these local committees, indeed, that the zemstvo movement, which had drawn up for the benefit of representatives engaged in them a considered programme, most clearly voiced the practical aspirations of educated society. Never again was the zemstvo leadership quite so realistic. Only one or two committees echoed the demand for a popular representative assembly, but there was an unexpected measure of sympathy with most of the zemstvo representatives' specific proposals. These included equal rights for the peasants with other 'estates' or classes, the liberation of the peasants from 'administrative tutelage', the abolition of corporal punishment for peasants, the obligatory alienation of state, appanage and monastic lands, together with part of the private estates, in the peasant interest, the introduction of universal primary education, the reform of taxation, the abolition of the system of separate 'estates' in zemstvo representation and the creation of a zemstvo unit for sub-divisions of the county.

It was a well-conceived programme, which touched peasant Russia more nearly than projects of parliamentary democracy. Characteristically, however, it ignored the central issue which plainly confronted the committees. Did the needs of agriculture require communal land tenure or individual peasant ownership? Although less than two hundred of the committees chose to express their views on the subject, the weight of evidence was clear. The great majority declared against the principle of the commune. Relatively few were in favour of its immediate abolition, if only because immediate abolition involved so much that was obscure and vaguely alarming.

These local committees, it is fair to say, spoke for a conservative landed interest, which had been made apprehensive by threats of expropriation of the private estates. Yet not all of them were illiberal and their argument against maintaining the commune did not proceed from self-interest only. This the liberals themselves recognized. But most of the intelligentsia preferred to ignore the argument, since it ran counter to their own cherished prepossessions. There was a small and extreme Marxist group, which had still to emerge from obscurity and which would have welcomed any means, the abolition of the commune included, of sharpening the class struggle in the village; but for the rest only Plekhanov in Switzerland and one or two more of similarly analytical mind had realized that the traditional Russian peasant economy was already in dissolution and that the ambition of most peasants, as Plekhanov put it, was to become capitalists themselves.

Though half impelled towards action by the work of the conference, the government for its own part hesitated, unwilling as yet to embark upon far-reaching legislation. On 26 February 1903, its irresolution was apparent in an imperial manifesto which at one and the same time proclaimed the inviolability of communal peasant tenure and pledged assistance to those peasants who desired to leave the commune. Positive action came a fortnight later in a law which abolished the collective responsibility for the payment of state dues and obligations of the members of village communes over the greater part of European Russia.

The person chiefly responsible was Witte, who would willingly have continued farther in the same reforming direction. But even before his dismissal from office in August he had already been worsted in the relentless struggle with the Minister of the Interior. Plehve—who owed his appointment to Meshchersky—was well attuned to both the intrigues and the policies of reaction of the highest imperial circles. His was the Sisyphean task, as Miliukov put it later, of saving autocracy.

4. The Industrial Proletariat

The progress of Russian industry during the previous couple of decades was demonstrated at the Russian Exhibition of 1896, which opened on 28 May at Nizhny-Novgorod, close to the site of the annual fair, which was held simultaneously. The exhibition had been devised by Witte to stimulate foreign investment and trade and at the same time to lend support to his protectionist policies.

In the same month the most formidable strike up to that time in Russian industry broke out among the textile workers of St Petersburg. It involved several large mills under different ownership and spread to one or two other enterprises in the capital; soon some forty thousand workers were out. Not the scale of the strike, nor yet the arrest by the police of about a thousand strikers, excited the public so much as the fact that this was the earliest organized mass movement of the Russian industrial workers. That it occurred in St Petersburg is to be explained first of all by the habitual dearth of labour in the region, which offered better opportunity than existed elsewhere for some form of workers' organization and which indeed served then and afterwards to make the St Petersburg proletariat peculiarly conscious of its strength.

Behind the strike was a small and shadowy labour union composed not of industrial workers but of members of the revolutionary intelligentsia. When, not long afterwards, workers themselves were drawn into secret local unions, the latter were still largely directed from outside by members of the revolutionary intelligentsia. It was in these controlling circumstances that strikes now broke out in other regions, notably the industrial centres in the south. Here, where mines, railways and factories were often state-owned and there were combined iron smelting works and blast furnaces which employed ten thousand workers, labour disaffection was necessarily directed against the government as employer.

The strikes, which gathered momentum against the general domestic background of peasant unrest, university disturbances, zemstvo agitation and the propaganda of Narodniks and Marxists, were as yet essentially economic in character; the political motives of those who organized them were still to some extent masked. Whether, in spite of a slightly rising level of wages in the nineties, there was any real improvement in the living standards of the industrial workers is open to question. Certainly the slump conditions of 1899-1903 tended to wipe out whatever gains there might have been. In the meantime, at any rate, the strikers' demands were largely aimed at a shorter working day, with a corresponding adjustment in rates of pay to maintain the level of earnings, and the withdrawal of various arbitrary forms of factory discipline and so on. These demands were imperfectly met on the government side by the legal enactment in 1897 of a maximum working day of eleven and a half hours and by a conciliatory pledge to recommend to employers an increase in wages. The law was widely disregarded (a fifteen-hour day was still not uncommon at the turn of the century), and Witte, however much he favoured good management in industry, could make relatively little impression on the run of capitalist employers.

From these strikes emerged an incipient working-class movement in Russia strongly penetrated by Marxist ideas. The form of Marxism that could be openly discussed in the press—'legal' Marxism, as it was therefore called—was one in which the economic analysis of capitalist development was divorced from all political issues. As such it appeared to the authorities to be of so abstruse a character that no objection was taken to the publication of articles on the subject by Plekhanov or the young economist Peter Struve. The forms of clandestine Marxist propaganda which were now circulated among the industrial workers, however, were a very different matter. Printed on secret hand-presses or smuggled into Russia from abroad, this was political literature expressly designed to foment revolutionary action.

It was a Marxist group, or rather an amalgamation of a score of small Marxist groups under the title of Union of Struggle for the Liberation of the Working Class, which had organized the St Petersburg strike of 1896. Its principal founders were Vladimir Ulianov, who took the name of Lenin, and Julius Martov, who was born Yury Osipovich Zederbaum. It is perhaps necessary here to speak of Martov only, since as the virtual begetter of Menshevism his record has been sadly distorted in Bolshevik historiography. Born in 1873 and three years younger than Lenin, he came of a

long line of eminent rabbinical scholars and combined in his person
something of the moral fervour and intellectual rationalism of the
Hebrew prophets. Slight and stooping of figure, handicapped by a
limp, his face thin and ascetic, Martov was a Jewish type of
impassioned talker and at the same time a singularly selfless,
courageous and determined spirit. Until 1903 Lenin's political
association with him was closer than any he formed afterwards.
Both had been caught by the police before the strike began; Lenin
was arrested in December 1895 and deported to Siberia, Martov
followed next month. But even in exile the two young men had
been able to maintain contact.

Under police vigilance, Marxist groups in the cities dissolved
or were broken up. Others took their place. Unity among them
was still lacking; there was an endless war of words between
Marxists and the 'legal' Marxists known as Economists, who
sought to transfer the weight of attack from revolutionary propaganda to the economic struggle of the workers against the
employers. The first practical effort to unite the groups in a Russian
Social-Democratic Workers' Party was made in March 1898,
when nine delegates from five local groups and from the Jewish
workers' union known as the Bund (of which Martov was one of
the original founders) met in Minsk, in White Russia. Their
three-day secret meeting on that occasion bears the historic title
of the founding congress of the Russian Social-Democratic Party.
The claim to the title is purely ritualistic, for eight of the nine
delegates were arrested as soon as the meeting was over and the
congress itself had no immediate sequel. Indeed, though a resonant
programme was drawn up for it after the event by Struve, the
party appeared stillborn.

It was not quite that; for Bolshevism still traces its descent
from these small beginnings in 1898. The fortunes of the Russian
Social-Democratic Party during the next five years belong to
Marxist scripture rather than to Russian history, and are of
negligible significance in this narrative. Nor indeed is it necessary
to follow in detail the history of Bolshevism during the fourteen
years after that, since Bolshevism played no decisive part in the
reign of Nicholas II. But it is essential at this stage to bear in mind
the conspiratorial character of Russian Social-Democracy, more
especially of its Bolshevik faction. A tiny underground organization, ruled by extremist dogma, ridden by ideological dispute,
directed almost entirely from abroad and maintaining itself within

Russia only with the aid of the properties of melodrama (secret presses, revolutionary pseudonyms, forged passports) and through the loyalty and courage of its following, the movement was driven forward in the pursuit of power by an intelligentsia with no very intimate experience of the life of the Russian masses.

Small though the number of active revolutionaries among the workers was in these years, their purposeful and untiring energies gave them a commanding influence. They were in touch with leaders outside, they circulated illegal literature in their plant or factory, they popularized slogans, they put themselves at the head of local strike movements. It was through their initiative that strikes and demonstrations took on a political character. The prolonged slump that settled on industry in 1899 and created large patches of unemployment did not weaken their militant propaganda, as in those years it might have done elsewhere; as always in Russia, economic discontent and underground agitation went hand in hand in the centres of industry. The Ministry of the Interior battled in vain with subversion in this form by the normal methods of arresting agitators and banishing them to their native village or farther afield.

For the ministry and the forces of security in general strikes were an unqualified evil. But if they could not be averted, economic strikes provided less cause for alarm than revolutionary propaganda. The technique of combating revolutionary socialism by a venture in what afterwards was ironically styled 'police socialism' could only have originated at the time in the mind of a Russian police official. It was in fact conceived by the head of the Moscow *Okhrana*, the security police, Sergey Zubatov, who had once professed revolutionary sympathies. To wean the industrial workers from the revolutionary leadership, it was necessary, Zubatov argued, to support their purely economic and relatively legitimate grievances. It was therefore desirable to encourage the formation of non-political labour unions, over which the police would exercise effective control. The idea did not commend itself to Witte, who saw no advantage in the prospect of even worse relations in industry, or to most other ministers, who vaguely sensed the risks involved. But Zubatov, a talker often taken in by his own cleverness, had the backing of other police officials and the scheme met with special approval from the governor-general of Moscow, the grand-duke Sergey Alexandrovich.

A start was made in promoting workers' associations in Moscow during 1900. Since mutual help and self-education figured largely in the early schemes, it proved possible to enlist the aid of various eminent professors of Moscow University, who were persuaded to give popular lectures on such subjects as friendly societies, consumers' co-operatives, factory legislation and trade unions in Great Britain. All this provided gratifying results: threatened strike action, assisted by discreet police pressure, secured the workers some gains, while for their part the *Okhrana* effected large-scale arrests of the revolutionary elements in the workers' midst.

It was the success of the Zubatov experiment which woke suspicion. Vehement criticism by the intelligentsia of the Moscow professors obliged the latter to withdraw their support, and those who replaced them were for the most part clergy, whose conservative sentiments carried less weight with the workers. But the venture, which was soon extended to several other large industrial centres, continued to receive full police protection. It reached a disturbing climax in Moscow on 19 February 1902, the anniversary of the act of emancipation, when the associations held a monster demonstration in the square overlooked by the memorial to the tsar-liberator. The mood of the vast crowd was undeniably patriotic, but this did not stand in the way of alarmingly high-pitched economic demands and threats of strike action. The industrial proletariat had indeed been given its head, and this, it should be remembered, at a time when the tide of Socialist-Revolutionary terrorism was still rising.

The prospect for 'police socialism' was somewhat dimmed. Plehve, as the newly appointed Minister of the Interior, though he was all for destroying nests of revolutionaries, was somewhat sceptical of the advantage of Zubatov's tactics. But they had proved successful up to a point in Moscow and elsewhere, and he was prepared to allow the labour associations to continue in being in the hope of undermining the position of his rival Witte, the patron of native and foreign industrialists. A methodical careerist, able and merciless, Plehve was all the more hostile to Witte because he himself had no grasp of the economic agencies of change in Russia, and because in his task of preserving the strict letter of autocracy he was often baulked by Witte's no less masterful and more flexible habit of mind. He was right, however, to count upon the growing indignation of the industrialists. These were now moved to angry protest by the strikes organized in the south by a body called the Independent Workers' Committee, which was controlled by a colleague of Zubatov named Shayevich. The committee, supported on one side by the police, on the other, with nice irony, by the Socialist-Revolutionaries, virtually dictated conditions of employment in the metallurgical plants and factories and even fixed wages. The immediate crisis came in November, when in Rostov-on-Don a strike which began in the railway workshops brought out almost every worker in the city. Amid a complete industrial standstill orators pressed for higher wages and a nine-hour day and then passed to inflammatory declamations against autocracy. It was necessary to call out a considerable body of troops to quell the disturbances and to make an appropriately large number of arrests.

So fantastically conceived a scheme as Zubatov's could scarcely fail to pass out of the control of the police into the hands of the active revolutionaries. 'Police socialism' not only stirred revolt where formerly there had been apathy but also provided a new model for revolutionary organization. In depicting this period of industrial unrest Soviet historians have seldom acknowledged the immense debt that the Russian Social-Democratic movement before 1917 owed to the *Okhrana*.

Complete disaster had still to overtake the Zubatov experiment. It came in the summer of 1903 in a general strike in the south. In the previous March, an ugly and tragic episode in the strike movement had roused bitter passions. A strike among the miners at Zlatoust, in the Urals, had turned to rioting, and the troops called to the scene, ordered by the provincial governor of Ufa to open fire, had gone on shooting after the crowd had dispersed. Though the killed and wounded had been avenged in May by the murder of the governor by a Socialist-Revolutionary railway worker, the bitter indignation which the episode aroused probably played a part in the outburst of strikes three months later. Starting simultaneously on 1 July in Odessa, Baku, Tiflis and Batum and then taking in Kiev, Nikolayev, Kerch, Ekaterinoslav, Elizavetgrad and other areas, within a short time they had enveloped the workers in the mines, in the factories, in the ports, on the railways and in the oilfields of the south. The strike of the port workers in Odessa had been a signal for the immediate dismissal of Zubatov and the withdrawal of police support from the recognized labour unions in various parts of the country, but the strike habit was not so easily broken. Workers streamed out of one factory to appeal to the workers of another to come out in sympathy with them. A week after 17 July, when a general strike was declared, nearly a quarter of a million men were out. The strikers' demands varied from higher wages and shorter hours to the right to form free trade unions and the summoning of a constituent assembly. Advanced cautiously at first, the political demands were taken up more boldly in public demonstrations. At this point the troops who had been brought in, more especially the Cossacks, became restive, above all in Odessa and Baku. By the middle of August the authorities had the upper hand and the general strike was over. Ruthless reprisals followed. In spite of some degree of organiza-tion, there had been no defined political strategy behind the strike movement, only an exasperated mass impulse of self-assertion.

The year 1903, in which—for the first time in Russia—the industrial proletariat asserted its strength, was also a year of decision in several other respects. It marked a dramatic new phase in the history of both Russian liberalism and Russian Marxism and a secret climax in the development of revolutionary terrorism.

For a generation anti-semitism, an endemic disease in Russia, had been stimulated by the conspicuous part played by Jews in the revolutionary movement. Every new form of anti-Jewish legisla-tion produced a new crop of Jewish revolutionaries. A report in 1905 from the commander of the Siberian military region gave the number of persons detained under political surveillance there as 5,426, of whom no fewer than 1,676 were Jews. But although both Alexander III and his son were as virulently anti-semitic as the most reactionary of their subjects, there had been relatively few pogroms after the outbreak of 1881. On 6 April 1903, however—Easter Day—after a long spell of calm, mob feeling was let loose in an outburst in Kishinev, in Bessarabia. Spurred on by a vicious campaign of anti-semitism in the local press which culminated in the story of a Jewish ritual murder, for two days the mob murdered and plundered and destroyed. There were considerable numbers of women and children among the hundreds of dead and injured. Not until the second day did the police make any move to check the savagery. In spite of the official ban on any reference to the subject in the press, anger at these events was so widespread in Russia, indignation abroad so unreserved, that the government hastened to add its own condemnation of the outrage. The governor of the province was dismissed, various officials were relieved of

their posts and transferred to other parts of the empire and some
of the ringleaders in the rioting were put on trial and punished.
But the anger did not die down, since all the evidence suggested
that the authorities had deliberately connived in the pogrom.
Plehve himself, in point of fact, had explicitly instructed the
governor not to resort to force against the rioters and thus inflame
the Russian population of the city against the government.

The pogrom had three immediate effects, which were in no way
lessened by a second pogrom in August in Gomel, in White Russia.
One was a further hardening of liberal opinion in the west against
the Russian regime, and with it perhaps a fresh access of sentimenta-
lity on the Russian problem; the second was a secret flow of Russian
funds in support of the underground revolutionary parties; and the
third—vividly illustrated in Andreyev's story, *The Governor*—
was the dissemination of an idea of 'revolutionary justice'.

Almost certainly the Kishinev outrage had its effect upon the
Jew Azef, an increasingly well-paid agent of the secret police during
the previous twelve years, who had found his way into the inner
circle of the Socialist-Revolutionary Party. There, for all that was
grossly insensitive and physically repellent in the man, he was
devoutly trusted. After the arrest in May of Gershuni,[1] betrayed
in the successful plot to murder the governor of Ufa, Azef had
become chief of its fighting organization. From that point, until
his fantastic double-dealing was exposed with resounding effect in
1909, he simultaneously helped to organize most of the principal
acts of terrorism against the regime and delivered up to his pay-
masters some of the most active of his fellow conspirators. Though
in his soulless cupidity he possibly did as much as any man to
debase the reputation and injure the prospects of the Socialist-
Revolutionary Party, it is hard to think that in his role of terrorist
Azef was not moved by racial sentiment.

Five years after the Social-Democrats had held their luckless
first party congress in 1898, the party scarcely existed in Russia.
But the exiles in Europe, inhabiting a tiny but scattered world of
their own, had not been idle. Lenin, who in Siberia had written *The
Development of Capitalism in Russia*, had escaped abroad and was
absorbed in inexhaustible Marxist polemics. With Martov he

---

[1]Incarcerated in Schlüsselburg, the death sentence passed on him there
commuted to a life term of *katorga* (convict labour), Gershuni was removed
to a prison near Irkutsk, in eastern Siberia, from which some months afterwards he effected an astonishing escape. He rejoined the party leaders in
exile and died in hospital in Switzerland in March 1908.

planned the publication of *Iskra* (*The Spark*)—'first the spark, then the conflagration'. Originally published in Leipzig, then in Munich, then in Stuttgart, the first number appeared on 1 December 1900. Edited jointly by Lenin and the three principal figures in the Liberation of Labour, all of them representatives of an older generation of Marxists—Plekhanov, P. B. Axelrod and Vera Zasulich—and smuggled into Russia, the paper was designed to create a common Social-Democratic purpose and a united party. But unity eluded so many groups and personalities, and the fateful second congress of the party was convened in an attempt to achieve it.

Since this is well-trodden historical ground, only the bare facts need be related here. Fifty-seven delegates (not all of them with voting rights), representing no fewer than twenty-five groups, were present when the congress opened in Brussels in July 1903. By the time they had left Brussels, at the request of the Belgian police, and moved to London, internal differences, deeper and more vital than was suspected at the time, had been accentuated by the habitually venomous discourtesies of Marxist debate. Almost the only ground held in common was that there were necessarily two distinct stages of revolution in Russia, a bourgeois-democratic stage and a proletarian-socialist stage. But on the theoretically correct Marxist tactics in pursuit of the first stage of revolution, on the distance in time and the difference in tactics which separated the first stage from the second, on the potentialities of the poorest peasants as a revolutionary force—on all these issues, as on the practical organization of the party within Russia, there was furious and often hair-splitting debate. In the end, the basic disagreement arose on Lenin's proposal to restrict membership of the party to a body of dedicated and professional revolutionaries. It was this disagreement which was reflected in the actual split on the composition of the editorial board of *Iskra*, which was to control the entire party apparatus and policy. In the result, the majority eventually sided with Lenin and took the historically incongruous name of Bolsheviks (*bolshintsvo*: majority); the minority, of Mensheviks (*menshintsvo*: minority). At the time the schism, though deplored by perhaps most of the delegates themselves, was not taken too tragically; it seemed largely the product of frayed nerves and bad temper. The abyss that had opened up in these refinements of Marxist scholasticism was not fully apparent until 1917.

Of far greater significance in 1903 was the political evolution of

Russian liberalism. From his official residence, the palace on the Fontanka, in St Petersburg, Plehve conducted an extensive campaign of civil espionage. He had greatly widened the ministry's normal practice of opening private correspondence. But there were limits to what could be achieved by surveillance of this sort. The nerve centre of the zemstvo movement was in Moscow, and there, from the early months of 1901, its leaders had evaded the government ban on formal conferences by holding private discussion meetings in which the hopes of achieving a constitutional form of government for Russia were canvassed in all high seriousness. Most of these meetings were held in the mansion of one of the most liberal spirits among them, Prince Peter Dolgorukov. Here, in that same year, the ranks of liberalism were reinforced by a notable convert from 'legal' Marxism, Peter Struve, the author of the Social-Democratic programme of 1898. It was Struve, a westernized Russian intellectual with all the abstract idealism of his kind, who now urged upon the zemstvo constitutionalists and their middle-class allies the advantages of publishing a liberal journal abroad. In June 1902 there appeared in Stuttgart the first issue of *Osvobozhdenie* (*Liberation*), edited by Struve in association with the historian Paul Miliukov. Like *Iskra*, it was smuggled into Russia. It advocated, as the basis of a liberal programme, the overthrow of autocracy and the establishment of a constitutional regime. As yet the precise means to be adopted in order to secure the overthrow of autocracy did not arise: this was the reef ahead which did not appear in the chart. But a crucial phase had been reached in the transformation of the zemstvo movement into an illegal political party.

For the Minister of the Interior the political pretensions of the zemstvos were a greater menace than the dialectics of the underground revolutionary factions to the system of autocracy of which he was the guardian. He had already discovered the hand of the zemstvos in agrarian disorders. In that same month of June 1902, Plehve forbade the further compilation of statistics on rural conditions in twelve zemstvos on the ground that 'politically unreliable' persons were engaged in it. 'Constant intercourse with peasants', he observed, 'gives a wide field to revolutionary propaganda.' There were, in fact, too many voluntary statisticians. The pages of *Liberation* now gave added proof that the zemstvos themselves were politically unreliable.

Yet neither the agitation of the zemstvo representatives nor the murmurings of society as a whole could be stifled by prohibitions of this kind. With growing unrest on all sides, the government adopted at least a show of conciliatoriness. The imperial manifesto of 26 February 1903, which in one and the same breath announced that the principle of the village commune was inviolable and promised to devise means of facilitating the peasant's right of leaving the commune, also touched upon other and more fundamental matters. While once more insisting that there could be no encroachment upon the autocratic prerogative, it hinted in the vaguest terms at the possibility of collaboration between the zemstvos and the central government. It offered, too, equally vague words of comfort to the religious minorities, spoke of the need for improving the lot of the Orthodox village clergy and implied that more money would be forthcoming to assist peasant purchases of land. But these small and dubious gestures of appeasement were without effect. Certainly they did nothing to halt the advance of the zemstvo 'constitutional' movement.

However restricted in their range of effort, the zemstvo liberals had been occupied with the everyday needs of the masses. In the process they had created a tradition of practical achievement in local self-government in Russia. The merging of this practical liberalism with the theoretical radicalism of a group of intellectuals, among whom some of the most influential had graduated from Marxism, was beyond question a misfortune in the Russian circumstances of the new century. Tsarist despotism, it is true, remained the great irritant, tsarist bureaucracy the great stumbling-block. As critics of the existing system, as social philosophers, as the voice of conscience, the radical intellectuals were irreplaceable. But as policy-makers they were totally without experience of government or administration. It might be true that conservative reform had reached a dead end, but what, precisely, did they mean by the abolition of autocracy in Russia? By what method did they propose to abolish it? And what consequences were likely to follow? Above all, what was to be expected from the alliance they had in mind with republican and socialist elements? In their want of realism, their failure to distinguish between ends and means, the intellectuals of Russian 'society' even at this stage were ruling out any solution of the problem of government in Russia other than the revolutionary one. And in this solution, which they envisaged as the triumph of constitutional democracy in Russia, their prospects of holding their own against the more extreme spokesmen of the illiterate masses were surely precarious.

It is arguable that in face of the recalcitrance of the autocratic regime the misfortune which overtook Russian liberalism could not have been avoided. A misfortune it remained. The original decision to form an underground Union of Liberation, comprising all opposition elements in Russia and with branches throughout the country, was taken at a small meeting of intellectuals in St Petersburg in April 1903. It was confirmed in the following July at a similarly small meeting in Switzerland attended by equal numbers of zemstvo representatives and intellectuals, the latter headed by Struve. In September, after prolonged and anxious debate, the radical zemstvo leaders burned their boats at a conference in Kharkov which addressed itself to the practical details of the organization of the Union, and in January 1904 the Union was formally established. Russian liberalism had been translated into an underground opposition party.

By that time Russia was on the eve of prodigious events in the Far East. Plehve himself had not been inactive. Witte had fallen in August, partly because of the industrial strike in the south, partly because of his opposition to the emperor's policy in the Far East, perhaps chiefly because of Plehve's adroit manoeuvres. The intellectuals abroad were beyond the latter's immediate reach, but at home he could visit his powers upon the zemstvo radicals in the assemblies and among the third element. On 17 January 1904, the entire zemstvo board of the province of Tver, notoriously liberal even before the opening of the reign, was suspended from duty. In an atmosphere of deepening opposition to the government from both society and the masses, the event passed in ominous silence. It was a day or two later that Plehve observed to the Minister of War, General Kuropatkin, soon to be appointed commander-in-chief in the Far East: 'What we need to hold Russia back from revolution is a small victorious war'.

5. War on Two Fronts

The war with Japan was in the making for at least a dozen years before 1904. Indeed, although in the last resort the causes of the war, as of so many other wars, were in part adventitious, its diplomatic origins are a principal thread in the unstable pattern of Russia's foreign relations from the 1880s. Alexander III, without too great effort on his part, had earned the rare distinction among Russian sovereigns of preserving the peace, but he had bequeathed to his successor a policy of unabashed adventure in the Far East.

Since the beginning of Nicholas's reign all had been quiet, on the whole, on the European front. The alliance with republican and democratic France held firm, though the barrier which separated monarchical absolutism from republicanism and democracy appeared to have grown higher and the *entente* was more correct than cordial. Emperor and president had exchanged visits in 1901 and 1902, but enthusiasm was conspicuously absent on the Russian side. For the rest, while Russia was still pledged to consult with Austria before recognizing any modification of the *status quo* in the Balkans, relations with Germany, Austria's ally, were wavering and ambiguous. They were maintained in the first place by correspondence between the two emperors and by three personal meetings between 1901 and 1903. In spite of the Franco-Russian alliance, there was as yet little taste in St Petersburg for anti-German policies, while the emperor William had by no means given up hope of winning Nicholas over to his own views on the balance of power in Europe. As a Russian imperialist Nicholas was in any case anti-British: his anti-British sentiments were harmonized with his anti-semitism in a classic remark, 'An Englishman is a *zhid*' (Yid). William's constant show of sympathy for Russian designs in the Far East played a leading part in his persuasions, which were further assisted, it would appear, by the frequent visits of members of the Russian imperial family to their relations in Germany.

If Russian diplomacy in Europe was cautious and even tinged with neutrality, it was precisely the opposite in the Far East.

Russian commercial appetites had been whetted by the construction of the Trans-Siberian railway, and Witte entertained large and opulent visions of an eventual Russian monopoly of Chinese trade. Enormous state funds were sunk on his initiative into projects of Far Eastern development. The return was so small, the prospect of any larger return so remote, that even the greater part of the commercial and industrial community were critical of this costly venture in economic imperialism. At the same time, however, the eyes of the empire-builders and the strategists were fixed on the vast regions beyond the Amur-Ussuri frontier. Nicholas's own feelings about Japan were of some consequence here, for on his tour of the Far East as heir to the throne he had narrowly escaped death at the hands of a member of a Japanese secret society. Under the repeated promptings of Prince Esper Ukhtomsky, who had accompanied him as guide on that occasion and who then and afterwards combined a magniloquent Russian nationalism and some knowledge of oriental art and religion with an intoxicated belief in Russia's Asiatic mission ('there are no frontiers for us in Asia'), he found it easy to entertain vast ambitions of conquest. What Russian diplomacy in China alone might not have achieved in its progress towards war with Japan was finally accomplished through the competition of all the Great Powers in their designs on the debilitated Manchu empire.

For Japan, emerging from behind her bamboo curtain, the natural bridgehead to the Asiatic mainland was Korea, which enjoyed autonomous status while owing allegiance to the Manchu emperor. Japanese pressure on Korea had been maintained since the seventies. It resulted in war with China in 1894 and China's total defeat. By the treaty of Shimonoseki in the following April, Korea was declared an independent kingdom, while China ceded to Japan not only Formosa and the Pescadore Islands but also the Liaotung peninsula, in Manchuria, with Port Arthur—a warm-water port long coveted by Russia's naval strategists—at its southern tip. Witte, who for all his extravagant notions of economic conquest foresaw clearly, and sought to avoid, the risk of war with Japan, was able to restrain the Russian demand for a slice of Chinese territory by way of compensation. Under the combined pressure of Russia, Germany and France, Japan was obliged to restore the Liaotung peninsula to China, ostensibly in return for a large indemnity. In July Russia came to China's aid by guaranteeing the loan—subscribed by French and Russian banks—necessary for that purpose. In December a Russo-Chinese bank was set up, once more mainly with French capital; its chairman was no other than Prince Ukhtomsky.

Chinese hesitations in making adequate acknowledgment of these marks of Russian favour were overcome in May 1896, when the elder statesman Li Hung-chang arrived in Moscow for the coronation. Handsomely bribed by Witte, he entered into a secret Russo-Chinese treaty of alliance against Japan and granted Ukhtomsky's bank a concession for the construction of a railway across Manchuria. By this means the Trans-Siberian line would run direct to Vladivostok, cutting off the six hundred miles of the loop of the Amur. Witte had hoped that the railway concession would be granted to the Russian government and had also proposed the construction of a branch line to the Liaotung peninsula. But in both matters he was worsted by the accomplished Li. However, the new Chinese Eastern railway, as it was called, though nominally a private venture of the Russo-Chinese bank, was in fact owned and controlled by the government in St Petersburg.

The next phase in China opened in November 1897 with the German seizure of the port of Kiaochow on the Yellow Sea as a potential naval base. In the exhibition of international greed and chicanery that followed Russia staked her claims to the Liaotung peninsula. Resistance by China was out of the question, and in March of the following year Russia secured a twenty-five years' lease of the peninsula and the right to construct a railway between Port Arthur and Harbin. In Tokyo there was an explosion of nationalist anger, since the Japanese had been defrauded of precisely those fruits of victory a couple of years earlier. Their sense of outrage was not wholly appeased by Russia's acknowledgment a few weeks later of Japan's special economic interests in Korea. At the time these were almost too self-evident to require acknowledgment. But as yet there was little that the Japanese could do. They were no more than spectators while the whole of the Manchurian railway zone was brought under the authority of the Russian Ministry of Finance—the town of Harbin became, in effect, an outpost of the Russian colonial empire—and protected by a permanent and armed Russian police force.

During these years of Far Eastern diplomacy without rein or scruple the German emperor, like Bismarck before him, had taken every opportunity to salute Russia's ambition in Asia. He had gone farther, indeed, in urging upon Nicholas Russia's mission to defend Europe from 'the yellow peril' and her destiny as a world power linking east and west. The German motives were patent to Witte, but other and more alarming influences upon the tsar were also at work. In addition to Witte himself, the Foreign Office, the War Office and the Admiralty, all of whom were inclined to urge different courses, there were the exhortations of an irresponsible and not always disinterested group of grand-ducal associates. First came the grand-duke Nicholas Alexandrovich, the emperor's uncle, and Admiral Alexey Abaza; later there was the vain and maladroit Admiral Alexeyev, reputed to be an illegitimate son of Alexander II; later still, a key figure, a former cavalry officer named Bezobrazov, who was related to Abaza, and around him an altogether shadier clique. All were fully prepared for war with Japan. The prospect, it may be said, in no way dismayed Nicholas, who shared their contempt for the Japanese *makaki* (little apes).

The Chinese Boxer rebellion against the 'foreign devils' in May 1900 gave the forward elements in Nicholas's entourage their opportunity. The extension of Chinese raids to the Chinese Eastern railway was a signal for the dispatch of strong Russian reinforcements to the railway zone and the virtual occupation of the whole of Manchuria.

In what followed the voice of the Russian government and the hand of the Russian military command were flagrantly at odds. The apprehensions of the interested foreign powers—Japan, Britain and the United States—were met by Witte and by Lamsdorf, a weak Foreign Minister whom Nicholas constantly overruled or ignored, with protestations of Russia's desire to respect the territorial integrity of China. Yet the Russian troops did not move from the cities of Manchuria and seemed determined to remain there. Tension mounted in Japan, where already a war party was in the ascendant, and anxiety grew in London and Washington, where the threatened principle of the 'open door' in China was of no little concern. The distance between Tokyo and London diminished rapidly: all through 1901 there were careful Anglo-Japanese discussions. At the same time an influential body of Japanese opinion, intent on cultivating Japan's destiny in Korea, did not as yet despair of reaching agreement with Russia through mutual recognition of their respective spheres of influence. With that object in view, towards the end of the year the Marquis Ito, the most distinguished of Japan's elder statesmen, left for St Petersburg. Though the talks progressed smoothly, nothing emerged from them; vacillating as always, Nicholas could not bring himself to strike a bargain over Manchuria at the cost of renouncing Russian designs on Korea. On 17/30 January 1902, therefore, the Anglo-Japanese treaty of alliance was formally concluded.

Diplomatic negotiations continued, however, and again the vagaries of Russian policy were beyond sober calculation. On 26 March 1902 St Petersburg formally recognized Chinese sovereignty over Manchuria and agreed to withdraw Russian troops from the country. Withdrawal was to be in three stages, at intervals of six months. The first stage of withdrawal was carried out successfully, but before the next was reached St Petersburg felt impelled to demand various guarantees. Since these, thanks to the weight of Anglo-Japanese and American support in Peking, were not forthcoming, the agreement broke down and Russian troops remained in possession.

It might still have been possible for Russia to reach agreement with the powers over Manchuria. But the critical area in the approaching conflict had shifted to the river Yalu, on the Korean frontier. While the Manchurian crisis was developing Nicholas had endorsed a singularly far-fetched and clumsy adventure sponsored by Bezobrazov. The latter had acquired an interest in an enormous timber concession on the Yalu as early as 1897. He had since succeeded in winning Nicholas's support for a melodramatic scheme of developing the concession in the emperor's personal interest. Development, in point of fact, was designed to serve as a cloak for the virtual annexation of Korea. Witte, under instructions from the emperor, reluctantly made over to the Yalu company thus formed rather more than two million roubles from the state treasury. Towards the end of 1902, on returning from a personal visit to the Far East, he gave emphatic warnings of the folly of the entire venture. The warning was coldly received by the emperor, whose ambitions now had the further approval of Plehve. Witte, indeed, was already near the end of his long term of office. In May 1903 the Yalu company, its composition and status discreetly disguised, started operations which afforded a pretext for deploying Russian troops on the frontier. The acute peril of the situation became visible that month, when Bezobrazov was appointed secretary of state for Far Eastern affairs.

Through all their dealings with Japan during the six or seven months before the outbreak of hostilities in January 1904, those in command in St Petersburg were convinced that the Japanese would not presume to attack. In Japan, on the other hand, final preparations were made in secret for a war which could not now be averted. Yet in July Tokyo made a further attempt at compromise which served also as a delaying device for the Japanese army and navy; in effect, the original proposal to live and let live in a Russian Manchuria and a Japanese Korea was repeated. No answer was received from St Petersburg for more than two months, and in the interval came the announcement from St Petersburg on 13 August that Admiral Alexeyev had been appointed viceroy in the Far East, with headquarters at Port Arthur. The appointment came as a bolt from the blue to the Foreign Minister, to Witte and indeed to every other minister except Plehve; all learned of it from the newspapers. Hard on its heels came Witte's 'resignation', which was made all the more wounding to him by his appointment to the purely honorary post of chairman of the committee of ministers. On 20 September/3 October the Russian reply was at last delivered: it evaded the issue of respective spheres of influence by once more hedging over the occupation of Manchuria and by reserving Russian rights on the Yalu. The negotiations, or the appearance of negotiations, dragged on, while on both sides military preparations continued. On 13 January 1904, after a last-minute attempt at mediation by France had failed, Tokyo once more renewed its offer to trade Russian rights in Manchuria for Japanese rights in Korea and pressed for an early reply. None had been received when on 23 January/5 February Japanese diplomatic relations with St Petersburg were broken off and formal mobilization was put in hand. No formal declaration of war had been made by Tokyo when in the small hours of 27 January/9 February Japanese torpedo-boats made a surprise attack on the Russian warships at Port Arthur.

The war was a humiliating disaster for Russia, or at least for the imperial regime, which never wholly recovered from it. From start to finish it was directed on the Russian side with the maximum of ineptitude and misfortune. Although total military defeat was avoided and by the terms of peace the country incurred what were relatively the lightest of penalties for catastrophic reverses in battle, long before the end the shock of failure had set in train violent disturbances in the mental climate of Russia. War is often a solvent of domestic crisis, as Plehve had rightly assumed, but all depends in the first place on whether it brings victory or not. In the event the ignominy of successive defeats by a despised Asiatic nation reproduced the effect of failure a half-century earlier in the Crimean War and brought a chastened government face to face with the pent-up demands of society. But now the demands were more fundamental, the challenge more formidable. It was a challenge by almost every section of the population to the autocratic power. As such, moreover, it afforded an opportunity to the handful of professional revolutionaries to rehearse their theories. Autocracy in 1905, like the monarchy in 1917, might well have foundered without the aid of war, but in both instances defeat in war made certain the internal upheaval that followed.

Not only in St Petersburg had it been taken for granted, in spite of warnings to the contrary by military and diplomatic representatives of other powers, that Japan would not take the offensive; until the last moment that comforting delusion was shared also by the new viceroy in the Far East and his staff. Yet the need for caution should have been apparent at a glance, for Russia was all too plainly ill-prepared to resist a Japanese attack. Less than a fortnight, indeed, before the Japanese opened hostilities, when it was far too late for St Petersburg to go into reverse, the Russian Minister of War, General Kuropatkin, declared at a meeting of ministers that the government must at all costs delay war for another sixteen months. Russian unpreparedness was reflected first of all in the condition of the Trans-Siberian railway. Its single track and limited rolling stock were ill-adapted to the heavy traffic of war, while there was still a gap of about a hundred miles in the section of the line running along the steep shore of Lake Baikal. In the period of grace for which Kuropatkin asked it was hoped to cut a score or more of tunnels in this section in order to complete the construction of the line. Until the line was completed it was necessary, as events proved, to employ a fleet of steamers on the lake—or, in the winter months, a light railway built on the ice—in order to bring reinforcements and supplies up to the front.

Reinforcements and supplies from European Russia were urgently necessary. The Russian army in the Far East, consisting of about a hundred and ten thousand regular troops and some thirty thousand railway troops spread out in pockets across Manchuria, was heavily outnumbered. The Japanese, who were immensely superior in artillery, already had a hundred and eighty thousand men in the field, while sea transport was in readiness for errying thirty thousand more troops to Korea immediately. At sea Russia was equally and fatally at a disadvantage. In spite of marked inferiority in the number of cruisers and a total inability to match the enemy in torpedo-boats, her strength in Chinese waters was possibly greater than the Japanese. But she had only two naval bases—Port Arthur, not yet completed, and Vladivostok, for part of the year icebound—and these a thousand miles apart. Japanese strategy, based upon establishing without delay command of the sea, was assisted beyond all expectation by the calamitous record of confusion and error of the Russian naval command. Not until the war was lost did Russia, pre-eminently a land power, realize that it had been lost at sea.

At the outset complete confidence in victory prevailed in St Petersburg. It was unaffected by the extreme nationalist view that Britain, the ally of Japan and the architect of Japan's naval power, was the real enemy, or by the knowledge that Russia had little to hope for from her ally France. There was no less confidence at Alexeyev's headquarters. But never was the conduct of a war so clumsy or so confused. Alexeyev, 'land admiral' though he was, had neither experience nor knowledge of military matters and had been obliged to cede command of the army in Manchuria to Kuropatkin. At once the problem of waging war without effective unity of command arose in an acute form. With what harmony, indeed, could viceroy and commander-in-chief be expected to work together? Alexeyev, spurred on by patrons and associates at court, was all for an immediate and general offensive. Kuropatkin, who like most of the senior generals had only contempt for the Alexeyev-Bezobrazov clique, was all for the classic Russian strategy of 1812. Anxious to husband his resources and to avoid a general engagement until he had built up his strength, he was prepared, if need be, to retreat to Harbin, or even farther. To the deputation from the St Petersburg city duma which on 27 February, on the eve of his departure for the Far East, visited him in the capital he observed only, 'Patience, patience, and once more patience, gentlemen!' It was the more realistic policy but understandably the less popular of the two. And while Alexeyev was still nominally Kuropatkin's superior there was little chance that it would be consistently carried into effect. During the whole of the critical phase of the fighting on land, indeed, the division of authority between viceroy and commander-in-chief necessitated constant appeals from both sides to the emperor and his advisers in St

Petersburg, who were themselves incapable of any sort of consistency of purpose.

In the Japanese torpedo attack on Port Arthur, where much the greater part of the Russian Far Eastern fleet, including all seven battleships, was assembled, three Russian ships were severely damaged. More significant was the brief trial of strength between the fleets on the following day, when after exchanges lasting little more than half an hour the Russian ships retired to the shelter of the harbour. During the night of 30 January/12 February, the Japanese launched a second torpedo attack, in which more Russian ships suffered damage. From this point, since the entrance to the inner harbour was now partially blocked and sown with mines, nothing stood in the way of the continuous passage of Japanese troops and supplies to the mainland. The Japanese pressed on without pause. The initial advantage secured at sea, their plan was to bring the enemy land forces to battle before the vast weight of Russian numbers could be brought to bear in Manchuria, and to sustain the campaign there by operations aimed at the investment and capture of Port Arthur.

At this as at every other stage of the war misfortune dogged the Russian fleet. The harbour had been partly cleared through the resource and energy of a newly appointed commander, Admiral Makarov, the single figure of genius in the Russian navy of the time, when on the last day of March his flagship, the *Peter and Paul*, struck a mine and blew up. Makarov and six hundred men went down, and with them the celebrated painter of battle scenes, V. V. Vereshchagin, who had gone to Port Arthur to observe the course of Russian victory at sea. On the same day another battleship, the *Victory*, was badly damaged. For the next two months the fleet was once more paralysed.

The fruits of the Japanese landings in Korea ripened steadily, but meanwhile attention was diverted to the Manchurian theatre of war. This was forbidding country, virtually roadless and almost equally treacherous in winter and summer. Both armies suffered an equal disadvantage in being supplied from distant bases. Equality stopped there. Though the Russian troops, lamentably ill-led though they were for the most part, never failed in courage or in those powers of bleak endurance which have been demanded of them during centuries of Russian war, they had nothing of the fanatical military virtue and self-abnegation of the Japanese, no

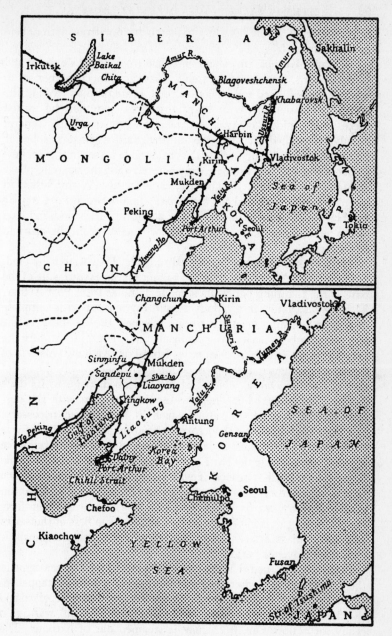

The Far Eastern theatre of war, 1904–5.

dedicated sense of Russian glory to match the idolatrous nationalism
of the enemy.

In March Kuropatkin, under pressure from both Alexeyev and
St Petersburg, established himself at Liaoyang, much farther south
than he had allowed for in his original strategic plan. While the
scattered Russian forces in Manchuria drew together, he waited
there. In the middle of April, contrary to his instructions, General
Zasulich launched an offensive on the Yalu against a superior
Japanese enemy. Flung back with considerable losses in this earliest
defeat of the war, the Russian army entered upon the opening phase
of Manchurian retreat. The penalty came swiftly. Within less than
a week the Japanese had cut the railway line between Port Arthur
and Harbin. The Russian garrison of about fifty-five thousand men
at the naval base and fortress was now isolated from the army in
Manchuria.

Promptly the Japanese proceeded to invest Port Arthur by land.
On 22 April/5 May they landed at a point on the eastern side of the
base of the Liaotung peninsula some forty miles from Port Arthur.
Three weeks later, in a bloody assault carried out with complete
disregard for life, Japanese troops stormed the defences at the
extreme southern neck of the peninsula and went on to capture the
port of Dalny, barely a dozen miles from Port Arthur. This was of
decisive importance in the prosecution of the siege. Only the use of
the harbour of Dalny, which had suffered no damage to its dock
facilities, enabled the Japanese to mount the siege with the desperate force and concentration which in fact proved necessary.
For their own part they had some reason for anxiety. There was
the prospect that sooner or later Russia would attempt to reinforce
her naval strength in the Far East with the lesser but still formidable
Baltic fleet. For that reason it was vital to Japanese maintenance
of the command of the sea to destroy the Port Arthur squadron in
good time—by sea or by land. On 25 July/7 August, therefore,
the encircled garrison of Port Arthur suffered the first of the series
of suicidal mass attacks on the fortifications which the Japanese
maintained over a period of five months.

It has been argued that the climax of the struggle at sea came in
the previous June—when, as matters turned out, nothing happened.
By that time the disabled ships at Port Arthur had been repaired and
the fleet, under its new commander, Admiral Witholf, was again
ready for action. On 10/23 June it steamed out of harbour. The
Japanese navy had meanwhile sustained considerable losses of its

own—two battleships had been sunk by mines—and the Russian squadron, it would appear, was at this moment more powerful than any force which Admiral Togo could bring to bear against it. But all through the fighting for Port Arthur, as indeed through every other phase of the war, Russian intelligence was hopelessly at fault on the strength of the enemy forces, and never more so than now. Witholf might have attempted either to give battle or to slip away under cover of darkness and join the Vladivostok squadron. Instead he did neither, but cruised aimlessly for a while and then returned to harbour. Not until 28 July/10 August did he stir in earnest, and then only on the personal instructions of the tsar, who at last was seriously alarmed by the breach which had been made in the permanent defences of Port Arthur three days earlier. On the morning of that day the force of six battleships and five cruisers moved out. In the afternoon it met disaster. The flagship, the *Tsarevich*, was disabled early in the fight and Witholf killed. In the disarray which followed all but one of the other battleships were so severely damaged that they also were only just able to regain harbour, while the surviving battleship together with most of the cruisers made their way to neutral ports and were interned. The ships of the squadron penned up within the harbour of Port Arthur never again put to sea, but waited helplessly to be reduced to wrecks by the Japanese land batteries.

During the months after the defeat on the Yalu the Russian forces had continued to fall back, giving ground stubbornly and fighting rearguard actions all the way, but always and inevitably lengthening the distance between them and the Port Arthur garrison. At Liaoyang, two hundred miles from the beleaguered fortress, the Russian positions were covered by strong fortifications. It had been Kuropatkin's intention nevertheless to draw back still farther, but Alexeyev and St Petersburg were insistent on his giving battle on the Liaoyang line in order to relieve the pressure on Port Arthur. In arduous and savage fighting during a week-long battle in August the losses on both sides were heavy, but in the result the Russians continued to withdraw northwards towards Mukden, some sixty miles away. It was an orderly retreat to a relatively favourable position on the line of the river Sha-ho, twenty miles from Mukden. There, in the last days of August, with the Trans-Siberian railway in improved order, considerable reinforcements began to arrive from Europe together with a newly formed Siberian corps. The effect was both to halt the Japanese in their forward tracks and to move Kuropatkin to a drastic reversal of his former strategy. On 28 September/11 October he launched a massive offensive on a wide sector of the river line. Some two hundred and twenty thousand Russian troops were engaged against a hundred and sixty thousand Japanese. The attack was sustained for ten days of furious fighting. At the end the Japanese had held every position and the Russians had lost thirty-two thousand men against Japanese losses of twenty thousand and had fought themselves to a standstill. Next month, in the calm of exhaustion that followed the battle, Alexeyev was recalled and Kuropatkin, though still subject to random instructions from the amateur strategists in the capital, was left in more or less full command.

One development on which extravagant Russian hopes were laid was in train at this time. Even before the Port Arthur squadron had been reduced to impotence St Petersburg was clamouring loudly for the dispatch of the Baltic fleet to the Far East. Against expert advice, Nicholas yielded. After Admiral Witholf's luckless bid for freedom, arrangements for the voyage of the Baltic fleet round the world to the Pacific were speeded up. In October it departed under Admiral Rozhdestvensky. On the night of 8/21 October occurred the famous and absurd Dogger Bank incident, when Russian ships opened fire on several Hull fishing boats in the belief that they were Japanese torpedo boats. War between Britain and Russia very nearly followed. But in the end the Russian ships were enabled to resume their voyage, though to catastrophic purpose only.

Before catastrophe overtook them, the harvest of disaster for 1904 was completed by the surrender of Port Arthur. All eyes in Russia had been turned for some time towards the garrison. Commanded by General A. M. Stoessel, perhaps the most inept of all the Russian commanders in the war, it acquitted itself throughout with great bravery. The general assault of the Japanese had opened on 7/20 August. In five days they lost fifteen thousand men. There followed a delay of several weeks, during which the Japanese began sapping operations and waited for the arrival of siege artillery, and then the assault was resumed by prolonged bombardments followed by successive waves of attack in mass formation. The Japanese losses were appalling, but the defences were being steadily reduced. On 13/26 November came the third phase of assault. During another five days Japanese losses in killed and wounded were twelve thousand. By comparison, Russian casualties in dead were trifling. But the proportion of wounded men in the garrison was rising, the warships in the harbour were wrecks and there was anxiety over both munitions and food. On 2/15 December the garrison suffered a grievous blow in the death of its ablest and most popular senior officer, General Kondratenko. From then onwards the command appears to have been divided on the merits of capitulation. Yet the actual surrender on 20 December/2 January not only came as an overwhelming shock to the entire body of Russian public opinion but provoked a section of expert military opinion in Russia to astonishment and anger. It is doubtful in the extreme whether the experts were right to be astonished. True, Japanese losses of nearly fifty-eight thousand proved to be more than double the total Russian casualties in Port Arthur, there were still between twenty and twenty-five thousand garrison troops able and willing to fight, and reserves of food and munitions were not so inadequate as had been thought. Stoessel, moreover, had acted on his sole initiative, without consulting a single senior officer in the garrison, and at the same time hopes of the eventual arrival of the Baltic fleet in the Yellow Sea still ran high. But it seems certain that the final capture of the fortress, and with it the opening of a tremendous new chapter in the history of the East, could not have been long delayed. Stupid though he was, in the hour of Russia's humiliation Stoessel was a scapegoat for the incapacity of his betters.

Five thousand miles to the west of the scene of war a singularly confused and agitated political drama was being played out in which Russian liberalism was to appear as both ally and rival of the forces of revolution.

An uneasy calm had settled on the home front in Russia after the shock of the Japanese attack on Port Arthur. Although scarcely anyone entertained the smallest doubt of eventual victory, scarcely anyone, even while patriotic sentiment had its fling, was visibly elated. The masses, indeed, because they could make nothing of the causes of the war and because in any case the war was so far away, were from the outset half indifferent as well as wholly uncomprehending. Intellectual society, even before there was any indication of military defeat in store, was itself not far removed from a mood of defeatism, although as yet it held no common ground with the openly defeatist revolutionary parties. Between the masses and intellectual society stood the main body of public opinion.

Its principal spokesmen were the zemstvo liberals. In spite of the link forged in the previous summer with the radical intelligentsia of the Liberation movement, they themselves were still moderates for the most part. But in the two or three months before the outbreak of war they had had renewed cause for doubting the benefits of moderation. After two years spent in compiling statistical abstracts and reports, the commission on the decline of the central black-earth provinces, on which the zemstvos were strongly represented, had held its final session in October 1903. Zemstvo and government representatives at once found themselves in sharp conflict over the terms of the commission's recommendations. The zemstvo representatives maintained that economic measures of amelioration were by themselves useless; little would be achieved, they argued, unless the distinctive legal status of the peasant was annulled and the powers of the land captain restricted. For themselves, moreover, they demanded the right to hold county zemstvo congresses. This, it was made clear to them, was an inadmissible 'political' demand, and the zemstvo representatives were promptly recalled by the chairman, Kokovtsev, to their duties. In the end, in the absence of agreement between the two sides, approval was given to a series of innocuous resolutions on the need for extending financial assistance to the zemstvos, developing cottage industries, improving peasant resettlement schemes, reducing redemption payments and so on. Press censorship at the time, under the direction of Plehve, was more than normally severe, and little public comment was possible on the irreconcilable differences between the two groups on the commission. But the intransigence of the government was very much in the minds of the zemstvo radicals—the 'constitutionalists'—who met briefly in Moscow in the following month.

With the country at war the liberal movement as a whole was prepared for the time being to call off its feud with the government and to put in cold storage the demand for a constitutional order of things. Even the newly formed Union of Liberation, whose first— and illegal—congress, held in St Petersburg almost at the moment of the outbreak of war and attended by a remarkable galaxy of political and intellectual talent,[1] was inclined to hold its hand in the

[1] It included, among the zemstvo radicals, Petrunkevich, Rodichev, Prince G. E. Lvov and Prince Peter Dolgorukov; among the zemstvo moderates, Prince Paul Dolgorukov, N. N. Lvov and Prince D. I. Shakhovskoy; among the moderate Narodniks, Korolenko, Annensky and Peshekhonov; among the Marxist revisionists or 'Economists', Kuskova and Bogucharsky; and, among the intellectuals proper, Struve, the economist Tugan-Baranovsky and the historian Paul Miliukov. V. A. Maklakov was not present.

war against autocracy until the war with Japan was over. But at the same time the most radical elements in the Union put their hopes in military defeat. 'The worse, the better' (*chem khuzhe tem luchshe*), they said of the war.

The truce between the forces of liberalism and the government was of brief duration. Although Plehve had thrown his weight against the proposal, the zemstvos had been granted permission to form a special association for the relief of the sick and wounded in the war and the families of the dead. Their work met with every possible obstruction from the Minister of the Interior, who in maintaining an ideal of police order drew no distinction between liberals and revolutionaries. In this clash with the zemstvo leaders, Plehve fell back upon the ministry's disciplinary powers in order to bring them to heel. The suspension of the zemstvo board of Tver, already mentioned, and the decision to set aside a zemstvo election in Vologda were followed in the middle of February by the refusal, on the grounds of 'political unreliability', to confirm the re-election of D. N. Shipov, for the fifth successive period of three years, as chairman of the Moscow provincial board. The entire zemstvo movement was up in arms. No figure in its ranks enjoyed greater respect or admiration than Shipov, who as a landowner leaned in all good faith towards the semi-socialist teaching of Henry George and who was in fact a slavophil idealist of the old type, a strong champion of zemstvo rights against the bureaucracy but also a declared opponent of the constitutionalists. Six weeks after war had broken out the liberal truce with the government was wearing thin.

Among the groups and parties to the left of the zemstvo-Liberationist movement there was no pretence even of conditional peace with the government. The Socialist-Revolutionaries were uncompromising in opposition. The war with Japan merely provided their terrorist organization with fresh incentives. Headed by Azef, with the bold, brilliant and oddly moving figure of Boris Savinkov as his principal henchman in the detailed planning of assassination, it had decided to turn from firearms to explosives. Plehve himself was marked down as the first victim. Early in 1904 an attempt on his life had miscarried; nothing, the terrorists were resolved, should now be left to chance. Hated throughout Russia, he was a subject of more than ordinary detestation among the Russian Jews and in those borderlands which were experiencing the intolerable rigours of russification—Poland, Lithuania and, most of all, Finland. From April 1903, when in face of the passive resistance of the entire population the Finnish constitution was suspended, Bobrikov had ruled as dictator. Nemesis caught up with him in June of the following year, when he was assassinated by the son of a Finnish senator named Shauman. The murderer, who committed suicide after the deed, was in no way connected with the Socialist-Revolutionaries, but it is probable that he was stimulated by their example. They, in turn, achieved their aim on the morning of 15 July, when Plehve was killed outright by a bomb hurled at his carriage while he was on the way to report to the emperor in the capital. The bomb was thrown by a young student named Egor Sazonov, who had been expelled from the university. It was characteristic of the mingled idealism and instability of Socialist-Revolutionaries of Sazonov's type that, sentenced to penal servitude for life in Siberia, he afterwards committed suicide in protest against the corporal punishment of political prisoners.

There were few regrets at the murder of Plehve; among the intelligentsia there was indeed open rejoicing, and more than that. In the interval before a successor to Plehve was designated, tension, which had mounted with the tide of defeat in the Far East, reached an acute pitch. The avenging blow aimed at the regime had been struck by the revolutionaries, but plainly 'society' could no longer hold its hand. In what circumstances, it was being asked, would the liberal war against autocracy be resumed?

At this stage the impressive and yet curiously disenchanting figure of Paul Miliukov assumes a dominant place in the fortunes of Russian liberalism. He embodies all its intellectual virtues and most of its practical failings. A fine scholar and a man of high personal integrity, somewhat cold in temperament and without charm or lustre in his relations with other men, as a politician Miliukov played an over-rehearsed part. From first to last his liberalism was derived from western thought and was in almost every respect discordant with Russian experience and tradition. In purpose and strategy Miliukov was as rigidly doctrinaire as the revolutionaries who eventually, and with good reason, defeated him. For while much of the strength of revolutionary doctrine may lie in its inflexibility, the one thing that liberalism in politics cannot accommodate is the doctrinaire temper.

Born in 1859, the son of a Moscow architect, Miliukov studied history under Vinogradoff and Kliuchevsky. In 1895 he was dis-

missed from his post at Moscow University on a charge of exercising a bad influence upon his students and was forbidden to reside
in the city. He was in exile from Moscow for the next ten years,
during which time he held a chair of history in Bulgaria, visited
France and England and lectured in the United States between
short spells in the provinces and in St Petersburg. Arrested and
imprisoned for six months in 1901 on the vaguest charges, in the
following year he was again arrested, this time because of an article
he had contributed to Struve's *Liberation* (he had originally been
offered, and had refused, the editorship). Through the intervention
of Kliuchevsky, he was released after a few months by Plehve. In a
strange interview on the occasion of his release which has something of the atmosphere of the treason trials of a later date, Plehve
appears to have offered him, whether mockingly or in earnest it is
hard to say, the Ministry of Education. With a grim humour that
comes unexpectedly from him, Miliukov declined and suggested
the Ministry of the Interior instead.

His intellectual distinction had earned for him a leading place
in the Liberation movement. More deliberately, perhaps, than any
other of the principal figures he looked for political opportunity
in the shattering reverses in the war with Japan. Clearly, since the
Liberationists were an all but negligibly tiny group in the vastness
of Russia, the tactical problem for them was where to find popular
support for their programme. It was here that Miliukov confronted
the all-embracing dilemma of the liberals. The small Russian middle
class possessed few of the instruments of power. Industry and
commerce, both of which subsisted largely on government patronage, were doubtful allies; though individual figures among them
might welcome the prospect of constitutional government in their
own interest, they would take few risks. Should the liberals therefore seek the support of the proscribed revolutionary parties? In
principle, the decision to do so had already been taken in the
previous year, when the Union of Liberation was formed. But
could they, in fact, accept Socialist-Revolutionaries and Social-
Democrats as temporary allies in the liberal cause? To Miliukov
it seemed plain that they could. An abyss, no doubt, lay between
the liberal reformers and the propagandists of a socialist revolution,
though how deep and devouring it was the former did not as yet
suspect, but for the time being were they not united at heart in
seeking to end autocracy and did not the regime lump them
together as enemies? What leaps to the mind here, amid all the

evidence of later years of how revolutions are made, is that Russian intellectuals of Miliukov's type were by no means wholly opposed to terror. Indeed, it seems to have held some psychological attraction for them. The crucial decision in the matter, at any rate, was taken by Miliukov and his associates towards the end of 1904, and the moderates—the realists in the movement—were outvoted by the intellectuals. It was this decision which more than all else clouded the prospects of Russian liberalism on the road to 1917.

Meanwhile the appointment of a new Minister of the Interior was delayed for some weeks. In August it was announced that the emperor's choice had fallen upon Prince Paul Sviatopolk-Mirsky. The rhetorical description of the latter's brief period of power as a 'political spring' points the contrast with the oppressive climate of Plehve's rule and conveys the extravagant degree of hope that followed his death. Though neither forceful nor clear-headed, Sviatopolk-Mirsky was, relatively speaking, an enlightened member of the bureaucracy. Assistant to Sipiagin at the Ministry of the Interior, he had been unwilling to serve under Plehve and had been appointed instead governor-general of the Vilna region. Perhaps because he stood fairly close to Witte Nicholas hesitated to appoint him; even then he would have preferred the servile and contemptible Sturmer, a principal agent in the dissolution of the empire a dozen years later. But in the rising temper of opposition to the government it was essential to choose a minister who would attempt to conciliate public opinion.

Sviatopolk-Mirsky's first gesture was to summon the leading officials of his ministry and impress on them the need for putting their trust in 'the forces of society'. He was, alas! as has been observed, ten years late. As an earnest of his good intentions, a manifesto of 11 August abolished the power of the cantonal courts to impose corporal punishment upon persons of peasant status. One of the last pages in the long history in Russia of class inequality before the law was turned. But there was even yet no sign that the regime was prepared to surrender any substantial principle of government. Sviatopolk-Mirsky revoked or amended various police regulations issued by his predecessor, lifted the restrictions on a number of political offenders and brought some back from exile, and pledged the government to strict 'legality', but otherwise sought the support of liberal society only on the basis of the maintenance of the 'existing order'. Plainly no concession was to be made to the demand for a constitutional order. Yet this was now the very essence of the demands of the radical opposition. There was no halfway house, Miliukov announced at this time, between autocracy and constitutionalism.

Other liberals or liberal-conservatives might doubt whether the co-operation of an elected body in the legislative task in the Russian empire necessarily implied the creation of a constitutional system. On that score Miliukov had no doubts. He had already come very near to advocating the destruction of autocracy by any means, and that final step he now proceeded to take. From 30 September until 9 October a conference of delegates of most of the radical and revolutionary groups in Russia was held in Paris. Summoned in the first instance by a left-wing Finnish group led by Konni Zilliacus, it included four representatives of the Union of Liberation—Struve, Prince Peter Dolgorukov, Bogucharsky and Miliukov (who was present under a pseudonym). There were also delegates from two Polish groups, nationalist and socialist respectively (the former headed by Roman Dmowski), together with delegates from Latvia, Georgia and Armenia. The Socialist-Revolutionaries were represented by Chernov and Azef, the latter in the guise of 'Ivan Nikolaevich'. As for the Social-Democrats, though Plekhanov had promised that they would take part in the conference, in the event neither Bolsheviks nor Mensheviks put in an appearance. The first and overriding purpose of the conference was achieved in the resolution approving the common aim of overthrowing autocracy in Russia and substituting for it 'a free democratic system on the basis of universal franchise'. The odd and instructive thing here is that Miliukov argued stubbornly for a time against 'universal' franchise; he was in favour of establishing some sort of educational qualification for the vote. But his objections were overborne by the other delegates. No less readily the conference proclaimed the right of national self-determination within the empire.

Lured by an abstract and anomalous ideal of Russian democracy and provoked by the rigidity and blindness of the autocratic power, the Liberationists thus set out upon the path of collaboration with the forces of social revolution. Since collaboration was for strictly limited ends, it did not as yet occur to them that they had gone for a ride on a tiger. There were dissenting voices among them; the most eloquent, though at this time he was heard infrequently, was the young lawyer, V. A. Maklakov, who was fully alive to the incompatibility of western modes of liberalism with the historic legacy of autocracy in Russia. Convinced of the necessity for a strictly constitutional order of government, Maklakov could not share the faith of men like Shipov in the liberalizing influence upon the bureaucracy of a consultative assembly of 'public men'. Yet at the same time he pinned his immediate hopes not so much on government at the centre as on strict 'legality' in administration and on the steady consolidation of the work of the zemstvos. In the liberal bid for revolutionary support he saw only a flight from realism. Such doubts as he possessed were swept aside, however, by the growing pressure of the radical intellectuals and by the disastrous news from the war front. Late in October the Union of Liberation drew up a programme. The zemstvos were urged to pass resolutions calling for constitutional government; special conferences and 'banquets' (the very word echoed the mood of preparation in France for the overthrow of the July monarchy under Louis-Philippe) were to be organized for the same purpose; and unions of doctors, lawyers, university teachers, other teachers, engineers and every other profession were to be formed to marshal the ranks of the opposition and swell the chorus of protest. Public meetings, it should be remembered, were unknown in Russia until this time.

Already educated society in a great many parts of the country was in uproar. Open criticism of the government had its heartening effect upon those who up to the present had held back. On 6 November a special conference of zemstvo leaders opened in Moscow with Shipov as chairman. It had not been formally sanctioned by the authorities, and the meeting-place was changed from day to day in order to guard against the possible intrusion of the police. Amid great excitement, the conference followed the lead of the Union of Liberation in a resolution composed of 'eleven theses'. The demand for full civil liberties (liberty of person, of conscience, of speech, of assembly), the democratic reform of the zemstvos and town dumas, the repeal of the state of emergency laws and the granting of a political amnesty was crowned, by a majority of nearly two to one, by the demand for a representative legislative assembly. The minority, led by Shipov, were content to ask for a representative assembly with advisory functions only. Not one of the hundred or so zemstvo leaders present approved the demand, long voiced by the revolutionary parties, for a constituent assembly. In this gathering at least hopes still lingered that reform would come 'from above', that the autocrat in person would confer a constitution upon Russia, as his grandfather had conferred liberty upon the peasants.

On 9 November, when the conference ended, its eleven-point resolution was forwarded to an incredulous and unhappy Minister of the Interior. Nicholas himself was outraged, and from this moment the dismissal of Sviatopolk-Mirsky awaited the emperor's convenience. But 'society' was enormously encouraged by this show of independence. Now joined in a common programme,[1] the zemstvo movement and the Union of Liberation set to work enthusiastically to organize 'banquets'—that is, public meetings. An orgy of speech-making on the theme of 'a constitution' marked the closing weeks of the year. The word, so long forbidden, was on everybody's lips. Zemstvos, city dumas and the new professional unions took up the refrain; the cant phrase of the hour was *Tak bolshe zhit nelzia* ('We can't go on living like this'). Even in the local assemblies of nobility formal declarations in favour of a constitutional system of government were sometimes loudly acclaimed.

Other developments were still more significant of the rising tempo of events. At many meetings, even at zemstvo meetings, the demand of a week or two earlier for a legislative assembly promptly gave way, amid the prevailing excitement, to the call for a constituent assembly. The taunts and the invective directed by the revolutionaries against 'frightened liberals'—a method of psychological attack constantly employed from this time onwards—were already beginning to tell upon them, A new 'legal' paper in St Petersburg, *Nasha Zhizn* (*Our Life*), founded with the support of one of the richest of Moscow's industrial-commercial million-aires, Savva Morozov, combined with Marxist agitation barely veiled propaganda against the war. In the middle of November mobilization orders in Poland evoked street demonstrations and clashes with the police. Towards the end of the month a crowd of several thousand people with red flags demonstrated in St Petersburg and for a few hours were in possession of the main street, the Nevsky Prospekt.

These were signs and symptoms that the government could not ignore. The clamour for constitutional reform was like a contagious fever, and beneath the clamour the police department caught the stir of more ominous preparations. A hint of alarm showed itself

[1] It is characteristic of Miliukov's cast of mind that to American audiences afterwards he described the eleven theses as 'the famous Petition of Right'.

now in the highest imperial circles. At the beginning of December Nicholas held a council attended by various members of the grand-ducal clan and high dignitaries of state. On 12 December an imperial ukase was issued on 'measures for the improvement of the state order'. Vague and non-committal in its instructions to the committee of ministers to devise appropriate schemes of reform, it marked no advance upon the imperial manifesto of June of the previous year. Rather it exacerbated the tense and expectant mood of the opposition by its warning that the zemstvos and town dumas were trespassing beyond their proper bounds and by clumsy censure of 'society' for its part in creating unrest. Anger was now joined to unrest. It would have been greater if the circumstances of the ukase had been generally known. The original recommendations drawn up for the emperor, partly on Witte's advice, by Sviatopolk-Mirsky had included a proposal that the State Council should be reconstituted to allow for the inclusion of members elected by the zemstvos. In spite of the opposition of Pobedonostsev, this recommendation had apparently been endorsed at a second imperial council. But at the last moment Nicholas had struck it out from the draft presented to him and had substituted for it the imperial warning and censure. Sviatopolk-Mirsky, who had known nothing of the decision before the ukase was published, vainly proffered his resignation.

Witte maintained ever afterwards that the day would have been saved and the revolution of 1905 averted if the original scheme had been executed promptly and in good faith. That, no doubt, is improbable, though not so improbable as may be thought; compromise in politics always appears to have been impracticable after it has been rejected. However that may be, when nine days later, on 21 December, news was received in the capital of the surrender of Port Arthur, the extreme of humiliation was added to unrest and anger. No potent ingredient was lacking now in what was undoubtedly a revolutionary situation.

One further event of the year 1904 must be recorded. On 30 July, after long years of disappointment and several false and somewhat hysterical alarms, the empress bore a son and heir to the throne of the tsars, the tsarevich Alexis.

6. The Revolutionary Year 1905

The gulf between 'society' and 'the people', which had been almost as wide as that between the ruling bureaucracy and the people, had narrowed a little, but the Liberation movement had made no genuine contact with the masses. Although loosely allied in the challenge to autocracy with some of the revolutionary groups, it had as yet no means of courting popular support. So far, indeed, there was nothing that resembled a popular political movement in Russia. Yet when the explosion came it was touched off not by any of the organized minority groups but by the masses. Or, rather, once more it was the lead given by autocracy itself which fired the mass revolt against autocracy.

At the time St Petersburg learned of the fall of Port Arthur a determined strike was in progress in the giant Putilov arms and metallurgical factory in the capital. It was an economic strike, which began in the locomotive shops, where the workers demanded a minimum wage and an eight-hour day. Within a fortnight it had embraced the entire Putilov plant and several other large industrial enterprises in St Petersburg. The rapid extension of the strike movement reflected not only the disturbed state of popular feeling but also the success, after a slow start, of a vestigial survival from the Zubatov venture of a year or two before. The strike was led by a body called the Assembly of Russian Factory and Mill Workers, which Plehve had sanctioned and provided with police funds a little while before his death and which was headed by a former associate of Zubatov, a priest and former prison chaplain named George Gapon.

Vain, unstable and seemingly power-hungry, possessed of an undoubted gift of oratory, Gapon had the mixed motives of his histrionic kind; he took sentimental colour from his surroundings and was not a police agent pure and simple. The plan of leading a mass demonstration in a petition to the tsar was not his own, but was urged upon him by elements in the workers' ranks more revolutionary in intent than himself. Gapon lent himself to it with reluctance. It is not certain whether Maxim Gorky, among others, had a hand in drawing up the petition. Magniloquent in form, this was appropriately humble in style. To the demand for ending the war, for full civil liberties, a political amnesty and a constituent assembly it added a miscellany of proposals for reform and the redress of grievances—the separation of Church and state, the introduction of universal education, the removal of all indirect taxation in favour of a graduated income tax, and so on. The apprehension in official quarters, where it was known that the day chosen for the demonstration was Sunday 9/22 January, was intelligible. A demonstration of any sort was illegal; a mass demonstration on these demagogic lines, in an atmosphere taut with menace, was an open invitation to violence. However loyal the terms of an otherwise extravagant petition, it was by no means certain that all the demonstrators would be unarmed. The strikes, moreover, were still spreading and had overtaken the printing establishments; from 7/20 January no newspapers appeared in the capital. Confused and divided in mind until the last moment, the authorities considered arresting Gapon. But he had apparently gone into hiding, and they fell back upon the routine expedient of additional security precautions. On the Saturday morning a self-appointed delegation of radical writers and public figures, who were no less apprehensive than the government of the prospect of violence, waited on Sviatopolk-Mirsky and Witte with a plea to avert at all costs a clash between the demonstrators and the security forces. An irresolute Ministry of the Interior could think of nothing more that might be done. Nicholas and the imperial family had privately removed themselves from the Winter Palace to the safety of Tsarskoe Selo, sixteen miles away, and the inclination in some official quarters to panic was countered in others by reckless thoughts of punitive action.

Early next morning, in bitter cold and amid a light fall of snow, five enormously long columns of men, women and children from the industrial suburbs of St Petersburg made their way towards the great square in front of the Winter Palace. Possibly some two hundred thousand people in all marched in procession, some carrying sacred icons and portraits of Nicholas and many singing the national anthem. As the columns approached the centre of the city their way was barred by detachments of police and troops. At all five stopping-points the procedure was uniform. There was no parleying: the processions were ordered to disperse, the front ranks, who had been marching with arms linked, did not stir, a blank volley was fired and the real shooting followed. The slaughter was on a considerable scale. The official number of casualties was a hundred and thirty dead and several hundred wounded. The true number was probably a good deal higher.[1]

The events of Bloody Sunday, as it was called, precipitated a popular outburst which had been secretly gathering strength since the earliest defeats in the war with Japan. The country was in turmoil: passions flared in demonstrations and riots; student disturbances once more reached a pitch of violence in which the universities closed down almost of themselves and remained closed; a great rash of strikes broke out in Nizhny-Novgorod, in Warsaw, in Riga, in the Caucasus and elsewhere. Abroad, where humane sentiment, shocked beyond measure, was in no way inhibited by ignorance of Russian realities, Bloody Sunday released a flood of protest. In Russia itself it did perhaps more than anything else during the whole of the reign to undermine the allegiance of the common people to the throne and to shatter the image of Nicholas as the father of his people.

While the Liberation movement resumed its hortatory appeal with renewed ardour and the strike movement continued to spread, Sviatopolk-Mirsky was released from duty and was succeeded by the colourless A. G. Bulygin, who only a fortnight before had replaced the grand-duke Sergey Alexandrovich as governor-general of Moscow. There was still no sign of a considered policy on the part of the government, though two intermediate steps were taken, one of them ridiculously inept. To reassure the emperor and to flatter his sensibilities, a small body of workers from the capital, carefully selected by the newly appointed governor-general of St Petersburg, General D. F. Trepov, was invested with the status of a delegation in order to convey the workers' devotion and loyalty to Nicholas at Tsarskoe Selo.[2] There was more substance in the appointment of a com-

---

[1]Gapon's subsequent history may be briefly recorded. Injured on the day, he took shelter in Gorky's apartment, and from a place of concealment afterwards launched a rhetorical judgment of wrath against 'Nicholas Romanov, formerly tsar and now destroyer of souls'. He then escaped abroad, where he enjoyed brief fame and glory, joined the ranks of the Socialist-Revolutionaries and proceeded to make contact once more with the police department before returning to Russia. The central committee of the Socialist-Revolutionary Party pronounced sentence of death upon him, and in March 1906 he met his end by hanging in a secluded spot across the frontier in Finland.

[2]The delegates were boycotted by their fellow workers afterwards.

mission, headed by a member of the State Council named
Shidlovsky and including delegates of both employers and labour,
to investigate 'the causes of the workers' unrest'. This, once more,
was Witte's idea. It came to nothing because tempers were rising
on both sides of industry and because the employers, who protested that the strike movement had largely been fomented by
the government itself, simultaneously resisted government
pressure upon them to increase wages by attributing the workers'
unrest to their lack of political rights.

As if to point their argument, a new wave of Socialist-Revolutionary terrorism broke in February with the murder of the
more than unpopular grand-duke Sergey Alexandrovich, an
uncle of the emperor married to a sister of the empress, who was
killed by a bomb thrown at his carriage by an expelled student
named Kaliayev. The murder appears to have touched Nicholas
on the raw. On 18 February, amid ever growing excitement and
confusion, the government bestirred itself. More precisely, on
his own initiative the emperor made three simultaneous and
somewhat contradictory moves, much to the astonishment of his
uninformed ministers. The first took the form of an imperial
manifesto, which had been drawn up in the first place by Pobedonostsev. It denounced those who violated the fundamental laws
of the Russian state and promoted disorder and treason, and
called upon 'all right-thinking persons of all classes and conditions' to rally to the support of the throne. The second, in the
form of a decree to the Senate, appeared almost to annul the
manifesto by affirming the right of every subject of the empire
to be heard by the crown and by inviting suggestions from both
individuals and institutions for 'improving the public well-being'.
In the third announcement, a rescript to Bulygin, Nicholas proclaimed at one and the same time the immutability of the autocratic principle and his decision to permit 'elected representatives
of the people to take part in the preliminary discussion of legislation'. The emperor was prepared, in short, to concede the
request for a representative assembly with consultative functions
only.

It is a universal truism that appetite grows in eating. A proposal that might have won a fair degree of support from the
moderates six months earlier now left most of them cold and made
less than no impression upon the intellectuals of the liberal
opposition. They had caught the scent of power; they were

farther than ever from being content with a consultative voice only. With every failure of the government to take up their challenge the Liberationists' programme had become increasingly libertarian and democratic. Nicholas's belated offer of a consultative assembly found them united in demanding a constituent assembly to be elected by universal, direct, equal and secret franchise. Their immediate need at this point was to make fresh converts to the liberal movement as a whole. On 23 February a congress of zemstvo constitutionalists opened in Moscow and formally approved the demand for a democratically elected constituent assembly. During the next couple of months the main part of the zemstvo movement, though anxiety at so extreme a course was not stilled, gradually swung into line with the Liberationists, themselves much strengthened at this point by the professional unions which Miliukov had taken under his wing. Government and society as yet avoided a collision: through all alarms and disturbances the opposition continued to engage in a battle of wits, while the government for its part continued to mark time. It made one unexpected concession, however, to liberal sentiment: in a decree of 17 April repealing various discriminatory laws against dissenters, of which the principal beneficiaries were the Old Believers, it came near to establishing a principle of religious toleration. But enlightenment in this form did not extend to the central issue of constitutional government.

If confidence nevertheless soared in the liberal camp, there was only confusion and uncertainty in the ranks of the extreme left. The Social-Democrats in exile had been thrown into great excitement by the events of 9 January. But they relapsed almost immediately into the devouring routine of internecine warfare and scholastic debate. At the beginning of the year, after the Mensheviks had gained possession of the central apparatus of the party, Lenin had struck out on his own with a new Bolshevik organ, *Vpered* (*Forward*). In April each faction held a separate congress; the Bolsheviks in London, the Mensheviks in Geneva. Personal rivalry and abuse spilled over in a continuing doctrinaire argument on revolutionary aims and tactics. For the Mensheviks a bourgeois revolution, which was all that could be hoped for in Russia at the moment, implied a long phase of liberal-socialist collaboration before 'objective conditions' became ripe for a socialist revolution. In the Bolshevik view, revolutionary pressure upon the bourgeois-democratic republic that would follow the overthrow of autocracy must be directed towards the dictatorship of the proletariat. In this brainspun and obsessive controversy the Social-Democrats in exile all but wore themselves out while waiting upon events in Russia.

It was the culminating disaster at sea in the half-forgotten war against Japan that ended the apparent deadlock on the political front. On land even the smallest local victory had eluded Russian arms. Except that at the beginning of 1905 railway communication with the armies in Manchuria had much improved and fourteen trains a day were carrying reinforcements and supplies along the Trans-Siberian railway in place of four at the beginning of the war, nothing had occurred to bring even the semblance of military advantage to Russia. In the last days of the old year a large-scale and audacious Cossack raid behind the Japanese lines petered out aimlessly. In the following month a Russian army under General Grippenberg was rashly committed to an out-flanking movement in the area of Sandepu, and, after a precarious initial success, was forced to retreat with heavy loss of life. The grim and prolonged battle of Mukden, one of the largest and bloodiest in history until our own period, followed. It lasted from 10/23 February until 25 February/10 March. The Russians, with more than three hundred thousand troops engaged, had a slight numerical advantage. But the skilfully mounted Japanese attack developed almost at once into a dangerous enveloping movement and the Russians were left with no alternative but to retreat. In savage and continuous fighting they withdrew to the north along the railway running to Harbin, losing day by day large numbers of prisoners together with immense quantities of stores and equipment. When on 25 February the Japanese occupied Mukden both sides had fought themselves to a standstill. The Russians had not suffered decisive defeat, but in so prolonged an ordeal under the cruellest conditions they had lost in all some ninety thousand men, a third of their total effective strength. Japanese losses were seventy thousand.

Embarrassed by constant interference from St Petersburg even more than by his own failure, Kuropatkin resigned the supreme command in favour of the elderly General Linevich, a soldier of more genuine ability. Though the fighting did not completely die down, for the rest of the war the Russian armies held more or less stationary positions north of Mukden. They were effectively building up their strength when Russia was overtaken by the climax and principal catastrophe of the war.

On the Russian side, the story of the naval disaster of Tsushima is one of crass muddle-headedness and tragic incapacity. In December 1904 Rozhdestvensky's fleet, having survived the Dogger Bank incident, had reached Madagascar. It stayed there for three months after the loss of Port Arthur while imperial circles in St Petersburg pondered matters of naval strategy. Extreme nationalist opinion, seized by the need to reinforce Rozhdestvensky at all costs, loudly urged the use of the Black Sea squadron in defiance of the international Straits convention. The plan was reluctantly turned down, but it was patriotic clamour that largely prompted the decision to send an auxiliary force of warships in the Baltic shipyards, several of them obsolete, to the Far East. On 9 May this doubtful reinforcement joined the main fleet in the China Sea, and on 14/27 May Rozhdestvensky attempted the passage through the straits of Tsushima on the direct route to Vladivostok.

Less than an hour after Admiral Togo's fleet had given battle the fate of the ill-assorted Russian force was sealed. The Japanese fire was overwhelming; almost simultaneously a dozen vessels were set alight and crippled or sunk. Within a few hours, indeed, the naval strength of Russia had been extinguished. Few of the Russian ships were a match for the Japanese in speed, and when darkness fell the Japanese torpedo-boats engaged in pursuit of the remnants of a shattered fleet. Of the eight Russian battleships four were sunk and four captured; of the twelve cruisers seven were sunk; of the nine destroyers five were sunk and one captured. A single cruiser and two destroyers were able to reach Vladivostok and a few more vessels made their way to foreign ports, but otherwise the Russian fleet had ceased to exist.[1] Japanese losses were a few destroyers.

The news of the scarcely credible disaster of Tsushima reverberated throughout Russia, reverberated more loudly even than the surrender of Port Arthur. It woke portentous echoes, too, through-

[1] Rozhdestvensky, taken prisoner by the Japanese in the engagement and released after the conclusion of the peace treaty, was eventually brought to trial along with other senior officers before a naval court-martial. The prosecution demanded the death penalty, but the demand plainly cloaked an attempt in the highest imperial quarters to find a scapegoat and Rozhdestvensky was acquitted.

out the world; the military and political potentialities of Asia, and with them the relations of east and west, were transformed overnight. Certainly the loss of the fleet stifled whatever faint belief survived among the educated Russian public that the war could be continued. True, there were still figures close to the emperor and among those in high command—they included Kuropatkin—who were all for prosecuting the war and who glimpsed victory at the end. But it was they, after all, who had already brought Russia a long way on the road to perdition. There were other and somewhat more realistic advisers in the emperor's entourage who could ignore neither the political ferment in the country nor the strategic consequences of the eclipse of Russia as a naval power.

The leaders of the radical opposition had long headed the peace party in Russia. Their opposition to the war had been fed not only by incompetent generalship and defeat but by the evidence of criminal jobbery and corruption in the Ministry of War. Yet even peace took second place in their thoughts to a democratic constitution. A week after Tsushima fourteen professional unions, all of them bent on making proposals for 'improving the public wellbeing' in response to the decree to the Senate in February, were associated in a central body, the Union of Unions, over which Miliukov presided. Almost at the same time a zemstvo congress made a final bid to establish confidence between the emperor and society. It chose a delegation of fourteen members, all of them recognized moderates and as such no longer representative of the mood of the majority, to proffer the loyalty of the zemstvos to Nicholas and to urge the necessity for a legislative assembly. Nicholas received them on 6 June, a day which marks his first meeting with the representatives of what in his own decrees and manifestos he termed society. It was, perhaps, a life-saving opportunity. He preferred to let it slip. 'My will', he announced, in courteous terms, 'to summon those persons elected by the people is unshakable.' The reference here was clearly to the Bulygin rescript. But in the same breath the emperor felt impelled to speak of 'essential Russian principles'. Here the reference to an immutable order of autocracy was no less plain.

If the temper of the zemstvo movement visibly hardened now, it was not because of this rebuff only. The delegation's gesture of loyalty had been a counter-response to a new surge of popular violence which threatened the very title of liberalism to lead in opposition to the regime. The passions aroused by Bloody Sunday had overflowed, and the mass movement of the summer of 1905 broke upon Russia in a spate of demonstrations, strikes, riots, terrorism and mutiny. The government was powerless to arrest it. General Trepov, who on 21 May had been appointed assistant Minister of the Interior, with complete control of the police, and who in effect was wholly independent of Bulygin and the virtual master of the country,[1] had no policy. Rigid in loyalty to the emperor but narrow, inconsistent and wholly lacking in judgment, he nevertheless sought to play a great part in affairs. His not very subtle cajolery of the industrial workers recoiled on him in an outburst of strikes early in June. There were fierce disturbances in Poland, particularly in Lodz, where the troops were called out and the number of killed during four days' fighting was officially given as a hundred and fifty. In Odessa there was a general strike; for a time the entire port area was in the hands of revolutionary groups. Agrarian riots broke out in several localities. On 14 June, in an episode which has been sung, pictured and poeticized to excess, the crew of the *Potemkin*, the newest battle-cruiser of the Black Sea fleet, hoisted the red flag and rose in mutiny; eleven days later they lowered the red flag in a neutral Rumanian port. On 28 June, in their campaign against government and police officials, the Socialist-Revolutionary terrorists claimed, among other victims, the military governor of Moscow, Count P. P. Shuvalov.

In this thickening atmosphere of popular revolt the zemstvo movement pressed on its attack. It now had the further support of a representative committee of the town dumas, or municipalities. At a congress attended by delegates from more than eighty cities which was held towards the end of June, the municipalities re-echoed the demand for civil liberties and a legislative assembly elected by universal franchise. A joint conference of zemstvos and municipalities, held in Moscow in defiance of the ban of both the governor-general and the chief of police, followed on 6 July. The tide of protest had by this time reached a point at which the law itself was in retreat. Instructed to attend the conference, the police duly made an incongruous appearance there. Only after

[1] On hearing of Trepov's appointment, which had been made over his head, Bulygin tendered his resignation. Nicholas declined to accept it and recalled him to the realities of government in Russia with the stern reproof that ministers did not resign but were dismissed by the tsar.

three days did they close the proceedings. Promptly the extreme wing of zemstvo constitutionalists took over at a conference of their own. It was they who were soon to give the liberal party in the making the title of Constitutional Democrats.

Another critical moment had arrived in the evolution of Russian liberalism. Where did the zemstvo leadership stand at this point in face of the revolt of the masses? All too faithfully the constitutionalists followed the lead of the intellectuals of the Union of Liberation in proclaiming their readiness to join forces with 'the broad masses' in the cause of political reform and the conquest of liberty. The declaration was made in slightly cryptic form, but the implied threat to resort to revolutionary violence was not open to doubt.

The liberal dilemma, it may be repeated, was real and for too long had appeared intractable. The most conciliatory approaches of the zemstvo leaders to the autocratic power had been met by an unvarying show of intransigence. How then could they reject the support of the 'broad masses' in the attempt to win constitutional government for Russia? There were still cautious or timid voices in their midst raised in warning against a revolutionary flood which might sweep liberalism away. But was it not reassuring that the extreme revolutionaries themselves maintained that only a bourgeois-liberal revolution was possible at this stage? In a demonstration of logic, therefore, which has so familiar a ring today, *Pas d'ennemis à gauche.* So the westernized intellectuals of the movement argued, blind to the consequences of their imminent surrender to forces more elemental than liberal and middle-class opinion.

Against this background of increasing political tension on the home front diplomatic negotiations went on for the conclusion of peace in the Far East. All the Great Powers had been sufficiently disturbed by the succession of Japanese victories before the crowning achievement at Tsushima. The German emperor entertained fears for the Russian monarchy, even for the life of the monarch. President Roosevelt felt concern at the altered balance of power in the Pacific and continued anxiety for United States interests in east Asia. Britain and France, whose common interests in face of Germany had been acknowledged in the *entente* of April 1904, sought to interpose themselves between belligerents who were their respective allies. In the event it was the German emperor who took the initiative and prompted Roosevelt's offer of mediation. The American invitation to a peace conference was issued on 26 May/8 June. Both sides accepted —the Japanese, in truth, had not dared to hope for total victory. But meanwhile hostilities did not cease; though the lull continued in Manchuria, the Japanese flung back the Russian forces in the north-eastern corner of Korea, the guns of the Japanese navy were pointed towards Vladivostok and two Japanese divisions occupied the virtually undefended and indefensible island of Sakhalin.

The peace conference opened at Portsmouth, New Hampshire, on 28 July/10 August. The principal Russian delegate was Witte, to whom Nicholas had turned at this juncture with marked reluctance. Witte acquitted himself in the negotiations with much adroitness, though the remarkably favourable terms which he was able to secure owed as much to United States support as to Japan's evident inability, through the total disruption of her economy, to continue the war at full stretch. Ironically enough, he was also aided by a show of obstinacy in Nicholas, who had set his face against the payment of an indemnity to Japan or any cession of Russian territory.

By the treaty of Portsmouth, signed on 23 August/ 5 September 1905, Russia formally acknowledged 'the paramount political, military and economic interests of Japan in Korea'. She ceded to Japan the lease of the Liaotung peninsula, including Port Arthur and the commercial port of Dalny, the stretch of the South Manchurian railway from Port Arthur to Changchun, and— Nicholas's instructions to Witte notwithstanding—the southern half of the island of Sakhalin. In addition, she made over to Japan all Russian industrial properties and rights in the Liaotung peninsula, and by this means was able to claim that she had paid no indemnity. Both powers undertook to evacuate Manchuria.

For Russia, who had first provoked war and then gone from defeat to defeat, these were by no means onerous conditions of peace. Nationalist opinion was nevertheless inflamed by them; in particular, the loss of the southern part of Sakhalin, an island which had chiefly served the uses of a penal settlement, was passionately resented. The country as a whole, however, remained unmoved.

For there were other and more immediate preoccupations nearer home. To every thinking person in Russia it was plain that a crisis in the all-consuming political struggle could not be long delayed. The claims of a united opposition had grown harsher and more peremptory and the nerve of the government was clearly shaken. On 6 August, when peace negotiations in the United States were in progress, the government had announced, in the so-called Bulygin project, the electoral procedure which was to be adopted for the consultative assembly—the State Duma —proclaimed in February. The project had taken shape during a week's conference (19-26 July) at the Peterhof palace which was attended by grand dukes, ministers and other chosen persons (the historian Kliuchevsky among them) and presided over by the emperor. It repeated over and over again the same dictum— that the principle of autocracy, in accordance with the funda- mental law of the Russian empire, was inviolable. But in labouring the principle while conceding an elected assembly the framers of the Bulygin project were upheld by the conviction that the peasantry—the *narod*—were body and soul loyal to the crown. Thus in a complex system of indirect voting in separate estates the peasantry were assured a considerable representation. In the towns, on the other hand, the vote was sharply restricted by property and other qualifications, with the result that both the industrial workers and the intellectual professions were virtually disfranchised. Elected on this basis, however, the representatives of the people would have the right of discussing all new laws and of presenting their conclusions, by way of the State Council, to the emperor.

Even this modest translation of the rescript earlier in the year horrified conservative opinion. At the other and revolutionary extreme it encountered mockery and contempt. Liberal opinion was still divided, though less divided than before. The majority were uncompromising in rejecting the Bulygin Duma and favoured a complete boycott, though curiously enough Miliukov and some of the principal zemstvo constitutionalists were not of their number; for a time they were prepared to use such a Duma as a stepping-stone to a democratically elected legislature. But Miliukov soon changed his tune, and the rest argued their case to no purpose. Vainly the moderates dwelt once more on the peculiarities of Russian historical development, vainly they insisted that Russia's masses were not prepared for the strict usages of democratic government, that the overriding liberal task was to serve the specific and practical needs of the population, that the necessary first steps in political reform in Russia mattered more than 'the ultimate rationalist goals'. As Maklakov noted much later in his memoirs, the liberal *mystique* of the summer of 1905 was such that it seemed blasphemy at the time to question 'the will of the people' as expressed in a representative assembly elected on the ridiculously styled 'four-tailed' formula (universal, direct, equal and secret franchise). Even to cast doubt on the efficacy of a constituent assembly as a means of resolving all difficulties was the mark of a reactionary.

Formulas, conferences, congresses, resolutions, programmes— in these matters the energy of the liberals, as of their allies on the left, was inexhaustible. But what, precisely, was the next step? The government was not yet so enfeebled that risks could be taken with impunity. Arrests, imprisonment, deportations and executions still served to quell the worst disturbances, while already there was talk among ministers and the higher bureaucracy of the need for presenting a united government front to the forthcoming Duma. Doubts—though not liberal doubts only— were resolved on 27 August, when to the general astonishment the government chose to establish by law full autonomy for the universities. Here was a miraculous opportunity. In the conditions promptly created or at any rate tolerated by the newly elected university authorities, in which the police were denied admittance to any part of the university buildings, free speech flourished in Russia as never before. Not university students only but men and women of every class and occupation, from factory workers and soldiers to artistic and fashionable society, crowded into the assembly and lecture halls of the universities and higher technical institutes. Every academic rostrum lent itself to the uninhibited devices of propaganda. The constitutionalists acquitted themselves bravely. But they could not easily compete with the raw and inflammatory eloquence, so much better attuned to the popular mood of pent-up expectation, of those of more extreme purpose. 'Down with autocracy!' met with roars of applause, but it was no longer sufficient to raise the roof. What kindled dormant passions was the call for an armed uprising. The St Petersburg Soviet, it was said by not a few who attended its birth, was the nurseling of university autonomy.

Tension broke at last in an empire-wide general strike. Historically, this was the earliest example in its revolutionary kind. Unpremeditated and unorganized, developing its own momentum through the mysterious contagion of mass feeling, it was an upheaval peculiarly in character with the elemental tradition of Russian revolt. It took the revolutionaries themselves almost by surprise. The cloud in the sky was no bigger than a man's hand when in the latter part of September the compositors in the printing establishments of Moscow went on strike for more pay.[1] Within three weeks a strike movement had enveloped the entire country.

The bakers had joined the printers, the workers of various factories had laid down tools, the infection had spread from Moscow to St Petersburg. In both cities there were street demonstrations and occasional clashes with the police. But all was still relatively quiet until on 7 October the Moscow railway workers on the Moscow-Kazan line stopped work. Within twenty-four hours the railway strike had reached Nizhny-Novgorod, Riazansk, Yaroslavl, Kursk, even the Urals railway system, and had also prompted a complete stoppage of the telegraph and telephone services of the central regions of Russia. On 10 October, when Kharkov and the Baltic port of Reval came out, Moscow was cut off from all normal communication and a general strike had been declared in the city. On the following day the strike engulfed the Polish city of Lodz and Smolensk and Ekaterinoslav; on the next day, Samara and Poltava; on the day after that, Minsk in White Russia and Simferopol in the Crimea. On that day also almost the last body of factory workers in St Petersburg who had not yet laid down tools did so. Undirected and irresistible, the impulse to strike swept every other consideration aside; no one was untouched, even the *corps de ballet* of the Marinsky Theatre in the capital walked out.

In the second week of that October the cities of the Russian empire presented, indeed, a strange spectacle. Not factories only but shops, schools, hospitals, law courts and local government offices had closed down. By day mobs were in possession of the streets, red flags flew from the housetops, processions formed, orators harangued. In the south, notably in Kharkov and Odessa, barricades were erected in the streets. Throughout all this the police were powerless to intervene—some indeed had gone into hiding—while there were constant scuffles and skirmishes with bodies of security troops. At night the cities were in darkness,

[1] They demanded a rate of two or three farthings more for setting every thousand words, with punctuation marks to be counted in future as words.

the streets deserted and silent; there was neither gas nor electricity, in some areas no water. Newspapers had ceased to appear.[1] Amid the sound and the fury of this revolt of the masses the mechanism of urban life in Russia had come to a complete halt.

At the highest levels of government panic was now undisguised. It was no longer possible to be blind to the threat the general strike offered to the fabric of state; no longer possible to doubt, since the radical opposition was now firmly united with the revolutionary parties, the necessity for political concessions. The preservation of the dynasty was clearly at stake. Once more, and for the last and most critical time, Nicholas turned to Witte. The latter, who for his services at the peace negotiations with Japan had been awarded the title of count, had returned to Russia (by way of France and Germany) on 15 September, at the start of the strike movement. Distasteful though he was to the emperor, Witte had two special qualifications for the task in hand: he had friends in the liberal camp and no little influence among the financial circles in the west to which Russia would of necessity soon be obliged to turn. In the extremity of the government's need, moreover, even in the eyes of a large section of the highly-placed bureaucracy he wore the likeness of a man of destiny. From Peterhof, therefore, which was now wholly cut off from St Petersburg except by the short sea voyage, Nicholas addressed himself with some urgency to Witte.

It seems certain that Witte originally under-estimated the full extent of the responsibility he was to assume. Though both the Union of Unions and various underground groups among the workers had proffered guidance, most of the strikes had originated in an entirely incoherent temper of revolt. Some strikes had the active support of the employers, for whom political freedom was an obligatory condition of economic enterprise and who in pursuit of a share in any constitutional regime that might emerge kept their workers on half-pay, sometimes on full pay. In the provinces in particular the strikers were all too often at a loss to formulate specific demands. But their aims soon crystallized. On 11 October, two days after Witte had virtually assumed charge again, Moscow leaders of the union of railway workers presented him with their demands. They were on normal enough lines: full civil rights, an eight-hour day, the repeal of the state of

[1] By 14 October only a single newspaper continued to appear in the whole of Russia—a Kiev daily.

emergency laws—and a constituent assembly. But almost immediately, in the accelerating tempo of revolutionary events, these
were stiffened by demands of an altogether more challenging
character. The railway workers' conditions for returning to
work consisted of nothing less than the proclamation of a democratic republic, the disarming of the troops and police and the
provision of arms for the forces of labour. To this programme
the professional unions, the vital link in the alliance of the
liberals with the left, gave their full support. Retribution was
indeed following hard on the heels of the tactics of Russian
liberalism.

On 13 October, when the strike in St Petersburg was for all
practical purposes complete, the St Petersburg Soviet made its
first appearance on the revolutionary scene. A body of elected
representatives of the workers of the capital, its organization
hastily improvised to give authoritative voice and leadership to
the masses, it was not the earliest of the numerous soviets which
came into existence at this time.[1] Some forty delegates, each
supposedly representing five hundred workers, were present at
the first meeting. Several belonged to the Menshevik faction of the
Social-Democratic Party, others were in sympathy with the
Mensheviks, but the majority were without party ties or connexions of any sort. The original chairman, a Menshevik, made
way a day or two later for another Menshevik, the lawyer George
Nosar, who hid behind the adopted name of Khrustalev. There
was no Bolshevik among the delegates; for some time after the
soviet had been formed the small Bolshevik group in St Petersburg
preferred to ignore it.[2] Yet from the start the soviets were the
principal formative influence in an otherwise inchoate mass movement of revolt in the cities. In the background from which they
had sprung stirred all the discontents, the insurgent passions, the
confused and desperate hopes which the railway workers had
translated into the demand for a democratic republic.

On the same day as the St Petersburg Soviet was born Nicholas
from his retreat at Peterhof sent a message to Witte formally
charging him with the task of co-ordinating the work of the various

[1] Soviet means no more than 'council'. The earliest soviet appears to have
been that formed in the textile town of Ivanovo-Voznesensk.

[2] Lenin, who at last had been unable to contain himself in exile, was still in
Stockholm, impatiently awaiting a forged passport that would enable him to
cross into Finland.

ministries in the restoration of order. Witte had not been idle in the meantime. His mind was made up. Coldly empirical in a crisis (and always inclined to arrogance because of his difference in this respect from the rest of the tsar's advisers), he had concluded that there was no choice but to concede the demand for a constitution. His was a politic decision only. He had never believed that parliamentary government or representative institutions in general were to be desired in the vast, disparate and undeveloped Russian empire. An absolutist regime, it seemed to him, could best guarantee order and progress in Russia. But in his celebrated memorandum on the zemstvos, in which he argued that they were incompatible with autocracy, he had left no room for doubt that autocracy could survive only by being enlightened. And though he erred lamentably in discovering, or in pretending to discover, the marks of enlightenment in Alexander III, beyond all doubt it was enlightenment that Nicholas's personal absolutism had so signally lacked. Witte thus saw no way out of the impasse created by the emperor's own weakness and deficiencies other than compromise with the liberal claims. Only by conceding the form and possibly the substance of a constitutional monarchy could the monarchy, in his view, be preserved.

In this conviction he had already instructed a permanent assistant named Gurliand to draw up a memorandum presenting in a favourable light the more moderate aspect of the liberal programme. It had been submitted to the emperor on 10 October with a covering report in which Witte dutifully posed the alternative of 'resisting the current'. For the next few days, while the country was in turmoil and its affairs still paralysed, there was much coming and going by steamer between St Petersburg and Peterhof. The situation in the capital, as in other parts of the country, was steadily becoming uglier; the demonstrations were growing larger, the revolutionary slogans louder, the clashes with police or troops more frequent. On 14 October General Trepov issued his famous provocative instruction to the troops: 'Do not spare the cartridges'. On the following day Witte was again received in audience at Peterhof. At this meeting he urged more bluntly than before the choice between 'a constitution and a military dictatorship'. He was prepared, he said, to assume responsibility for a fully co-ordinated government under a constitutional monarchy, but he could take no part in a government established under the protection of a military dictatorship.

Nicholas, who did not despair of a military dictatorship as a temporary solution, still hesitated. He requested Goremykin to produce an alternative plan and at the same time cast the grand-duke Nicholas Nikolaevich, his uncle, for the role of military dictator. The latter begged to be excused; the story—imperfectly authenticated—is that he produced a revolver and threatened to shoot himself if the emperor insisted. Witte for his part refused to endorse Goremykin's alternative scheme, which proved to be a watered-down version of his own proposals. Nicholas was left with no further choice.

What in the last resort forced the hand of both the emperor and the ruling bureaucracy was not the general strike, not the St Petersburg Soviet, not the rising revolutionary temper in the towns, but the imminent danger of peasant revolt throughout the length and breadth of Russia. The ghost of Pugachev walked again. It was necessary at all costs to lay that familiar and formidable ghost; for without the tacit support of the peasantry the dynasty was indeed lost. Already the countryside was lit by the flames of anarchy in a dozen provinces. Earlier in the year, in February and March, and again in the early summer, there had been serious agrarian disturbances in the central regions, but disorder had gradually died down. The congress of peasant delegates which had met in Moscow in May, and which brought to birth two months later a Peasants' Union for the whole of Russia, was not itself a peasant body; the delegates, for the most part Socialist-Revolutionaries, all belonged to the urban intelligentsia, and the Peasants' Union was designed by them as an organized counterpart to the Union of Unions. But in October it was undoubtedly the peasants themselves who had resorted to arson and murder in the countryside. The worst and most horrifying excesses were still to come, but even at this early stage the 'red cock' was crowing lustily on the roofs of burning manor houses in Samara and Saratov, in Tambov and Chernigov, and throughout the Baltic provinces. If the fever raging in the industrial centres spread with a similar intensity to the whole of the countryside, nothing would be left of either the autocratic state or the private estates of Russia. Surrender was the only course, indeed, because for the first time the revolt of the industrial proletariat coincided with the greater menace of revolt of the peasant masses.

The imperial manifesto of 17/30 October 1905, which transformed Russia, however imperfectly, into a constitutional monarchy, was essentially Witte's work. He had urged strongly that its provisions should be incorporated in a 'most loyal report' by the new head of government (himself, that is), not in a manifesto; if the tsar subsequently changed his mind, responsibility would thus fall not on him but on the chief minister. But Nicholas, with the sense of his absolute prerogative always in mind and the example of Alexander II in the decree of emancipation before him, chose otherwise. He may well have repented afterwards, not only in later years when he planned to disembarrass himself of the State Duma, but immediately after the event, when in letters to his mother he expressed his profound shame and mortification at the compulsion laid upon him.

The manifesto conferred upon the population of Russia all essential civil liberties—freedom from arbitrary arrest and imprisonment without trial, together with liberty of conscience, of speech, of meeting and of association. It promised to extend the franchise in the forthcoming elections to the State Duma to the classes which had been deprived of it in the Bulygin project of August and to entrust further measures of enfranchisement to the Duma. It established 'the immutable principle that no law may come into force without the approval of the State Duma', which was also vested with rights of control over the authorities appointed by the crown. Simultaneously with the manifesto a report by Witte, duly sanctioned by the emperor, enlarged upon the scope of these provisions. According to V. N. Kokovtsev, Minister of Finance at the time and eventually chief minister, neither manifesto nor report had been shown to other members of the government. Two days later, on 19 October, the committee of ministers was formally translated into the council of ministers and by imperial rescript Witte was designated chairman.

The October manifesto, as it was called, swept with a great stir through the ramshackle structure of Russian society. It was a gale blowing in all directions, a gale which had long been awaited but had nevertheless sprung up suddenly. For much the larger part of the body of the educated or half-educated who made up Russian public opinion it brought an intoxicating breath of liberty, an unconfined joy in the promise of a newer and cleaner world. In St Petersburg and elsewhere there were fresh demonstrations in which men wept in hope and relief and strangers kissed in the streets. The gates of the prison-house, it seemed, were open and the people of Russia might now walk in freedom.

This exhilarating sense of release was not felt everywhere. It was a bleak and bitter wind that blew about the heads of those monarchist and nationalist elements for whom the dogma of 'unlimited' autocracy was the stuff of Russian patriotism. Their response to the manifesto was similarly instantaneous. While the streets overflowed with jubilant crowds and rang with revolutionary oratory, rival processions were formed of men and women carrying the portrait of the emperor and singing the national anthem. The police played their part in organizing these counter-demonstrations, but in some degree they reflected a genuine and angry protest by a large body of people, among them numerous petty tradesmen, who had lost their livelihood or suffered economic injury through the general strike. In recurring episodes of street violence turbid passions were let loose on both sides and political brawls often shaded off into gang warfare. Less spontaneous than these street clashes were the pogroms launched against the Jews throughout and even beyond the pale. There had been numerous minor pogroms in the previous spring and summer, but this was a methodical campaign of murder and robbery directly instigated by local monarchist groups or even by the police authorities. For a week after the promulgation of the manifesto anti-Jewish riots raged unchecked. They were largely the work of Black Hundred[1] gangs, which usually contained a strong criminal element.

What of the liberal movement during these days? The constitutionalists had won a famous victory: so much was beyond doubt. There was rejoicing in their ranks, as there could scarcely fail to be, but there was also active suspicion. How complete was their triumph? Between the promised State Duma and the regime of parliamentary democracy to which they aspired lay a no-man's-land strewn with risk and uncertainty. Had the autocratic power surrendered in good faith? Or was the manifesto a manoeuvre only? Never was the liberal opposition so divided in spirit as in this moment of victory. It represented, after all, a coalition for making war on the tsar's government, and whether in war or peace coalitions rarely survive the emergency which has called them into existence. Contrary to all appearances, indeed, the amorphous liberal movement had already dissipated much of

[1]The name goes back to the guilds of petty tradesmen in medieval Muscovy.

its potential strength with the formation of the Constitutional Democratic Party, or Party of the People's Freedom (*Narodnaya Svoboda*), in which were united the Union of Liberation, the zemstvo constitutionalists and the Union of Unions.

The circumstances of the congress at which the party was founded are perhaps characteristic of the fate and fortune of Russian liberalism. Opening in Moscow on 12 October, when the revolutionary strikes were at their height, the congress was greatly weakened by the absence, through the breakdown of communications, of the entire body of delegates from St Petersburg. It closed on 17 October, on the very day that the delegates, only vaguely forewarned by rumour, learned the terms of the manifesto. And it was accompanied by a formal split in the liberal ranks, with two wings of left-wing dissidents rejecting the programme of the new party and a strong right wing hesitating to commit itself and passing soon afterwards into opposition as a separate party. Miliukov, the appointed leader, nevertheless spoke for the organized body of liberal opinion as a whole when on the evening of 17 October he expressed strong suspicion of the purposes of the manifesto and declared that the war against the government would be continued. 'Nothing', he announced, 'has changed, the struggle goes on.'

If on 17 October the main body of liberals were still resolved to fight for the strict letter of a parliamentary regime, the revolutionaries on their left were still dedicated to the cause of revolution. Manifesto or no manifesto, the temper of the St Petersburg Soviet was uncompromisingly warlike. Not for the Soviet of Workers' Deputies, as it styled itself, the empty reward of a sham parliament. It had grown considerably in numbers, and both its membership and the membership of the executive committee elected on that same day were now largely at the disposal of the underground Mensheviks and Socialist-Revolutionaries. The supreme orator in their midst, a rhetorician of genius, was Trotsky, who had secretly returned to Russia early in the year and had only just made his appearance in St Petersburg. It was Trotsky, still reputedly half-Menshevik, who imposed upon the soviet his audacious vision of an all but immediate transition to the proletarian revolution. On that same day, 17 October, appeared the first of the somewhat irregular issues of *Izvestia* (*News*), the official organ of the St Petersburg Soviet. It was in *Izvestia* that Trotsky threw out his challenge to the forces of government behind the manifesto. In the brilliantly evocative and virulent phrases which make him one of the greatest of political journalists and pamphleteers, he wrote: 'Witte has come, but there is still Trepov. . . . The proletariat knows what it wants and what it does not want. It wants neither the police thug Trepov nor the liberal financial shark Witte, neither the wolf's snout nor the fox's tail. It spurns the *nagaika* [police whip] wrapped in the parchment of a constitution.'

This, more than liberal suspicion, was the challenge Witte had still to meet. It did not stand alone. The whole of Russia was in ferment. There was nothing in the manifesto to appease the passions of the oppressed nationalities of the empire. Its effect was rather to exacerbate them. It was the divine right of autocracy which had held the empire together, the virtual surrender of the unifying principle of autocracy which now intensified the demand throughout the borderlands for autonomy or for complete independence. In Finland the general strike grew imperceptibly into a nationalist movement so menacing that the Russian governor-general fled from Helsingfors to the protection of a Russian warship in harbour. Within a day or two it was left to St Petersburg to rescind almost all the restrictions of earlier years upon Finnish constitutional rights. The demand for autonomy echoed loudly in the Baltic provinces, in the Ukraine, in the Caucasus, even among the peoples of central Asia and north-eastern Siberia. Only in Poland, where since the early summer rival nationalist and revolutionary movements had fought together for Polish freedom, did the authorities resort to unqualified repression, proclaiming martial law towards the end of October.

In his attempt to ride the storm Witte was reduced to a more precarious and helpless condition than he had bargained for. He was hampered in the first place by the guarantee of civil liberties which he himself had endorsed. Though as yet these liberties lacked all substance in law, much of the existing law was a dead letter, ostentatiously derided by the revolutionary intelligentsia and by the mob. Not law but the extreme of revolutionary licence prevailed in the press. The police were powerless, the official agencies of censorship equally so; their place was usurped, indeed, to wholly contrary purpose, by the printers' union, which in practice exercised a right of veto over all matter for publication. In all that concerned the restoration of order Witte found himself checked and paralysed by the risks of coercion. As chairman of the newly formed council of ministers he could only temporize. On 21 October, when both the St Petersburg Soviet and the liberal leaders were pressing hard for a political amnesty, he met them somewhat short of halfway by revoking numerous sentences of political exile, thus restoring a number of notable figures to the active leadership of the revolutionaries. On the following day the emperor parted from Pobedonostsev, for so long his most intimate adviser, without any apparent regret or sense of loss. Witte also, in spite of his professed admiration for Pobedonostsev, bore the parting with equanimity. Together with Pobedonostsev most of the other ministers and heads of departments were dismissed. On 27 October Witte set up a Ministry of Industry and Trade. Not one of these moves lessened in any way the disastrous consequences of his inability to restore order. As Maklakov was to observe long afterwards, 'society attacked Witte for his inactivity against reaction, reaction for his inactivity against revolution'.

The diverse forces of reaction in the country had not waited long to form a united front. Upper-class and ecclesiastical elements had been loosely organized as early as 1900 in the Russian Assembly (*Russkoe Sobranie*), but all elements were drawn together in the Union of the Russian People (*Soyuz Russkago Naroda*), founded towards the end of October. It was headed by Alexander Dubrovin, a physician of some ability but as a person given to pathological hatreds and prejudice. The principal target of his Great Russian nationalism was the Jews; his secondary targets, the Poles and the Finns. This was patriotism after the heart of many notable figures at court and among the higher bureaucracy, and very much to the taste of the emperor himself. Nicholas was soon to shock even an element of conservative opinion, and to enrage Witte in particular, by his open declaration of support for the Union of the Russian People, but even before then Dubrovin was able to count upon a lavish supply of funds. Branches of the union, in which the local clergy were often active, were established throughout the country to promote monarchist propaganda, and the outrages of the Black Hundred gangs which they stimulated met with the unabashed approval of the sponsors of the movement. Witte himself had not long to wait before two attempts were made on his life.

The knottiest part of his immediate problem, however, was the St Petersburg Soviet. On 21 October it had reluctantly called off the general strike in the capital (Moscow and other cities followed suit a few days later) in face of the changed attitude of the employers after the publication of the manifesto and the bewildered or sullen drift back to work by hungry men. But it had yielded no ground over the demand for a democratic republic. Its leaders had no intention of allowing the strike weapon to rust, and meanwhile there were secret if necessarily small-scale preparations in the industrial suburbs for an armed uprising. The socialist-liberal alliance, in spite of Miliukov's declaration that nothing had changed, had all but broken up. Trotsky heaped scorn upon the liberals for their cowardice, protesting that they were more afraid of revolution than of the tsar, but he did not yet despair of them. For the St Petersburg Soviet had astonishingly maintained itself as in some sort a rival authority to the government. It was to the soviet that the working population turned for advice or aid in the chaotic conditions in the capital; it was the soviet which gave instructions in the workers' quarters. Its executive committee negotiated directly with Witte on problems of transport and food supplies. The government's orders to the postal and tele-graph workers could be issued only through the soviet. Even the city duma was obliged to carry out the instructions of the soviet, most conspicuously in allocating funds for the relief of the strikers' families.

For the time being at least the government could not but acquiesce. But so paralysing a form of dual power in the capital could not continue indefinitely. Witte bided his time, convinced that the revolutionary impulse of the masses· must flag. And indeed their leaders were soon hard pressed to discover means of satisfying the hopes and rewarding the sacrifices of the industrial workers. On 29 October the soviet announced the introduction of an eight-hour working day. The employers promptly retorted with a series of lock-outs. Three days later the soviet declared a second general strike. But the spirit of the factory workers was visibly failing and their response was all too noticeably incomplete. Three days later still the second general strike was called off. The campaign for an eight-hour day was abandoned soon afterwards.

There was still no thought of surrender, however, on the part of the handful of tireless and determined men in command. By the middle of November the number of workers' deputies had swelled to nearly six hundred, and among the executive com-mittee of about thirty there were now three representatives from each of the three main revolutionary factions—Mensheviks, Bolsheviks, Socialist-Revolutionaries.[1]

They were heartened in their hopes of insurrection by renewed outbursts of mutiny in the armed forces. Not merely in St Petersburg and Moscow but in half a dozen garrison areas and naval bases disaffection had once again blazed into something more. On 26 October the sailors in the naval barracks at Kronstadt had mutinied and for two days were in virtual control of the fortress. On 11 November there were disorders among both army and navy units in Sevastopol which culminated two days later in the resounding episode of the cruiser *Ochakov*. Taken over by a retired naval officer, Lieutenant Schmidt, the *Ochakov* raised the red flag in a dramatic gesture of 'non-recognition' of the government and hauled it down only after the ship had been set on fire by salvos from the coastal batteries.[2] More heartening still were the rumours of the widespread rioting of the troops in the Far East awaiting their return to Russia and stretched out in dangerous confusion, amid contradictory orders from their own officers and from newly formed strike committees, along the overloaded Trans-Siberian railway.

Even now the government as a whole still delayed and temporized, exhibiting in the process an almost freakish inconsistency. On 24 November, for instance, it issued 'provisional' rules for the conduct of the press which for all practical purposes did away with the censorship. Yet Witte himself was more nearly in control of the situation. Two days later the police arrested Khrustalev-Nosar, chairman of the St Petersburg Soviet. In his place the soviet immediately elected a ruling body of three (among whom was Trotsky) and boldly announced that 'preparations continue for an armed uprising'. On 2 December it issued a manifesto calling upon the nation not only to refuse payment of taxes but also to withdraw all bank and savings' bank deposits and to demand payment in gold. Designed to prevent the government from raising a foreign loan with which to combat the revolution more successfully, the manifesto had the support of the Socialist-Revolutionaries, both Social-Democratic factions, the Peasants' Union and the Polish Socialist Party.

[1]Lenin, who made an appearance in St Petersburg at this time, was an active but still hidden figure behind the deliberations of the soviet.

[2]Lieutenant Schmidt, who holds a dubiously authentic place in the Bolshevik revolutionary myth, was arrested and shot.

The government, however, had at long last prepared itself. On the following day, 3 December, the building in which the St Petersburg Soviet had its headquarters (it had taken over the premises of the highly reputable Free Economic Society) was surrounded by troops. Some two hundred and seventy deputies, including Trotsky, were present at the time. All were arrested.[1] At the same time the offices of the eight papers in the capital which had published the manifesto were occupied by the police. Whatever defiance the workers of St Petersburg might still offer, the strength of the soviet was broken, its remarkable period of power over.

For the Ministry of the Interior the duel between the government and popular authority in St Petersburg had not been the crucial issue. Formidable though the soviet was, it was overshadowed by the growing lawlessness and violence of the peasantry. The October manifesto had had little or no effect in the villages of Russia. It had done nothing to end peasant disturbances. Immediately after it was issued, indeed, agrarian risings on the Volga and in the western regions, above all in the Baltic provinces, where Russian peasants felt implacable hatred for their German masters, had reached a pitch of savagery more extreme than any that had attended agrarian unrest since the emancipation.

The government had no choice but to attempt to conciliate the peasantry also. An imperial manifesto published on 3 November called on the peasants to end all disorders and pledged the government to measures of relief 'without injustice to the other landowners'. At the same time, as an earnest of the resolve to satisfy the 'urgent needs' of the peasantry, redemption payments for 1906 were reduced by half and formally abolished as from 1 January 1907.[2] The disorders did not cease. Within a few days they reached a fearful climax of murder and destruction. In one province after another the government declared a state of emergency and directed punitive expeditions to the affected areas.

At precisely this time, 6-12 November, the Socialist-Revolutionary intellectuals of the Peasants' Union gathered once more in Moscow, openly this time and with a sprinkling of genuine

[1]Fifty-two were brought before a civil court in September of the following year on charges of revolutionary conspiracy. The trial, conducted with exemplary legality, lasted ten weeks. Trotsky, with fourteen others, was sentenced to exile in Siberia for life. He escaped *en route*.

[2]Certain small categories of peasants were excluded from the operation of this decree.

peasants in their midst. Under the pressure of recent events, they had modified their views on the strategy by which socialism in peasant Russia was to be won. They rejected the October manifesto and repeated the demand for a constituent assembly. The campaign of terrorism was temporarily called off, though the suspension (which was not everywhere observed) was bitterly condemned by a sizable minority led by Savinkov. In general, the emotional aspect of Narodnik doctrine was now abandoned for a more coherent revolutionary policy and a specific programme of mass action.

The policy and the programme were largely the work of Victor Chernov, a remarkable figure in many ways though without the obdurate force of personality of other revolutionary leaders of the period. Born in 1873, the grandson of a serf—his father, like Lenin's father, was an official who had been ennobled—Chernov inherited the insurgent peasant tradition of the Volga black-earth lands. His feeling for the peasantry as the living and suffering body of Russia was unaffectedly deep. Since the summer months of 1905 (he had left Russia four years before) he had recognized both the futility of mere individual terror and the need to divert Socialist-Revolutionary propaganda from the urban intelligentsia to the village. His socialist ideas had always owed a good deal to Marxism, though with his conception of the village commune as a potentially socialist form of organization went a sincere and exalted vision of the free development of human personality. But he was always a theorist, and a somewhat woolly theorist at that. The history of the Russian revolution might well have been different if Chernov had been able to interpret the ideals of agrarian socialism with more flexibility and force in 1905. For although the peasantry throughout European Russia still maintained their right as a class to possess all the cultivable land and thus continued to demand the partition of the private estates, this was not, in point of fact, the basic cause of the agrarian riots of 1905. In the Volga provinces in particular, the peasants' immediate and severely practical demands were for reduced rents on the land they temporarily leased from the local squires and for the exclusion of rich tenants in favour of the poor and the land-hungry; the alienation of all private land came afterwards. It may be observed in passing that by this time nearly a quarter of the total amount of privately owned land in European Russia was in peasant hands.

Under Chernov's guidance, the second congress of the Peasants'
Union proclaimed its solidarity with the industrial proletariat
and demanded the transfer of all land to the peasants within a
system of state ownership and the early summoning of a constituent assembly. These demands were to be furthered by,
among other things, refusal of conscript military service and
peasant strikes on the large landed estates. The government's
response to a threat of this character, which touched the great
landowning aristocracy at its most vulnerable, was not long
delayed. On 14 November, nearly three weeks before it came to
grips with the St Petersburg Soviet, all the members of the
central body of the Peasants' Union were arrested. The prospect
that the peasantry might join forces with the proletariat in
organized revolt was thus removed at a blow.

After the arrest of the St Petersburg Soviet nothing remained
to be done except to stamp out the embers of revolt among the
industrial workers. Or so by this time the revived forces of
authority assumed. This was to leave out of account the valedictory
blaze of revolution in Moscow. On 6 December, a newly improvised St Petersburg Soviet, no more than a faint copy of the
original, had issued a summons to a third general strike. The
summons wakened scarcely an echo, except in one city in the
south and, more loudly, in Moscow. There, on the prompting of
Lenin, who was still convinced of the imminence of proletarian
victory, the last and sacrificial scene of the revolution of 1905 was
played out. Hastily the decision was taken to launch an armed
uprising in the old capital on 9 December. There was never the
faintest prospect of success. The temper of the garrison troops,
it is true, was so unreliable that the authorities hesitated to use
them, while official requests for reinforcements from St Petersburg had met with the plea that no troops could be withdrawn
from the task of protecting the lives of the emperor and the
imperial family. But neither the garrison nor the population of
Moscow was in the mood to support a revolutionary insurrection.
Confronted by so much evidence of popular apathy, the insurgents
adopted the tactics of 'partisan' warfare. Over several days there
were sharp spells of guerilla fighting, accompanied by much
desultory shooting, until on 15 December the Semenovsky
regiment of Guards arrived in response to the urgent representations of the new governor-general of Moscow, Admiral F. V.

Dubasov. The regiment made light work of crushing resistance in the central parts of the city, shooting all who were found in possession of arms. The last insurgent stronghold, the workers' quarter of Presnia, high up over the Moscow river, surrendered after a sustained artillery bombardment.

The Moscow insurrection of December, in which perhaps no more than two thousand men on the rebel side were actively engaged and which may have cost in all half as many lives, was largely but not entirely a Bolshevik occasion. Several hundred Socialist-Revolutionaries contributed their quota of heroic folly, and it was one of their number who blew up the building of the Moscow *Okhrana* (security police). The insurrection produced in later years an inflated crop of myths and legends and was eventually celebrated by Lenin in a melodramatic misreading of history as 'the general rehearsal' for the Bolshevik seizure of power in 1917. The motives and forces which had animated it lingered after defeat, but the rising was altogether too reckless to deserve that title. Plekhanov, the founder and teacher of the Russian Social-Democratic Party, who had already begun to discover in Lenin a limitless want of scruple in the pursuit of power, was nearer the mark in describing it as criminally premature.

Though the immutable principle of autocracy had gone the way of other immutable principles, the monarchy had so far survived the events of the revolutionary year 1905. Its willingness to work the new and qualified constitutional system had still to be tested. Meanwhile the face of society had barely changed: the ruling bureaucracy had recovered its nerve and its authority, the greater part of the educated classes had drawn even farther away from the masses, the scope of local self-government remained as restricted as before and no real limits had been set to the arbitrary power of the police. For the liberals, doubtful of what they had gained and compromised by the alliance with the defeated forces of revolution, the future was ambiguous and uncertain. Yet even now they had not exhausted their capacity for error.

7. *A Demi-Semi-Constitutional Monarchy*

The most dangerous moment in the life of a bad government, said Tocqueville, is that in which it begins to change for the better. That was undoubtedly the experience of the absolutist-bureaucratic government of Russia at the close of 1905. If the extreme of danger had apparently passed, all the difficulties of making a change for the better remained. Russia was still boundlessly vast, racially and culturally diverse, the masses still clamant. Where in the absence of the divine right of absolutism was the vivifying new principle of unity? Where in a Russia ridden by armies of despotic officialdom were the forces of legality and consent which would be required to translate the October manifesto into a democratic system of government?

If the liberals had some cause to suspect that what the country was being offered was only the illusion of representative government, nothing could have strengthened the grounds of their suspicion so much as the consequences of their own behaviour. It was their want of proportion which helped in no small degree to cloud the prospects of the State Duma. The revolutionary challenge of the St Petersburg Soviet and of the Moscow insurrection, which had united sincere conservatives and open reactionaries in defence of autocracy, had also damaged almost beyond repair the political reputation of the liberal leaders in bureaucratic circles. Yet even after the December rising the liberal leaders were no more prepared than they had been before to forgo the strict letter of their demand for a parliamentary regime on perfected western lines. In maintaining so stubbornly this doctrinaire attitude they delivered Russia once more, as will be seen, into the hands of the old ruling caste.

Their first and irretrievable error was to refuse the invitation of Witte to enter the new government. This, once again, was to be wilfully blind to the commonplaces of the country's need. Whatever his personal shortcomings, Witte was fighting a difficult battle in the cause of constitutional government and a first instalment of democracy. From the beginning it was plain that his initiative in securing the October manifesto had earned for him the unforgiving hostility of the emperor. He had drawn the fire of the old order, too, in promptly removing from the post of governor-general of St Petersburg the hated Trepov, who still retained the confidence of Nicholas and who continued to function as palace commandant. That early gain achieved, Witte's attempt to enlist the support of the liberal opposition was genuinely designed to assist the transition to a constitutional order of government. Although the new council of ministers had been conceived as in some sort a cabinet, he was not yet in command of the situation. Liberal support would help to make him so.

In a flurry of negotiations after 17 October he approached, among others, several of the leading zemstvo and city duma representatives. He urged Shipov to accept office as State Comptroller and was willing to nominate Alexander Guchkov, a wealthy Moscow industrialist and public figure, as the new Minister of Trade and Industry; he had the eminent jurist and liberal senator A. F. Koni in mind as Minister of Justice and the liberal professor Prince E. N. Trubetskoy as Minister of Education. But all these proposals came to nothing because the opposition leaders in the background were obdurate in demanding more than Witte could concede. Shipov, who had behind him only a right-wing minority in the zemstvo movement, was prepared to enter the government only with their sanction. And for the majority the price of co-operation in any form with Witte was a constituent assembly—that is, the opportunity of preparing in all democratic formality still another and different constitution for Russia.

Witte did not give up hope of liberal co-operation. On 6 November another zemstvo congress opened in Moscow. Though there were faint murmurs of protest at the opposition leaders' intransigence, even the arguments of Struve in favour of participation in the government on limited and strictly defined terms failed to touch the congress as a whole. Once more it was Miliukov's attitude at this juncture that was decisive. In an earlier interview with Witte he had flatly refused support unless the October manifesto was expressly interpreted by the emperor to mean a 'constitution'—a word which even now Nicholas would not permit to be used in his presence. (As Maklakov said afterwards, Miliukov insisted on 'the use of the word and ignored the content'.) It was Miliukov who now prevailed on the zemstvo congress to declare that the government could count on its support only if it upheld faithfully 'the constitutional principles' of the manifesto.

The opposition, it may be repeated, had lively and continuing cause for distrust. It takes two to pursue a quarrel if not to pick one, and provocation came not only from the influences near the throne but from Witte himself. For the liberals as a body the last straw had been the appointment as Minister of the Interior of P. N. Durnovo, a reactionary of evil and ruthless temper. Though Witte repented of his decision afterwards, he appears to have been in some way mysteriously bound to Durnovo and was at the same time prompted by the need for a strong man in a key ministry. For different reasons Nicholas himself was reluctant to endorse the appointment and at first made it only provisional. Certainly the measures adopted by the new Minister of the Interior in the task of restoring order lacked nothing of punitive zeal. It was Durnovo who commissioned the two expeditions which, with the aid of the gallows and the firing squad, put down the rioting among the troops awaiting demobilization in the east. The name of General Meller-Zakomelsky was remembered with loathing in this connexion long afterwards. Executions apart, Durnovo's policy of reprisals involved the deportation from their homes of some forty-five thousand 'agitators'.

He had done nothing to commend himself to the Constitutional-Democrats at their second congress in St Petersburg in January 1906. It was the savagery of Durnovo's means of restoring order, indeed, which fortified the resolve of Miliukov, the acknowledged party leader, to keep in reserve the renewed threat of a mass revolutionary appeal. The Constitutional-Democrats—the Cadets, as they were beginning to be called—were more than ever intransigent in face of Witte's appeal for support.

In these circumstances, the only type of government that Witte could form was one composed (with a single exception) of bureaucrats of the old school. No worse introduction to the new constitutional order could have been conceived: the consequences of the deadlock between Witte and the liberals were felt in the widening breach between government and liberal society right up to the revolution of 1917. The exception, however, was significant and projects not the least momentous of the 'ifs' of the reign. As Minister of Agriculture Witte chose an official of enlightened stamp, N. N. Kutler, who spent his short term of office in drafting a carefully devised scheme for the alienation of the large private estates in the interests of the peasantry. Witte himself was by this time converted to the necessity for something not far short of complete alienation. But the scheme was withdrawn amid an explosion of angry protest from the landed aristocracy, and Kutler resigned in March 1906.[1] With his departure all hope vanished of winning the active support of the peasant masses for the system of constitutional government in the making.

The October manifesto had provided only a formula for the new order in Russia. It had still to be elaborated by the unreformed apparatus of autocracy. From December until the very eve of the opening of the State Duma on 27 April/10 May 1906, the new order was clothed in a succession of legal enactments, decrees and provisional regulations. These were the secret fruits of bureaucratic planning and of recommendations from high quarters even more effectively screened from the public gaze.

Through the great rents they made in the proffered system of representative government the October manifesto was still visible. But the chastened spirit of those October days was no longer in evidence. The emperor's weakness had passed; the pledges he had given were not so much dishonoured as profoundly qualified. The legislative order of things devised during the four or five months before the Duma met dispelled whatever small hope lingered of a strictly parliamentary regime. On 11 December, before the Moscow insurrection had been put down, a decree was issued which set forth the procedure for elections to the Duma. In planning to widen the franchise beyond the limits of the Bulygin project Witte had been obliged to delay the opening of the Duma, originally fixed for the middle of January. Two new projects for the electoral law had been presented to him, one—which was turned down—by a representative group of 'public men', the other prepared by a subordinate on his instructions and duly published. This project, since it provided for something appreciably less than universal suffrage and for a system of indirect voting in three or four separate colleges, played havoc with the liberal 'four-tailed' programme.

[1]He afterwards joined the Cadet Party and was elected to the State Duma, where for some years he proved a formidable critic of government agrarian policies. Later still he served in the Soviet Ministry of Finance.

Yet would anything other than a system of indirect voting have been practicable in a country so vast, so new to the doctrine of representative government and so largely illiterate as Russia? The provisions of the electoral law were not, in fact, by any means unenlightened and were not unfavourable, as events proved, to the 'public men' whose own project had been rejected. The Duma was to sit between elections for a period of five years. There would be four hundred and twelve deputies in all for the provinces of European Russia, thirty-six representing the ten Polish provinces, twenty-nine representatives from the Caucasus, deputies from western and central Siberia, from central Asia, from the Far East; even the pastoral Kirghiz nomads would return a deputy. The electorate, based on a manhood franchise at the age of twenty-five, was divided into three separate categories—peasants, urban voters and landowners. The last, or those at any rate with a property qualification of approximately four hundred acres, voted directly at a county election assembly. The peasants voted in three stages, choosing delegates for the canton (a group of villages), who chose delegates for the county, who chose the actual voters for the province. The number of urban voters was drastically restricted by property qualifications, with the result that relatively few factory workers were enfranchised. Twenty large towns enjoyed separate representation; eighteen of them each returned a single deputy, Moscow returned four and St Petersburg six. In all, the system of representation was so weighted that the landowners provided thirty-one per cent of the total number of effective voters, the peasants forty-two per cent, the towns twenty-seven per cent.

The electoral law stirred the leaders of an opposition committed to the doctrine of parliamentary democracy to vehement indignation. Here was the betrayal of pledges received which they had always feared. But their feelings rose still more sharply when on 20 February, six days after the date of the opening of the Duma had been announced, an imperial manifesto set forth the legal provisions of the developed constitutional system. The opposition now learned in the first place that the legislative rights of the State Duma would be shared by an upper house in the shape of a transformed State Council. Half the members of this second chamber would be appointed by the crown; the other half would be elected by the zemstvos, the nobility, the clergy, commerce and industry, the Academy of Sciences and the universities. All laws required the consent of both houses as well as the imperial sanction. All powers not specifically conferred upon the Duma and the State Council in common belonged to the crown.

Worse was to come. On 4 March, at the height of the election campaign, the pledge of full civil liberties was qualified by provisional regulations which, while ostensibly they guaranteed the right of assembly and of association, hedged them in with stringent police powers of supervision. Four days later the Budget rules were published. They excluded from the legislative competence of the Duma not only the expenditure of the Ministry of the Court but also the army and navy estimates and the payment on all state debts—more than a third of the national expenditure. On 23 April, four days before the opening of the Duma, all the various enactments relating to the new order of constitutional monarchy were codified in the Fundamental Laws, which will be considered shortly.

Within two or three weeks of the announcement of the electoral law in December the campaign of election to the new Duma was in full swing. It lost nothing of excitement during the period of piecemeal construction of the constitutional system. This was, in truth, a momentous occasion. For the first time in Russian history political parties functioned openly under the protection of law.

The most active and determined of the parties was that of the Constitutional-Democrats. It had wholly absorbed the liberal vanguard of the zemstvo movement, which now faded from the political scene as a distinctive force in 'society'. In the absence of the parties of the revolutionary underground, the Socialist-Revolutionaries and the Social-Democrats, who had reasons of their own for boycotting the elections, the Cadets stood farthest to the left. The party had shed two splinter groups of distinguished figures on its right and a small group of semi-socialists on its left, but it still had the support of the greater part of the non-revolutionary educated classes of the country. It numbered among its upper- and middle-class spokesmen intellectuals of considerable note and orators of impressive quality. The original Cadet programme, in which the issue of constitutional monarchy or democratic republic had been left in abeyance, was clarified by the Moscow insurrection. At the party congress in January the Cadets finally abandoned the demand for a constituent assembly.

They took their stand on a policy of winning full parliamentary rights for the Duma and on wide-ranging social and economic reforms. Strongly impelled by the number of former Narodniks in their ranks, they favoured the alienation of the large private estates, on a basis of fair compensation, in the interests of the peasantry.

To the right of the Cadets and, like them, in opposition to the government, was the Party of the Union of 17 October—the Octobrists, as they were called—who proclaimed their adherence to the principles of the October manifesto and dissociated themselves from what they regarded as the extremism of the Cadets. Formed in the first place by Shipov and Guchkov and composed originally of landowning zemstvo moderates, their ranks were filled out by small groups drawn from other 'public men', from commercial interests and from the more progressive bureaucracy. The Octobrists sought, in their own phrase, to develop and strengthen the foundations of constitutional monarchy; they professed themselves convinced supporters of a system of popular representation and stood for the maintenance of civil liberties. But economic and class interest visibly qualified their liberalism. It was this more than any depth of realism which prompted the belief of the majority that the strict letter of a parliamentary regime was neither practicable nor as yet desirable in Russia. Their Russian nationalist bias made them specially critical of Cadet doctrines of national self-determination within the empire. Though they did not rule out the eventual resort to some degree of alienation of the private estates if all other agrarian reforms failed, the Octobrists were equally hostile to this part of the Cadet programme on the grounds that the break-up of the large estates would inevitably lower the productivity of Russian agriculture. The mixture of enlightened selfishness and specious argument in this attitude towards the agrarian question was perhaps characteristic of the Octobrists and of the more calculating and less sympathetic of the two founders of the party. Grandson of a serf, Alexander Guchkov was an energetic and somewhat mercurial character, who had travelled along the Great Wall of China during the Boxer rebellion, fought as a volunteer with the Boers in South Africa and served with the Russian armies in Manchuria. A leading figure in industry, he had little support from other industrialists, who in so far as they carried any political weight as a class threw it largely on the side of the Cadets.

The extreme right was grouped round the Union of the Russian People. It refused to recognize the Duma as a legislative body and demanded the restoration of the emperor's 'unlimited' autocracy.

The attitude of the underground revolutionary parties towards the elections may be recorded briefly. In the closing days of December the Socialist-Revolutionaries held their first formal congress in Finland. It endorsed a maximum and a minimum programme, both specifically socialist, which were drawn up for the party by Chernov. The maximum programme was for the day of complete and final revolutionary victory; the minimum served immediate and practical ends. It had four main planks: an armed uprising; a federal republican structure of the Russian state; the expropriation of all private estates, without compensation, and the socialization of the land; and the use of individual terror by sanction of the highest party organ.[1] With these ends in view the Socialist-Revolutionaries, or at least their principal leaders—there was doubt and hesitation among their following—decided to wash their hands of the election. Votes, after all, could do nothing to bring the revolution nearer.

The Social-Democrats, contemptuous in principle of 'constitutional illusions' and 'the parliamentary comedy', seemed even more inflexible in rejecting any part or lot in the election campaign. In point of fact, there was a sizable group among the Mensheviks, possibly a majority, who were in favour of assisting the Duma to a fair start. Even among the Bolsheviks there were some who shared this attitude. But Lenin was never so dogmatic in error as at this time. Amid the continuing strike movement of the early months of 1906, during which martial law or a lesser form of emergency legislation was in force over the greater part of the country, he was still convinced that Russia was ripe for an

---

[1] At no time did the Socialist-Revolutionaries positively renounce terror. But this qualifying condition was strongly opposed at the congress by an extreme wing of the party, who, inspired by the indomitable sixty-year-old Breshko-Breshkovskaya among others, urged the maximum use of terror and thus became known as the Maximalists. They were responsible for the most notorious terrorist outrages of the next two years. On the other hand, a moderate group, the Narodnik-Socialists, composed largely of writers and public men associated with the Narodnik journal *Russkoe Bogatstvo* (*Russian Fortune*), were equally resolute in opposing both the doctrine of armed uprising and the use of terror in any circumstances. This group detached itself from the party.

armed uprising and awaited only a timely signal. It would be fatal, in his view, to blunt the edge of the revolutionary aspirations of the proletariat by involving the party in the sham of a parliamentary campaign. Revolutionary tactics demanded a boycott. A boycott, therefore, went hand in hand with the continued watch and wait for insurrection.

The elections began in March. It was a novel experience for both educated society and the government, and both were in a mood of some anxiety as the first results came in. They surprised the one and reassured the other; in province after province the elected representatives of the people proved to be peasants. The electoral law had been designed, as has been indicated, to give the peasants, traditionally loyal to the throne, a commanding representation, and the government now congratulated itself on its wisdom. 'Thank God', Witte exclaimed in the council of ministers, 'the Duma will be peasant!' He spoke too soon. The loyalty of the peasant deputies had still to be demonstrated. And the election results that followed later in the month and in April showed that the Duma would be not so much peasant as an opposition Duma, all but completely dominated by the Cadets.

At the beginning of April, when there were unmistakable hints of the probable temper of the Duma, an imperial council was held at Tsarskoe Selo to discuss the draft of the new Fundamental Laws[1] of the empire. During almost the entire period of five months that had passed since the tsar set his signature to the October manifesto one supreme question had been debated anxiously in court and ruling circles. Did the manifesto imply any limitation of the imperial prerogative? Could the existence of the forthcoming Duma affect the unlimited autocratic power (*neogranichennaya samoderzhavnaya vlast*) of the sovereign? The question was answered on 23 April, when in the Fundamental Laws issued on that day only the word 'unlimited' was omitted. 'To the emperor of all the Russias', the first article declared, 'belongs supreme autocratic power. Submission to his power, not from fear only but as a matter of conscience, is commanded by God himself.'

In the midst of loud rejoicings at their electoral victory the Cadets were required to swallow this bitter draught. On top of all that had gone before the taste was indeed noxious. The Fundamental Laws disabused the liberal opposition of the last shred

[1]The original Fundamental Laws were issued by the emperor Paul in 1797.

of belief in the government's good faith. Miliukov denounced them vehemently, charging the government with 'conspiring against the people'. The Fundamental Laws left no loophole for doubt that the tsar's prerogatives were in substance untouched by the new forms of constitutional rule. To him was reserved the right of declaring war and making peace. In him resided all authority over the Orthodox Church. It was at his will that the precise length of annual sessions of the Duma was determined. At his will the Duma might be dissolved at any time; all that was necessary was that the decree of dissolution should bear the date for new elections and for the convening of a new Duma. As for opposition hopes of a responsible ministry, all ministers were appointed by the emperor and were responsible to the emperor alone. A vote of censure on the government which secured a two-thirds majority might be submitted to him, but it did not necessarily entail the resignation of the government.

The deepest hopes of the liberal opposition were thus destroyed. As matters now stood the function of the council of ministers differed little if at all from that of the former committee of ministers and a unified administrative policy was beyond the reach of any new government. What was most damaging and most galling was that these Fundamental Laws were immutable except at the instance of the crown itself. There was, therefore, no legal means available to the Duma of amending the constitution. In the moment of victory it was precisely the prospect of amendment that had swelled the hopes of the parliamentarians of the Constitutional-Democratic Party.

On the same day that the Fundamental Laws were published Witte was dismissed. During the six months of his term of office as quasi-Prime Minister his position had grown steadily more intolerable. His own opportunism and want of scruple, together with an unaccustomed confusion of mind, had helped to make it so. But the difficulties he encountered owed most to his political enemies. He had been fighting simultaneously on three fronts, and in each instance unsuccessfully. Having earned, as he knew, Nicholas's lasting rancour for his leading part in the October manifesto, he had since aroused the jealous fears of both emperor and empress, who were persuaded that he planned to make himself a Prime Minister on the British model and thus to reduce them to the constitutional level of reigning sovereign and consort. The election results did nothing to reconcile them to him.

As for his relations with the liberals, once they had rejected Witte they were uncompromising in opposition to him. And for their part the conservative bureaucracy and conservative opinion throughout the country were bitterly hostile. In their personal reports to Nicholas the other ministers, led by Durnovo and apparently aided and abetted by the foolishly scheming Trepov, were unsparing in criticism of Witte.

Confronted by the repeated evidence of the emperor's distrust, Witte had more than once proffered his resignation. The odd thing is that at the same time he neglected no means of trying to regain Nicholas's favour. It was he himself, as he explains with perverse satisfaction in his memoirs, who amended the original draft of the Fundamental Laws so as to reserve still larger areas of power to the crown. Yet on 14 April he once more tendered his resignation, listing among other reasons his outspoken differences with Durnovo over agrarian policy and the Jewish question. It was accepted and announced nine days later.

Was he prepared for his own dismissal? Or did acceptance of his offer of resignation come as a mortifying shock? It is hard to tell. Certainly he had been goaded into a condition of nervous exasperation by the intrigues of highly-placed officialdom against him. But it is unlikely that a politician who in later years showed himself as avid and as unprincipled as Witte in seeking a return to power could ever have wished whole-heartedly to surrender it. All his efforts to re-establish himself were in vain. Appointed at the time of his dismisal a member of the State Council, Witte found it impossible to mend his political fences and from this moment completely dropped out of the picture of Russian policy-making.

It is perhaps foolish to speculate whether he might not have averted the revolution of 1917 if the tsar had reposed greater trust in him. So vast an issue did not rest with him or with any other man. There is some reason for asking whether, with Nicholas's consent, he might not have saved the dynasty. In one sense, indeed, it was he more than any other man who preserved it for a further eleven years after his dismissal. He had helped to defeat the revolutionary general strike and to bring back from the Far East a defeated and dangerously demoralized army. It was he who, a few days before his dismissal, negotiated the loan from France of 2,250 million gold francs—the largest foreign loan ever made to Russia—with the aid of which Nicholas was able to face the opening of the State Duma with some confidence. The loan was made at the price of Russian diplomatic support for France against Germany at the Algeciras conference, but it is doubtful whether anybody other than Witte could have secured it. Its internal significance in Russia was plain to liberals and revolutionaries alike. 'I spit in your eyes, beautiful France!' exclaimed Maxim Gorky when the news was announced.

Before Witte's resignation took effect Nicholas had been in communication with Prince Meshchersky and had consulted, among others, his former Minister of the Interior, I. L. Goremykin. It was Goremykin who was now chosen to succeed Witte as chairman of the council of ministers. Of all the errors of judgment which Nicholas made this was one of the deadliest. Elderly and indolent, by no means a fool but completely self-centred and cynical and at the same time slavish in his submission to the throne, Goremykin was the type and pattern of servile courtier of an older generation. He was almost the last person in Russia who could be expected to turn to public advantage the first meeting of government and Duma. A clean sweep of the ministers who had served with Witte had produced successors who in quality were not markedly different from them. One face, however, was wholly unfamiliar in bureaucratic circles in the capital. The new-comer was P. A. Stolypin, an experienced provincial governor, who was appointed Minister of the Interior.

From the government's point of view, the grievous and startling result of the elections had been the eclipse of conservative opinion. Before the Duma met there was still a little uncertainty about the attitude of some of the forty or so separate parties and national groups represented in the new assembly, but already it was plain that not a single deputy of unimpeachably conservative views had been returned. The extreme right—the Black Hundred zealots of the Union of the Russian People—stood outside the first Duma; their spell of power was still to come. But of the two hundred peasant deputies elected out of a total of five hundred and twenty-four, there was not one, it appeared, who could be relied upon to support the government. The entire Duma was patently and solidly an opposition Duma. Precise figures of party strengths are not easily established since the affiliations of various small groups were tenuous at the opening of the Duma and there were several shifts of allegiance afterwards. But the Cadets formed by far the largest organized party with a membership of about a hundred and eighty. To their right were two separate groups of between thirty-five and forty liberal moderates, who habitually voted with the Cadets. Still farther to the right was a group of a dozen Octobrists. Of the rest the national minorities had about seventy deputies, half of them Poles, who were concerned above all else with autonomy under the Russian crown. As a rule, they voted with the Cadets. So did most of the peasant deputies, of whom more than a hundred coalesced into a Labour (Trudovik) group, a body with no organization outside the Duma which stood for radical agrarian reform in the peasant interest.

In the event there were eighteen Social-Democrats in the Duma. There might well have been more—and fewer Cadets—but for the party leaders' original decision to boycott the elections. However, although the Bolsheviks for the time being continued to spurn the 'parliamentary comedy', the official Menshevik leadership had had second thoughts. At the last moment, when most of the election results had already been declared, the Mensheviks took the field in Transcaucasia, always one of their strongholds.[1] In the result all the Transcaucasian deputies in the Duma proved to be Mensheviks.

On 27 April Nicholas opened the State Duma, the new legislature of the Russian empire. The ceremony, historic enough in all conscience, took place in the magnificent St George's Room of the Winter Palace in the capital. Even here the outward show of unity was lacking. Suspicion on one side, defiance on the other, darkened the occasion. On one side of the great chamber, flanked by the tsar's ministers, stood the luminaries of the court and the state dignitaries, all gold braid and decorations, the women splendid and glittering with jewels. Opposite them were first of all the members of the State Council, behind them the massed ranks of the Duma; some deputies in uniform, others in evening dress, bearded peasants in long-skirted caftans, socialists in workers' blouses, most of the minority representatives in national costume. The court was deliberately at its most brilliant; the radical opposition, incensed by the promulgation of the Fundamental Laws, was no less deliberately hostile and challenging. Preceded in solemn procession by the officers of state bearing

[1] The elections in Transcaucasia in early April coincided with the Social-Democratic congress in Stockholm, where the Mensheviks were in the majority and where the two factions were ostensibly re-united.

the imperial regalia which had been brought from Moscow, Nicholas entered the chamber, bore himself with customary dignity in reading a brief and colourless address composed for the occasion and withdrew. He had said nothing that could offend, but he had also said nothing in keeping with the role of a constitutional monarch at the opening of parliament.

For even now what the Cadets had looked for was the sort of King's speech to Parliament that might have been spoken by Edward VII, or one at any rate in which the emperor announced a programme of legislation for the session. As the largest of the parties in the Duma they had not waited for the opening ceremony to stake their claim, if only for appearance sake, to form a government. That claim still represented the party point of view on matters constitutional when the Duma re-assembled in its appointed meeting-place, the Tauride Palace. Here, in the magnificent building put up by Catherine the Great for Potemkin, the most celebrated of her favourites, the Cadets were as unmoved by the logic of Russian history as they had been outside it. Not for a moment did they pause to consider even at this stage the possible advantages to Russia of compromise with the government. They were obsessed by English parliamentary ideas, or rather by the notion that English parliamentary usage could be imported into the climate of St Petersburg. With every appearance of confidence they addressed themselves first of all to the proper formalities. From the Cadet ranks came the president or speaker of the Duma, Sergey Muromtsev, and every other elected officer. Muromtsev did not fail them. A professor of jurisprudence and a most majestic figure of a man, who had apparently prophesied in youth that he would preside over a Russian parliament and had held himself in readiness for the event ever since, he brought a severe dignity if nothing more to his conduct of Duma procedure. In a ceremonious gesture he called upon the veteran Ivan Petrunkevich ('the patriarch of Russian neo-liberalism', in Miliukov's phrase) for the opening speech. But Petrunkevich, somewhat agitated by the great occasion, confined himself to the demand for a political amnesty.[1] Together with the agrarian

---

[1] On their way along the Neva from the Winter Palace to the Tauride Palace the Duma deputies had passed the Kresty prison. From its casements scores of political prisoners had waved to them and their cry of 'Amnesty!' had been taken up by the crowd. Durnovo's regime at the Ministry of the Interior had indeed filled the prisons to overflowing.

problem this was the chief practical preoccupation of the short-lived first Duma.

The full Cadet programme, which was adopted without a dissenting voice in the Duma, took the form of an 'address to the throne'. Its proposals and recommendations included a political amnesty; the obligatory alienation of the large private estates; a ministry responsible to 'the elected representatives of the people'; universal and direct franchise; abolition of the State Council; abrogation of the emergency laws; abolition of the death penalty; and a lengthy series of reforms of administrative procedure. With humble duty the Duma desired leave for a deputation to present the address to the emperor in person.

Nicholas's eventual reply was to instruct Goremykin to inform Muromtsev that the proposed address might be handed to the Minister of the Court. This somewhat elaborate exchange of courtesies boded no good. And indeed the temperature on the Cadet benches and in the chamber as a whole was rising from day to day. For ministers were under no obligation to appear in the Duma and in their absence deputies could only continue the game of parliamentary make-believe. In exercising their right, however, to expose abuses or to question the legal propriety of ministerial action, they grew increasingly vociferous. The government was not alarmed. Equipped with delaying expedients of every kind, it could always shelter behind the Fundamental Laws. Goremykin, foxy beneath all his indifference, had the situation well in hand. He appeared before the chamber on 13 May, a heavily bewhiskered man with a pale expressionless face and a feeble voice, and delivered the government's reply to the demands of the opposition. All were 'inadmissible', the agrarian proposals especially so since 'the principle of the inalienability and inviolability of property is the fundamental rule of government throughout the world'. As for a responsible ministry and the abolition of the State Council, these matters could not be raised on the initiative of the Duma. Finally, although an amnesty was the prerogative of the crown, the council of ministers for their part were entirely opposed to it.

By the time Goremykin had finished the Cadets were in uproar. They were contending with the government, it seemed to them, for the most elementary rights of the Duma, indeed for its very existence. The Cadet Nabokov, the son of a former Minister of Justice and not the least eloquent member of his party, rose to his feet and vehemently put forward the doctrine that 'the executive power must bow to the legislative power'. The remark was greeted with a storm of applause and the debate continued on the same impassioned level. In the end the Duma, in an all but unanimous vote of no confidence, demanded the resignation of the government.

The first Duma lasted in all seventy-three days. Long before the end Goremykin had decided to ignore it until an opportunity arose for the emperor to dissolve it. Those nearest to Nicholas were not of one mind on the subject, but what else but dissolution, it may be asked, was possible in the circumstances? Goremykin preserved a wearied equanimity while opposition speeches grew still more inflammatory and the chamber rang at every sitting with cries of 'Resign!' These Duma speeches, it should be borne in mind, were published and circulated throughout the country, and this at a time when police reports spoke of renewed revolutionary agitation, agrarian riots and terrorist acts. At the other political extreme, too, there was a resurgence of violence, and the liberal opposition was further inflamed by the connivance of the police in Jewish pogroms, by police treatment of political prisoners, and most of all by the vicious attacks of the Union of the Russian People. As the spokesmen of the extreme right the latter had a considerable ally in the Council of the United Nobility, a reactionary association of landowners which had been called into being by the threat of expropriation of the private estates. Both bodies rained addresses and telegrams upon the emperor protesting their loyalty and the loyalty of the masses to the autocratic principle and urging the dissolution of the Duma.

A pretext for dissolution was eventually found in the technically unconstitutional position taken up by the Duma on the issue of agrarian reform. The government had announced the broad lines of the agrarian scheme it proposed to introduce, but had not yet prepared specific legislation. The scheme flatly rejected the idea of expropriating private land. By way of answer the Duma appealed to the country to await the publication of its own project of reform based upon enforced expropriation. An appeal in these terms was, in the strict sense, unconstitutional. Dissolution, in point of fact, followed two days afterwards.

Before the curtain was brought down on the first Duma, however, an extraordinary scene, apparently half earnest, half make-believe, was played out off-stage between the forces near the throne and leading opposition figures. Two different schemes to bring

about a *détente* between crown and opposition were launched
with every display of sincerity. The first was canvassed by Trepov,
who was still in Nicholas's confidence, and involved the formation
of a Cadet ministry. To this end Trepov sounded Miliukov—who,
though the acknowledged Cadet leader, was not a member of the
first Duma.[1] Trepov's motives are by no means certain. Was it in
his somewhat muddled mind that a Cadet ministry would either
be obliged to crush the extreme left or else demonstrate its total
incapacity to govern before being dismissed? Or was he bent on
rescuing the Duma from the ministerial plot which had been hatched
from a separate and simultaneous scheme put forward by the Foreign
Minister Izvolsky? Whatever Trepov's motives, Miliukov was
his normal and inflexible self and returned only impossible
conditions.

Izvolsky, monocled, flower in buttonhole, dilettante-ish in
politics as in all else, had proposed a coalition ministry of opposition
and bureaucratic talents. Nicholas had seemed to warm to the proposal and Izvolsky and the new Minister of the Interior, Peter
Stolypin, had been deputed to approach opposition leaders. Their
first contact was with the still moderate and still universally
respected Shipov, who had been elected by the zemstvos of Moscow
province to the State Council. Towards the end of June, when
Shipov was received in audience by the emperor, it was already being
rumoured that he would head a coalition ministry. But Shipov had
had time to acquaint himself with Miliukov's terms. Opposed by
some members of his party but supported by the majority, these
were precisely what might have been expected from Miliukov—no
coalition but a free hand for the Constitutional-Democratic Party.
Thus forewarned, Shipov ventured to urge upon Nicholas the
advantages of a Cadet ministry under Muromtsev, arguing
reasonably enough that responsibility would temper the extremism
of the party. He came away from the audience convinced that
Nicholas had been won over to the idea.

Here, once more, was a possible turning-point in the reign. If
the emperor had in truth been willing to consent to the experiment,
if he had chosen to entrust the liberals with temporary responsibility in a half-autocratic, half-constitutional order of government, Russia could scarcely have failed to travel a somewhat

[1] He had been disqualified on a technical point of residence from standing
as a candidate and thus survived, unlike almost the entire body of Cadet
deputies in 1906, to serve in later Dumas.

different road in the years before 1917. But indecision in Nicholas was stronger than all else. He hesitated, sought further counsel, leaned to this opinion and then that. He may never have contemplated putting the opposition on trial; or perhaps the vigorous manoeuvres against the scheme of several of his ministers, with Stolypin at their head, were too much for him. At all events while Muromtsev waited for a summons to Peterhof which never came the emperor instructed Stolypin to complete his preparations for the dissolution of the Duma. The commandant of St Petersburg gave every assurance that there would be no disturbances; several cavalry regiments of Guards had been specially posted, in fact, in the capital. Early on 9 July, a Sunday, the Tauride Palace was surrounded by troops and the imperial decree of dissolution was displayed outside. In contravention of the Fundamental Laws, no date was announced for the holding of new elections. On that same day Stolypin replaced Goremykin as chairman of the council of ministers.

The short life of Russia's first quasi-legislature, the deformed offspring of Russian practice and western theory, closed on a note of comedy. Nicholas apparently vacillated until the end. On the night of 8-9 July, or so the story goes, a note was sent from the emperor at Tsarskoe Selo to Goremykin instructing him to suspend for the time being the decree of dissolution. But Goremykin had gone to bed after leaving orders that he was on no account to be disturbed. He was not disturbed. By morning the decree had been put into effect.

8. *Necessities of State*

There was something unteachable, it must be said once again, in Russian liberalism throughout its short history. However well its leaders meant, and in much that they thought and said they meant superlatively well, they deceived both themselves and others in claiming to represent so much more considerable a part of Russia than in fact they did. The trite but historic remark of the British Prime Minister, Sir Henry Campbell-Bannerman, on learning of the dissolution of the Duma, 'The Duma is dead. Long live the Duma!' like so many historic remarks, was conceived in ignorance. The Duma was not a democratic parliament, as the British Prime Minister had assumed and as Russian liberals with less excuse had chosen and still chose to pretend.

A self-deceiving obstinacy prompted their behaviour immediately after the notice of dissolution. Miliukov in his memoirs declares that the Cadets had fully expected that the government would dissolve the Duma and had determined nevertheless to remain in their places and resume the parliamentary debate. Unfortunately, the entrance to the Tauride Palace was guarded by troops. With artillery in the side streets and other troops posted elsewhere in the city there were, in fact, in spite of hopes of a popular revolt in sympathy, no disturbances. For the disinherited Duma the cup of bitterness overflowed. Some hundred and eighty deputies, two-thirds of them Cadets, crossed the frontier into Finland and assembled in the Belvedere Hotel in Vyborg. 'The session of the Duma', announced Muromtsev, speaking as weightily as ever from an improvised rostrum, 'is hereby resumed.' In an atmosphere over-charged with excitement, the deputies launched the rash 'Vyborg appeal'. Drawn up by Miliukov, it called upon the people of Russia to refuse to pay taxes or to provide recruits for the army until the Duma had been re-convened.

The significant thing about the Vyborg appeal is that once more the standard-bearers of Russian liberalism were resorting to much the same tactics as the extreme revolutionary factions. They seemed bent, indeed, upon disproving their fitness for the constitutional responsibilities to which they laid claim. The appeal followed the same lines as the 'financial manifesto' of the St Petersburg Soviet in the previous December, which had similarly urged the population to refuse to pay taxes and to withdraw savings' bank deposits. It was characteristic of Miliukov on this occasion to lose sight of the fact that direct taxes formed a relatively trifling part of the budget and that the next recruits would not be summoned until the following November, four months away. These considerations were not wholly absent from the minds of the assembled Cadets, many of whom were uneasy at so extravagant a gesture and who signed the appeal with undisguised misgiving. In the event, as might have been expected, it met with scarcely a flicker of response. Neither did the simultaneous and somewhat cynical appeal of the Social-Democratic Party for a general strike in defence of the Duma. Liberal misgivings, in truth, were not groundless. At a party congress later in the year the Cadets in effect repented of the decision to launch what was so plainly an unlawful appeal. But this did not save the signatories from the penalty of legal trial towards the close of 1907, when they were sentenced to a term of three months' imprisonment. Thus disqualified from standing again for election, the leading cadres of the Constitutional-Democratic Party were henceforth lost to the Duma. With all their failings they included most of the brains, the ability and the force of idealism in the party. Miliukov, for all that he was the author of the appeal, suffered no penalty.

The first Duma had vanished from the scene, but the government carried on. It did so without undue difficulty while preparations were made for summoning a second Duma. The stage was set for the new chairman of the council of ministers, Peter Stolypin, who during the next five years played the part of the ambiguous Russian equivalent of Prime Minister. Of commanding presence, a man of strong and in many respects impressive personality, clear-headed and courageous, he was as well fitted for the part as any member of the Russian bureaucracy. Yet it is hard to warm to him except in sympathy with his thankless task in serving so jealous and unresponsive a sovereign. And even sympathy is diluted by a sense of Stolypin's unbridled conviction of his own political virtue. His defects as a conservative statesman, who might have succeeded where Witte failed, were that he could not conceive it possible he was mistaken, and that he was therefore scarcely ever flexible enough in his approach to persons or to problems.

Increasingly he was driven by a rigid sense of state necessity into courses which were innocent of scruple or even violated the law in both letter and spirit.

Born (in Dresden) in 1862 of a solid Russian landowning family, he had served as marshal of the nobility and then as governor in the western provinces before being appointed governor of the Volga province of Saratov in 1904. This was the scene of some of the worst agrarian disturbances in the following year. As governor Stolypin travelled from one affected area to another and discharged his 'tranquillizing' duties with ruthless efficiency. His talents were of a forthright kind. Without breadth of intellect, he had a tremendous capacity for work, was a forceful speaker with an unaffected turn of rhetoric and was not wholly wanting in generosity. The generosity went with a realism of mind which is summed up in a trenchant and imperfectly appreciated aphorism that he addressed to the Poles in the second Duma: 'In politics there is no vengeance, there are only consequences'. His experience in the western provinces with their mainly Polish and Catholic nobility had strengthened in him an aggressive vein of Russian nationalism. An experienced landowner, he combined with a sound knowledge of peasant farming the class instinct of the landowning nobility. Yet neither his Russian nationalism nor his class bias saved him from a certain unpopularity in those highest circles of state to which he was a newcomer. As chairman of the council of ministers he was never taken to the bosom of the court or of the aristocratic ranks of the bureaucracy. Nicholas, however, in the first flush of discovery of a new servant of autocracy, expressed unbounded admiration for Stolypin and, very characteristically, abandoned Trepov without any sign of regret.

In his evident desire to work with the Duma Stolypin stood apart from the higher ranks of the bureaucracy. He was determined to keep the Duma in its place, but, unlike many of the highest officials and unlike Nicholas himself, he had no thought of reducing it to a purely consultative assembly. In all apparent sincerity he declared himself anxious to abide by the rule of law. His first impulse had been to win some degree of co-operation from the moderate liberals or liberal-conservatives. With this object in view he approached a number of them—Shipov and Guchkov, the high-minded and honourable Heyden and Stakhovich. But they suspected him, no doubt with justice, of attempting to make use of them for an essentially bureaucratic ministry. As a condition of their support, therefore, they demanded that 'society' should have seven seats in the government. This was inevitably refused, and Stolypin could only resume the bureaucratic task where Goremykin had left off. Never again would the government make overtures of this kind to the opposition.

Stolypin's conduct of affairs involved even freer and more extensive use than Goremykin's of the powers of emergency legislation conferred by article 87 of the Fundamental Laws. This sanctioned legislation by decree while the Duma was not sitting but required that all such enactments be duly submitted for confirmation to the Duma within two months of its re-assembly. Stolypin used these emergency powers for an extraordinary variety of purposes, some trifling but others of the greatest moment. It was through article 87, for instance, that he effected the conservative but far-reaching agrarian reform which on the eve of war in 1914 appeared to hold some hope of solving Russia's land problem. Article 87 was a thorn in the flesh of the opposition, for the interval of two months was frequently prolonged and the Duma, whatever its theoretical rights in the matter, could not easily reverse a law which had already been in force for some considerable time. More than seven months passed between the dissolution of the first Duma and the opening of the second, and in that period Stolypin set in train measures of great substance which the Duma was afterwards powerless to undo.

In mitigation of Stolypin's resort to the *fait accompli* and of the harshness of his administrative policies in general, it should be borne in mind that, in this period between the first and the second Duma, a resurgent revolutionary terror reached formidable proportions. Official figures of the number of victims of Socialist-Revolutionary outrages, from governors of provinces and generals to gendarmerie officials and ordinary village police, are some sixteen hundred for 1906 and over two thousand five hundred in the following year. It was only in the intervals between combating revolutionary terrorism with a not dissimilar government terror that Stolypin found time for more constructive measures. Within a week of the dissolution of the Duma he had been confronted by renewed rioting in the armed forces, first in the island fortress of Sveaborg, in the Gulf of Finland, then in Kronstadt and again on board a battleship of the Baltic fleet. Immediately afterwards Moscow had briefly erupted again in an attempted general strike; the possibility of a second venture in armed insurrection there could not yet be dismissed. And then followed a spate of Socialist-Revolutionary murders and the first wave of terror of the extreme Socialist-Revolutionary faction, the Maximalists.

On 12 August 1906, while Stolypin was receiving officials and petitioners in his summer residence on Aptekarsky island in the capital, two men in police uniform threw a heavy bomb into the reception-room. The villa was demolished, twenty-seven people, including both terrorists, were killed outright and thirty-two more were wounded of whom six died on the following day. Stolypin's young daughter and a two-year-old son were injured, but Stolypin himself, who had maintained extraordinary composure, was unhurt. Amid the revulsion at these tactics the central committee of the Socialist-Revolutionary Party dissociated itself from an exploit which had been planned by the Maximalist Solomon Ryss. At the emperor's request Stolypin took up quarters with his family in the Winter Palace. The next day General Min, who had finally put down the Moscow insurrection, was assassinated. During the next few months the list of assassinations included the governors of two Volga provinces, the governor-general of Warsaw, the military commandant of St Petersburg and the chief military prosecutor. Two unsuccessful attempts were made on Admiral Dubasov, who had been in command in Moscow during the insurrection—and who had done his best to dissuade the emperor from bringing the insurgents to trial before military instead of civil courts.

The growing scale of terrorist attacks was a reprisal in some sort for the measures taken by the government to restore order. Terror, counter-terror, more terror—that progression has always borne witness to the Russian faith in violence. On 19 August, a week after the attempt on Stolypin, a state of emergency was declared in the greater part of the country and, under article 87, special powers were vested in the provincial governors or in other delegated authorities to dispense criminal justice through field courts-martial. At the discretion of the local authorities a suspected person might be tried within twenty-four hours of the commission of a crime by a military court, whose sentence must be executed immediately. Once more, the idea, which was flatly opposed to Stolypin's profession of 'legality', seems to have originated with Nicholas or within the narrow imperial circle. The courts-martial, simultaneously directed against acts of 'revolutionary justice' and peasant disorders, were designed as instruments of terror, and such they proved to be. They seldom imposed anything but the death sentence. Between September 1906 and April 1907, when they ceased to operate, the official number of death sentences carried out under this summary procedure is given as six hundred and eighty-three. It is probable that the real figure was a good deal higher.

One further type of crime fell within the province of the field courts-martial. It consisted of 'expropriations'. This was the name originally given to the raids on banks and state offices which were carried out by small squads of revolutionaries bent on securing funds for their party. Such raids and armed hold-ups multiplied rapidly immediately after the dissolution of the Duma. All too often the term 'expropriations' served to dignify the exploits of criminal gangs who were innocent of any political motive, but both the Socialist-Revolutionaries and the Social-Democrats were heavily involved in this type of armed robbery. In October 1906, outside a bank in the centre of St Petersburg, the Maximalists, directed by Solomon Ryss, staged an attack with bombs and revolvers on an official carrying state funds under military escort and made their escape with four hundred thousand roubles. It was no change of heart but rather police espionage and terror that brought these Maximalist robberies to an end. The Social-Democratic—or, rather, the Bolshevik—robberies lasted longer. They owed a great deal to the ingenuity and resource of one of Lenin's principal agents at this time, outwardly the image of bourgeois respectability, the engineer Leonid Krassin. At the party congress in Stockholm in April 1906, the Mensheviks, temporarily in the ascendant, had denounced the expropriations vehemently, protesting that they dishonoured the name of the party and opened its ranks to criminal elements. Lenin had stoutly justified these partisan actions, as they were called, as a regrettable necessity. And indeed they continued for quite some time afterwards, more especially in the Caucasus, where the almost legendary Kamo, a bank and train robber of genius, who brought off a particularly daring exploit in Tiflis in June 1907, had as his immediate superior Josef Djugashvili, who became Stalin.

Stolypin's rejection of 'legality' became all too vividly apparent in the wholesale resort to the verdict of military courts. It was discreetly veiled in his circular instructions as Minister of the Interior—a post he retained throughout his five years as chairman of the council of ministers. Governors of provinces were expressly urged to enlist the aid of informers in combating sedition, while gendarmerie officials, already vigorously supported in their rights of administrative arrest and deportation, were encouraged to make extensive use of agents-provocateurs. These instructions had deadly consequences. From now onwards the security forces and the revolutionary underground were interlocked at key points, and remained so almost until the end of the tsarist regime. Only a degree less infamous than the case of Azef, of whose activities Stolypin was fully aware, was that of Solomon Ryss, who was similarly both revolutionary and police spy. He was unmasked and executed in 1908, but the system he represented continued unabated and Stolypin himself was fated to suffer the penalty.

The negative aspects of Stolypin's policy between the first and the second Duma chilled and antagonized liberal society. But this preliminary phase of his tenure of power, in which so much of the government's energies was necessarily concentrated, with whatever punitive excess, on the restoration of order, had also its spectacular aspect of reform. It was Stolypin who assumed responsibility for a thoroughgoing attempt to resolve the peasant problem in Russia.

The Russian peasantry had waited in vain for the fulfilment of the pledge given in the imperial manifesto of 3 November 1905 to alleviate their conditions—without injury to 'the other landowners'. The total amount of redemption payments which had been written off by the decree issued on the same day was about 1,100 million roubles. But the peasantry had looked, and still looked, for something more than the cancellation of their debts to the state. And not the peasants only shared this expectation. As the debates in the first Duma had proved, except on the issue of compensation the liberals were all but indistinguishable from the Socialist-Revolutionaries in demanding the expropriation of the large landed estates. The Social-Democrats, too, had abandoned their former programme of restoring the 'cuttings-off' to the peasantry for a policy of socializing the land. And even among the conservative landed gentry there were not a few who by this time favoured some degree of alienation as a means of averting a resurgence of agrarian disorder. Stolypin's purpose, initially outlined in the government declaration of agrarian policy in the first Duma, was to achieve reform without expropriation and thus to maintain the essentially conservative character of the regime. He proposed to abolish communal tenure in order to allow the peasants to enclose their scattered strips into compact holdings.

By this means he hoped to create in the countryside a stable class of peasant proprietors in whom the government could repose confidence. For the commune was now politically suspect. In the words of the landowning caste of the Council of United Nobility, it held a 'socialist bacillus .

Herzen, mixing his metaphors, had said that the commune was 'everything' in Russia, a key to her past, the germ of her future. That faith, still shared by an older generation of socialist intellectuals, could no longer be maintained by anybody else. Stolypin's view of the matter was soberly pragmatical. In pursuing necessity as he saw it, he was willing to weight the scales for 'the sober and the strong' and ruthless enough to drive the millions of weaker peasantry to the wall. He owed a great deal to the conclusions of the various agricultural committees and commissions which had reported earlier in the reign, but he also showed conspicuous boldness and practical good sense in devising the details of a fundamental transformation of rural Russia. How long a period of time would have been required to make it effective is one of the many hypothetical questions which spring from the collapse of the existing order in 1917.

The principal instrument of the entire scheme of agrarian reform was the law of 9 November 1906, which formally conferred upon the peasant the right to leave the commune and to consolidate his holding as individual property. It was prefaced by a series of earlier measures designed to increase the total amount of land available for peasant ownership and to ease the transition to the new order of peasant society. A law of 12 August transferred to the Peasants' Bank for purchase by the peasantry the appanage lands (the estates held by members of the imperial family) which the peasant communes already rented. Another law of 27 August dealt similarly with state lands, consisting for the most part of great forest areas in the north and north-east, which were suitable for cultivation. A decree of 19 September brought into the field of resettlement in Siberia the Altay lands held in the name of the emperor. The new order in the village was acknowledged in the decree of 5 October, which abolished most of the surviving legal restrictions upon the peasantry as a class: internal passports, for instance, though still obligatory, were removed from the discretion of the village assembly, while in a dozen other matters the peasants, though not their elected officers, were freed from the administrative control of the land captain. A fortnight later

peasant rights of ownership were recognized by a law empowering
the Peasants' Bank to make loans to individual peasants for the
purchase of separate allotments. Finally came the decree of 9
November.

Painstakingly adapted to the varying circumstances of peasant
tenure, it established different methods of claiming the right to
individual ownership. In the great majority of communes—about
three-quarters or more of the total, representing some nine million
peasant households—the tradition of periodical redistribution of
the land presented formidable obstacles to the new dispensation.
These were overcome in the communes where household tenure
was hereditary by the mere declaration that hereditary tenure had
reverted to individual ownership. In both instances, the old principle of joint family tenure was abolished and ownership was vested
absolutely in the head of the household. This process of dis-
inheriting the junior members of the family was one of the cruellest
features of the entire scheme. It worked both hardship and mischief,
more especially because the junior members continued to be held
responsible for a share of the taxes levied on the household.

The scheme did not begin to come into operation until 1 January
1907, when the county committees who were to supervise the
necessary arrangements began their work. It was carried through
energetically in face of opposition from both the left and the
extreme right. Socialist denunciations were bitter in the extreme.
'Agrarian Bonapartism' was Lenin's characterization of a conservative reform designed to end four centuries or more of peasant
collectivism.

Early in December it was finally announced that the Duma would
be convened on 20 February 1907. This was a signal for the start
of a new election campaign. The number of distinct parties and
groups was this time larger than before, and in the result the
fragmentation of the opposition played no little part in reducing
its effectiveness. On this occasion both the Socialist-Revolutionaries
and the Social-Democrats openly took the field, Lenin in particular
being now convinced that the Duma could be used as a sounding-
board for revolutionary propaganda. The Cadets, though their
cadres were severely depleted by the legal consequences of the
Vyborg appeal, threw themselves into the campaign with un-
diminished vigour. Even now, in spite of all that they had learned
or should have learned, they still thought of forming, in union with

all groups and parties to their left, a single opposition bloc—a proposal which the Bolsheviks rejected with some virulence. For in the fashion that has since become standard Communist practice it was liberalism which the Bolsheviks recognized as the principal enemy. In this they were at one with the forces of government. The Ministry of the Interior intervened ingeniously in the election campaign. As a first measure, all parties to the left of the Octobrists were declared 'illegal', and only 'legal' parties were permitted to issue election literature. The Cadet pre-election congress was itself illegal, and was therefore held not in St Petersburg or Moscow but in Helsingfors. Next, special discrimination was directed against the liberals and the parties of the left by denying employees of public bodies (that is, the 'third element') the right to take part in the elections, while Senate interpretations of voting procedure and ministerial circulars to the provincial authorities were directed to the same end. During the campaign the Cadet clubs in Moscow and elsewhere were summarily closed down and opposition meetings were arbitrarily terminated by the police.

Nor did obstructive measures of this kind mark the limit of government intervention. The full weight of the Ministry of the Interior was thrown on the side of the Union of the Russian People and various smaller groups of similar persuasion. Equipped with arms from secret government sources, the Black Hundred gangs had kept up their campaign of murder and intimidation. In July 1906, shortly after the dissolution of the first Duma, they had been responsible for the murder of the Cadet deputy Herzenstein, an eloquent exponent of the party's agrarian policy. In January 1907 they had made the first of two attempts on the life of Witte (the second followed in May). From now onwards, right up to the end of the regime, these reactionary groups and their leaders were in receipt of regular and substantial payments from the secret funds of the ministry. The leaders were closely linked with anti-semitic notables of the Church, and a government decree of 12 December 1906, issued through the Holy Synod, summoned the clergy to take an active part in the elections. Perhaps mention may be made at this point of the fate of the proposals submitted by the council of ministers to the emperor in the previous October for ending the crudest forms of discrimination against the Jews. They were conceived in no sudden access of liberalism, but were meant to close a source of rank corruption and to blunt the edge of anti-Russian feeling in the west. Even so, they came under furious criticism from the Union of the Russian People. On 10 December, two days before the Orthodox clergy were instructed to shoulder their responsibilities in the election, Nicholas returned the draft of the proposals to Stolypin. No doubt they were entirely reasonable, he said, but in refusing to endorse them his heart told him he was right.

Government pressure in the elections secured for it relatively small gains only. The results brought into existence a party on the extreme right and simultaneously strengthened the extreme left; the chief losses were sustained in the centre by the Cadets. There were, too, thanks to Stolypin's ruthless dragooning of the peasants in the first Duma, somewhat fewer peasant deputies. By comparison with the first Duma, the second was more variegated and less cohesive. On the opposition side, counting from the extreme left, there were sixty-five Social-Democrats, among them a dozen Bolsheviks, thirty-four Socialist-Revolutionaries, fourteen Narodnik-Socialists, a hundred and one Trudoviks, ninety-two Cadets. On the extreme right were twenty-two deputies of violent reactionary views. Between them and the opposition proper were between forty and fifty more, for the most part priests or peasants, who could be relied upon to vote with the right, and thirty-two Octobrists.[1] The representatives of the national minorities were mostly without party affiliations, and the Poles, the largest group among them, once more enjoyed a strong bargaining position with forty-seven seats. In all no more than ninety deputies could be expected to give their support to the government.

A conspicuously divided and somewhat incoherent assembly, the second Duma was self-condemned at the start. It endured for no more than three and a half months and was never in a position during that time to influence government policy. The revolutionary parties were not concerned to assist in legislation but only to address their following and to stir the country by unwearied agitation. The extreme right, led by the recklessly inflammatory V. M. Purish-

---

[1]Before the elections Guchkov had pledged the Octobrists to somewhat more than qualified support of the government. Shipov thereupon resigned from the party which he had largely founded. With his support a small group of former zemstvo moderates united in the Party of Peaceful Reconstruction. Liberal reformers who had rejected 'constitutionalism', they now stood somewhat closer to the Cadets in almost everything except the tactics of the Cadet leadership, which they distrusted. But they did not return a single deputy. Another new liberal group which stood slightly to the right of the Cadets, the Party of Democratic Reforms, had a single representative in the second Duma.

kevich, a dangerous little man with a remarkable gift of abusive oratory, and P. A. Krushevan, who bore a heavy responsibility for the Kishinev pogrom, were resolved to obstruct all serious discussion. From the outset, indeed, they clamoured for the dissolution of the Duma. Between them both party extremes, and more especially Purishkevich, produced constant uproar during the Duma sittings. The new president, F. A. Golovin, who had succeeded Shipov as chairman of the Moscow zemstvo board but was elected as a Cadet—almost all the available knowledge of parliaments and parliamentary procedure was concentrated in the Cadets—kept order with difficulty and was frequently obliged to suspend sittings. As much as all else it was the anxiety of the Cadets, and indeed of most of the opposition as a whole, not to provide a pretext for dissolution which kept the Duma going for as long as it did. Even before the elections the Cadets had tried to reckon with the possibility that the government would look for such a pretext; after the political murder in March of Iollos, another of their prominent figures in the first Duma, they showed marked restraint in meeting the provocative violence of the extreme right.

But they were now led in the chamber itself by Miliukov, and Miliukov, though he showed almost a touch of genius in finding formulas which smoothed over internal party differences, was not equipped for effective leadership in the Duma. In purpose and temperament, V. A. Maklakov, who entered the Duma at the same time, and who differed sharply from Miliukov while serving him loyally in three Dumas, was altogether less intransigent and much more realistic. Among all the remarkable orators on the Cadet side he was the least rhetorical. Lucid and courageous in mind, he had argued against establishing even the loosest ties with the forces of revolution. Now, after the chastening liberal experience of the first Duma, Maklakov stood for relations with the government other than those of mere opposition. There were all too few in the Cadet ranks to follow his lead in desiring some degree of co-operation with the government for limited and defined ends.

In the course of the Duma's review of the legislation enacted since the previous summer under article 87, the first clash between government and opposition inevitably arose over the field courtsmartial. The opposition hotly condemned the whole procedure as both unconstitutional and evil. The government retorted with denunciations of the revolutionary terror, vainly inviting the

Cadets to add their voice in the Duma in condemnation; while for their part the paladins of the Union of the Russian People hurled loud and reckless charges against every other group in the chamber. These charges and counter-charges did not die down. But the fundamental issue between the government and Duma arose on the question of Stolypin's land policy, which ran counter to every principle of agrarian justice that the Cadets and the parties to their left professed. Since there was no means of securing a majority for this most vital part of the government's programme, the second Duma was no less ripe for dissolution than the first.

The government's scheme of legislation was introduced in the lower house by Stolypin on 6 March 1907. Besides the agrarian bill, it included various items, such as a modified system of cantonal self-government, the reform of the lower courts and the 'legalization' of trade unions, which were much less substantial than Stolypin endeavoured to make them appear. His statement was received by the liberals with hostility and by the left with derision. It was on this occasion that Stolypin, in reply to the Menshevik leader, the Georgian Hercules Tsereteli, brought off one of his noted turns of rhetoric: 'These attacks are calculated to paralyse the mind and will of the government. They can all be reduced to two words addressed to the government: "Hands up!" But to those two words, gentlemen, the government can only reply, in complete calm and integrity, with [two] more words: "We are not intimidated!" '

Intimidated Stolypin certainly was not: he was brave to the point of theatricalism. But the question of integrity scarcely entered into the anomalous relationship of executive and legislature. The good faith, at any rate, of a government which, while professing strict legality, is prepared to throw legality overboard in order that it may carry on, is of dubious quality. Part of the difficulty, without doubt, was that the extreme left denied Stolypin even a remote opportunity to come to terms with the rest of the opposition. When the state budget was introduced in the Duma, for instance, both Social-Democratic factions and the Socialist-Revolutionaries sought to vote its rejection without a preliminary word of discussion. This time the Cadets came to the government's assistance in enabling the budget proposals to be handed over to the Duma's finance commission. But the mischief on the extreme left remained. And it was not only the approaching dissolution of the Duma which now became evident. The darker threat was of a revised system of

representation aimed at securing the return of a more amenable
Duma.

In telegrams and addresses to the emperor the local branches of
the Union of the Russian People had repeatedly petitioned for
the dissolution of the 'rebellious' Duma. The small group of
confidential advisers around the emperor and empress were of
similar mind. Stolypin had larger plans in view and brought
patient craft and calculation to their execution. He was reluctant
either to risk an open conflict with the Duma over his agrarian
legislation or to resort to dissolution on those grounds; in either
event, the reaction in the countryside would be unwelcome. Here
the Social-Democrats played into his hands. During the budget
debate one of their deputies by the name of Zurabov voiced a
bitter and quite uninhibited criticism of the army which by imp-
lication touched the emperor and incensed not the nationalists
only. Dissolution very nearly followed there and then. Expressions
of conservative feeling against the extreme left had in turn become more than normally intemperate when a few days later the
government issued a vaguely worded statement that it had un-
earthed a plot to murder the emperor. The Duma could not
misinterpret this warning. In the debate on army affairs in the
middle of next month the temper of the opposition as a whole
was specially cautious. On 4 May, however, the apartment of
another Social-Democratic deputy named Ozol was raided by the
police. It was announced that documents discovered on this
occasion proved the complicity of the Social-Democratic members
of the Duma in a conspiracy to provoke mutiny in the armed forces.
Since the documents in question were in fact a forgery and were
supplied by a woman agent of the secret police, Catherine
Shornikov, the government's own complicity in the affair is beyond
dispute. But the fact should not be ignored that both the Social-
Democrats and the Socialist-Revolutionaries were deliberately
engaged in trying to create their own cells in the armed forces
for the purposes of insurrection. It is relevant to note, too, that
the Social-Democratic congress held in London during this month
of May 1907 laid down for the party member in the Duma the
primary role of agitator in the cause of violent revolution.

The Duma debate on the arrest of Ozol left matters in abeyance:
the government charges against the Social-Democratic deputies
were not withdrawn. On 1 June Stolypin formally moved that their
immunity be waived. The Duma refused immediate consent and

appointed a commission of twenty-two members to investigate the charges and to report in two days. The forgery was proved beyond all doubt, but on the morning of 3 June, before the report was quite ready for submission, the doors of the Tauride Palace were closed. The imperial manifesto dissolving the Duma which was posted up outside announced that new elections would be held on 1 September and the new Duma be convened on 1 November. Sixteen Social-Democratic deputies had already been put under arrest and all those who had not gone into hiding were now similarly taken in charge. The emperor celebrated the occasion with a telegram to Dubrovin, the presiding figure of the Union of the Russian People, endorsing its aims and congratulating himself on its support.

The dissolution of the Duma did not stand alone. Simultaneously came the promulgation of a new electoral law. It is hard to acquit Stolypin in this connexion of extreme duplicity, for until the last moment he kept up the appearance of casting about anxiously for a means of reconciliation with the Duma. In point of fact, the new electoral law had been in secret preparation since his tenure of the Ministry of the Interior in the first Duma. The original draft, prepared by his assistant at the ministry, the methodical and versatile Kryzhanovsky, had been laid before the council of ministers months before the elections to the second Duma, and had been held in readiness since. Issued over the head of the legislature and therefore in flagrant contravention of the Fundamental Laws, the new electoral law was essentially a *coup d'état*, and was promptly and bitterly recognized as such. The invocation of the historic rights of the throne in an emergency masked once more Stolypin's view of state necessity. In a political system newly emerged from absolutism into the deadlock of two successive ventures in popular representation, it was not to be expected that this view would coincide with the view of the opposition.

The key to the change in the electoral system was the disillusionment of the ruling bureaucracy in the peasant voter. Far from being the soul of Russian conservatism and the prop of an ostensibly limited autocracy the peasants had proved themselves only a degree less radical than the urban population. To the government it was therefore clear that popular representation, which for the most part was peasant representation, must be reduced. The new law retained the old system of indirect voting in several stages; deputies were still elected by colleges of electors who were chosen separately by groups of landowners, peasants, urban residents and industrial workers. But the proportion of voters for each group represented in the electoral college was now drastically readjusted. Under the electoral law devised in 1905, itself conspicuously inequitable, the landowners in European Russia had contributed thirty-one per cent of the total number of electors and the peasants forty-two per cent. Under the new dispensation, the relative handful of landowners contributed no less than fifty and a half per cent of the total number and the peasant masses only twenty-two and a half per cent; while the representation of the industrial workers was reduced from about four per cent to two per cent. Seperate representation was retained only in seven cities, in place of the previous twenty; in five of them (St Petersburg, Moscow, Riga, Kiev and Odessa) direct election was tried out for the first time. Elsewhere urban residents were divided, according to property qualifications, into two separate categories, the smaller of which had the larger number of electors, and the urban vote was assimilated to that for the provincial constituency. In the result, an elector in a provincial college represented, it is estimated, two hundred and thirty landowners, a thousand members of the trading and industrial community, fifteen thousand members of the rest of the urban bourgeoisie, sixty thousand peasants or a hundred and twenty-five thousand industrial workers.

This basic manipulation of voting strengths apart, the Ministry of the Interior was empowered to carve up existing electoral areas into separate constituencies according to the nationality of the local population. By this means among others the representation of the national minorities was severely reduced. The Poles and the Caucasian peoples, in particular, returned no more than a third of the former number of deputies allotted to them. This was in keeping with the newly proclaimed principle that 'the Duma must be Russian in spirit. Other nationalities . . . must not and will not possess the power to be the arbiter of questions purely Russian'. There were no representatives, incidentally, from central Asia, which was now declared to be unripe for elections.

Conducted on these principles, the elections to the third Duma afforded the bureaucracy satisfactory results. This was a deeply conservative assembly, and for that reason it endured for the full term of five years. Although to outward appearance they were neither government fish nor opposition fowl, the Octobrists had in fact affirmed their support of Stolypin and were returned as the largest single party. Figures of party strengths varied during the lifetime of the third Duma with numerous small shifts of allegiance in the centre and on the right; but, out of the total number of four hundred and forty-two seats in the new chamber, the Octobrists had more than a hundred and fifty, while between them the three nationalist and ultra-conservative groups to their right, who were essentially the puppet creation of the government, had only a few less. Cadet representation fell to fifty-four, though the Cadets could normally count upon the votes of half as many so-called Progressists. There were thirteen Labour members (Trudoviks) and fourteen Social-Democrats, the latter led by another Georgian Menshevik, Nicholas Chkheidze. The Socialist-Revolutionaries had once more boycotted the elections. The opposition strength came mainly from Siberia, the Caucasus, Poland and the Lithuanian provinces. There were no fewer than forty-four priests[1] in the third Duma, all of them notoriously right-wing.

Loyal at one and the same time to the monarchy and to a class version of the constitutional idea, the Octobrists were elevated to a dubiously mediating role between government and opposition. They provided the new president of the chamber, N. A. Khomiakov, a son of the celebrated slavophil philosopher. Their undisputed leader was Alexander Guchkov. Half-liberal in theory but wholly conservative in economic interest, rather vain but well-meaning, possessed of few ideas but a good organizer, he fairly sums up the qualities of what was perhaps the least unhopeful element in the gloomy third version of a popular Russian legislature.

[1]The Ministry of the Interior had empowered provincial governors to establish at their discretion a separate electoral college for the clergy.

9. For the Sober and the Strong

'Give the state', Stolypin exclaimed on one occasion in 1909, 'twenty years of quiet at home and abroad, and you will not recognize the Russia of that day!' It was, no doubt, a complacent and perhaps not very remarkable prediction, but it bore witness to both the restored confidence of the government and a widespread sense of relief in the country that the turmoil of the years of revolutionary struggle was over. The people of Russia had had their fill of revolution for the time being. Though the composition of the third Duma scarcely reflected the mind of educated society, let alone of the masses, it did reflect a certain swing to the right in public opinion. This was reproduced not in the Duma only. From the summer of 1906 the violence of peasant disturbances and the agrarian programme of the first Duma had left their mark upon the zemstvos also: many of the zemstvos with a sustained record of liberal faith and works passed into the hands of the conservative gentry, who in most instances retained control until the close of the regime. The reaction, in the simplest sense of the term, was normal enough. Russian energies, as so often in the past, had been consumed too quickly, and amid a prevailing lassitude of spirit people looked for tranquillity almost before anything else.

Politically, the third Duma hovered between two worlds. It was neither wholly emancipated from a pre-Duma order of government nor had it taken firm root in an order of 'legality'. At the outset it was embroiled in angry debate on the proposal of the nationalists and the extreme right to employ the term 'autocrat' in the address to the throne. What was at issue was, of course, the constitutional character of the monarchy. Significantly, a majority in the Duma rejected the use of the term. But in April of the following year, when the Duma had demanded the appointment of a commission of enquiry on the railways, the retort of the Finance Minister, Kokovtsev, 'Thank God we have no Parliament yet!' was no less significant. The words infuriated more than one group in the chamber and Kokovtsev himself afterwards regretted them, but they fell not far short of the circumstances and ruling sentiment of the time.

Even before the third Duma met, the revolutionary parties had virtually acknowledged defeat. The Socialist-Revolutionary leaders, finally reduced to impotence by the arrest or flight of the principal terrorist groups in the summer and autumn months of 1907, chose the road of exile in western Europe. In January 1909 their philosophy of terror was exploded, at least for the remaining years of the tsarist regime, by the exposure of Azef. The revelation—the work of an *émigré* revolutionary journalist named Burtsev—convulsed Russia and all but shattered what remained of the party. It had its damaging effect upon the government, too, drawing from the incriminated Stolypin only clumsy evasions of the truth.[1]

As for the Social-Democrats, they also had suffered shipwreck. At the party congress in London in May 1907, held in a most unbrotherly atmosphere in a Christian Socialist Brotherhood Church in Whitechapel, some three hundred delegates—Bolsheviks, Mensheviks, Polish and Lettish members and representatives of the Jewish Bund—had disputed furiously for three weeks and then fallen apart. Between Bolsheviks and Mensheviks argument still raged bitterly on the expropriations in Russia, which provided Lenin with the funds that enabled him to maintain Bolshevik initiative. A further cause of strife was that Lenin almost alone still retained faith in the revolutionary potentialities of the Socialist-Revolutionaries. But even these and other comparable differences of ideology, though once more they split the party into warring sects, dwindled in importance beside the complete disruption of the movement in Russia. The arrest of the Social-Democratic deputies, who had been sentenced to convict labour in Siberia for four or five years, had been followed by mass arrests in the cities and factories. The surviving rank and file were leaderless. When in December 1907 Lenin started out once more on the chastening road of exile, it was in the conviction that a 'revolutionary situation' no longer existed in Russia. Dispersed widely, singly or in twos and threes, in Zurich, Geneva, Berne, Paris, Munich, Vienna, Cracow and elsewhere, the expatriates waited for the most part in failing hope until the end of the road was in sight.

It was partly because conservatism now seemed so strongly

[1] In the first gruesome shock of public—and party—incredulity Azef tried for a time to hold his ground, but then thought it wiser to disappear. He died in Berlin in 1918.

entrenched in Russia that educated society as a whole suffered so marked a loss of faith in politics. The Duma aroused few expectations; all too obviously its function was to endorse decisions already taken. The remarkable thing in the circumstances is that its potentialities as a legislative chamber were not wholly stifled. The Tauride Palace continued to serve as in some sort a training-ground for the parliamentary idea, and, however incomplete the process, the training nurtured even in conservative bosoms a feeling for parliamentary liberties. A section of the Octobrists remained noisily conservative and contributed to the rowdiness of the chamber for a time, but slowly a more tolerant attitude prevailed among the majority. Within a couple of years of the opening of the third Duma not a few Octobrist deputies had moved a little closer towards the Cadets and the government could no longer count with complete confidence upon the support of the party as a whole. The budget commission of the house rose steadily in importance, while in response to Guchkov's lead the defence commission, restricted in membership though it was by a ban on all parties to the left of the Octobrists, showed growing independence and initiative in face of the claims advanced for the emperor's prerogative. On 8 March 1910 Guchkov was elected president of the chamber in place of Khomiakov, who desired to be relieved of responsibility. At the audience granted to him on the following day Nicholas struck the note of icy displeasure which he maintained throughout Guchkov's brief term of office. Thanks in part to this assertion of Duma rights, however, public interest in politics revived a little. The municipal elections in St Petersburg and Moscow registered small Cadet gains, and even the elections to the zemstvos showed a slight swing, if not to the left, at least away from the extreme right.

The sweeping scheme of agrarian reform on which he had embarked in 1906 remained Stolypin's chief preoccupation. Though it was not formally endorsed by the Duma until June 1910, he pursued it with relentless vigour. The poorer peasantry suffered in the process, but it is certain that their situation must in any circumstances have grown worse before it could become better. For the land hunger of the poor was but a single aspect of the general poverty and backwardness of Russia, and for this no remedy could be devised which did not entail cruel consequences. The prospect which Stolypin hoped to gain for Russia is summed up in his much-quoted words to the Duma on 5 September 1908: 'The government has put its wager not on the drunken and the weak but on the sober and the strong—on the sturdy individual proprietor'. The words raised a storm of controversy; understandably so, since they involved the biggest issue in peasant Russia in the years immediately before 1917. It has generally been accepted that they implied a deliberate intention, or at least a willingness, on Stolypin's part to sacrifice the interests of the majority of the peasants to a prosperous *kulak* class. On the other hand, since the debate in the Duma turned on the particular question whether ownership should be vested in the household or in the individual, it has been maintained that in championing the individual against what he called 'the small family commune' Stolypin meant to identify 'the strong' with the majority of peasants. There is something of special pleading here. The remorseless political bias of the reform is not open to doubt. All that need be said in extenuation is that in the last resort both repartitional and hereditary tenure within the commune stood in the way of progress for richer and poorer peasant alike.

The original law of 9 November 1906, which signposted the road to a society of peasant proprietors, was rounded off by two further principal measures, both of some complexity. On 14 June 1910 the condition of hereditary tenure was formally extended to repartitional communes where no redistribution of peasant allotments had taken place since the emancipation, and at the same time a simple majority replaced the two-thirds majority required to exercise the right of consolidating individual holdings. By a law of 29 May 1911 rights of individual ownership were extended from arable land to pasture.

The fruits of Stolypin's labours had scarcely begun to ripen when the Stolypin era was brought to a close. But so far-reaching and fundamental a reform had not been undertaken in the expectation of swift results. Though slowed down by the war, progress towards the petty-proprietor ideal was maintained almost up to the eve of revolution. The number of land surveyors employed by the supervisory local committees rose from two hundred in 1906 to five thousand in 1911 and seven thousand in 1914. The available statistics illustrating the rate of progress are of the most disconcerting variety, though the broad changes are not in dispute. It is estimated that in 1905 some two million, eight hundred thousand peasant households in European Russia—about one-fifth of the total—enjoyed hereditary rights of ownership of their allotment of land. Ten years later the number had risen to more than seven million, or over half of the total. Consolidation—the crux of the reform—even though in too many instances it was assisted by a brutal disregard for the hereditary holdings of other peasants, went at a much slower pace. At that same date, the end of 1915, less than one-tenth of the number of peasant holdings had been fully consolidated into small farms of the western variety (with farmhouse or the Russian equivalent close to the fields or still set some distance away in the village) and a similar proportion had been partially consolidated by a reduction in the number of scattered strips. But nearly three million more requests for consolidation still awaited the attention of the land committees. However slowly, the face of the Russian countryside was changing: the infinitely patched and subdivided land was assuming a newly coherent agricultural shape.

By itself the process of conversion from communal tenure to individual ownership could do nothing to assuage land hunger. Throughout the operation of the reform, at least during the remaining years of peace, the continued increase in peasant numbers was reflected in under-employment in the village. But from 1906 onwards the pace of two complementary processes was quickened to notable advantage. Every expedient was adopted to encourage the sale of private land to peasants and to facilitate colonization in Siberia. The amount of land acquired by the Peasants' Bank rose from year to year. The state and appanage lands made available for peasant purchase represented only a fraction of the total area of the private estates surrendered in this way. In 1913 about half of the cultivable non-allotment land in European Russia was mortgaged to the Peasants' Bank. Conditions of peasant purchase were progressively eased: loans were advanced for the full amount required, not for part only, and the rate of interest was reduced to a lower figure than that offered by any other credit institution. Even so, Stolypin considered the policy of the Peasants' Bank much too cautious and sought to quicken the pace by transferring the administration of the bank from the Minister of Finance to the Minister of Agriculture. Kokovtsev, always prudent to excess in financial matters and indeed in all else, strongly resisted the proposal and found an ally in the emperor.

As for Siberia, it was only now that the government hailed it in earnest as a land of opportunity. Resettlement east of the Urals had had its ups and downs since the nineties, but in spite of waverings of government policy migration had continued fairly steadily until the war in the Far East. It was resumed on an altogether more intensive scale, through wider schemes of government assistance, after freedom of internal colonization had been proclaimed in March 1906. The great trek eastwards during the next three or four years caught up not only the land-hungry from the over-populated central provinces but also the adventurous and the restless among a traditionally migrant people. In each of the three years 1907-8-9 close on three-quarters of a million people uprooted themselves from European Russia to start a new life in Siberia. After 1909 the numbers significantly fell away, dropping to just over two hundred thousand in 1911 and rising slightly again after-wards. For there was also a considerable movement back. One out of every six new colonists returned westwards in 1908 and one out of every five in the year following. As in the earlier years of resettlement, expectations were often pitched too high and the pioneering rigours of existence in the new lands defeated the less industrious or the less enduring; while the government for its part wasted much cost and effort through the faulty organization of aid and the failure to provide temporary colonist dwellings. Neverthe-less between 1906 and 1915 three and a half million people migrated to Siberia. The argument that peasant numbers were increasing at a much faster rate, and that the colonists represented only a drop in the ocean of the land-hungry, is true; but it is also true that no short-term solution of the land problem in Russia was conceivable in those years, or is perhaps conceivable today.

The Stolypin remedy, it may be repeated, was designed in the first place not to confer immediate benefits upon the peasant majority but to assist the progress of peasant agriculture and to create more stable conditions in the village. For these purposes it required the twenty years of quiet that Stolypin had asked for—and continued industrial expansion besides. Cruel though many aspects of the reform undoubtedly were, it is hard to believe that anything less drastic would have overcome the force of peasant inertia. At the outset incentives were necessary, and individual ownership provided them. Where consolidation of peasant holdings took place there is clear evidence of better agricultural methods and of higher yields.[1] In both respects, moreover, the relevant comparison is with eastern Europe and not with the west.

[1] It may be noted that the Ministry of Agriculture greatly extended in these years the work started by the zemstvos in setting up experimental agricultural stations and model farms.

That the effect of the sales of allotment land, which until 1906 had been inviolable, was to sharpen class differences in the village may be taken for granted. The countryside could not be insulated from capitalist development. Following the lead of Plekhanov, it was the 'legal' Marxist economist, Tugan-Baranovsky, who observed that in the twentieth century 'the dream of every peasant is a profitable farm of his own'.

The position of the chairman of the council of ministers, which to an appreciable extent was one of responsibility without power, was at all times ambiguous and difficult. It became especially difficult for Stolypin. As has been indicated, Nicholas had begun, as so often in the past, with expressions of unbounded trust in his new discovery. 'I cannot tell you', he wrote to his mother, the dowager empress, in October 1906, 'how much I have come to like and respect this man.' That note of enthusiasm was short-lived. Though he could not fail to recognize Stolypin's abilities or his service to the monarchy, it was no less certain that Nicholas would eventually become jealous of him. There were never lacking in the highest circles of state those who played upon this jealousy and who once more conjured before the emperor's eyes the menace of a pretender to the constitutional powers of a prime minister.

No less dangerous to Stolypin was the Frankenstein's monster he had helped to create by raising the forces of reaction to a position of power in the Duma. In the eyes of the extreme right Stolypin was no better than a liberal. Throughout the country the agencies of the extreme right flourished in the noise and stir of patriotic and nationalist associations, all of which enjoyed the patronage of exalted names. The Union of the Russian People and, after the quarrel between Dubrovin and Purishkevich, the latter's Union of Michael the Archangel, had become a power in the land. Increasingly it was their representatives in the Duma, not the parties of the centre or the negligible left, with whom Stolypin was obliged to reckon first. Their threats, their blackmail, their Black Hundred gangs, their anti-semitic propaganda steadily undermined his authority. In 1909 the inflammatory agitation conducted by a monk named Iliodor among the population of the province of Saratov caused grave anxiety. Backed by the powerful bishop of Saratov, Iliodor reduced the civil authorities in the province to complete helplessness. From unmeasured abuse of the governor he passed on to denunciations of the ministers in St Petersburg—

'Yid-Freemasons', he styled them—and of government policy. In the background of events in Saratov was a Siberian peasant named Rasputin. It was this situation, as will be seen, which provided a growing cause for the coolness on the emperor's part towards Stolypin.

There were other and for the time being weightier causes of Stolypin's loss of favour. Plans for the reorganization of the army and the navy were being put in hand in the light of bitter experience in the war with Japan. Under article 96 of the Fundamental Laws, the emperor enjoyed unrestricted authority in this sphere so long as no question of further credits arose. The high-handed government interpretation of this provision had drawn forcible protests from Guchkov, and these Nicholas in turn had denounced as unwarrantable interference. With the support of the majority of his party, however, Guchkov had gone on to request the dismissal of various 'non-responsible' persons holding higher appointments in the army and the navy as a condition of extending the necessary credits. In the Duma debate in June 1908 he boldly called upon various grand-dukes to resign their posts as inspector-general or the like in the armed forces. The appeal went unheard, and the clash was renewed in the following March, when Nicholas dismissed the Minister of War, General Rediger, for his inability to silence Guchkov. Inevitably Nicholas's dissatisfaction over the whole affair extended also to Stolypin.

A further instance of the ambiguity of Stolypin's situation is worth recording. His policy of repression notwithstanding, he was anxious not to sever every link with the liberals. When Peter Struve, impressed by the magnitude and promise of Stolypin's agrarian policy, established informal contact with him in order to urge the wisdom of instituting political reform, Stolypin consented to discussions on the subject. But Struve could visit him only in secret and at dead of night. The position of the chairman of the council of ministers would have been still more gravely compromised with the extreme right if his personal contacts with Struve, the ex-Marxist Cadet, were generally known.

A further link between the two men was their extreme Russian nationalism, which in Struve ran to heady liberal-imperialist ambitions in the Balkans. Always an integral part of Stolypin's habit of mind, under conservative pressure his Great Russian nationalism was translated into harsh and inflexible policies of russification. From May 1909 he embarked upon a campaign of repression of the national minorities that revived the worst features of the years before 1905. The liberties which the minorities had won in that year were now almost entirely revoked. Once more, Finnish affairs were brought under the direct control of St Petersburg. By a law of 17 June 1910 the Finnish Diet was given a consultative voice only in whatever belonged to Russia's 'imperial interest' and was thus reduced to impotence in matters involving army service, taxation, the press, teaching in the schools and a great deal more besides. The passion of Finnish resentment and a spate of foreign protests (they included a protest to the Duma signed by some four hundred members of the French Chamber of Deputies and Senate) were without effect. On the eve of war in 1914 no part of the empire was more obdurately anti-Russian than Finland.

Still blinder and more senseless was the assertion of Great Russian chauvinism in the Ukraine. Across the Austro-Hungarian frontier, in Galicia, were several million people of Ukrainian stock, and among intellectuals on both sides of the frontier an awakened feeling for their cultural inheritance—for the poetry, for instance, of Shevchenko—had assumed mildly nationalist forms. These were now countered so vigorously from St Petersburg that fears of a Ukrainian separatist movement which until then were largely imaginary at once acquired greater substance. The ban on the use of Ukrainian in Ukrainian schools bred a deepening resentment and bitterness which flared amid the horrors of the years of civil war to come.

As always, however, the brunt of Russian nationalist persecution fell upon the Poles. Nothing made this more certain in the present instance than Stolypin's personal experience as landowner, marshal of the nobility and governor in the western provinces. The resurgent policy of russification had been foreshadowed, indeed, by his approval of a project designed to reduce still further Polish representation in the Duma. This aimed at dividing the body of voters in the western provinces into two separate colleges, Polish and Russian, and by this means ensuring a majority of seats for the Russian minority. It provided the model for the scheme which Stolypin later adopted for introducing zemstvos in the western provinces.

The zemstvo bill, which was eventually confined to six provinces only—in the other five it had to be admitted that the Russian population was all but negligible—was brought before the Duma in May 1910. Unexpectedly, it ran into heavy weather. It disfranchised the Jews and allowed for separate electoral colleges for Poles and Russians in order to ensure Russian supremacy. Together with an obligatory Russian majority on the zemstvo board and a Russian chairman it required a Russian majority among zemstvo employees. All this was immensely gratifying to the extreme nationalists. It was less relished elsewhere. Even though the bill favoured the Russian peasantry against the Polish landowners, it met with hostile criticism not from the left only but from the centre. The bill received a relatively small majority in the Duma, but only after its grossest forms of anti-Polish discrimination had been toned down. The separate electoral colleges were retained, but the number of representatives of the Orthodox clergy was reduced and the condition that the chairman of the zemstvo board and the majority of zemstvo employees must be Russian was struck out.

The measure had still to be approved by the State Council, which did not turn to discussion of the bill until 1 February 1911, eight months later. And now a strained and increasingly tense situation arose in Stolypin's relations with the upper house. Never before had he been involved in substantial differences with the deeply conservative State Council. Its opposition to the smallest flicker of liberalism issuing from the lower house, more especially to 'democratic' projects of popular education and to proposals to extend the zemstvo system to Siberia and to set up cantonal zemstvos, had earned for it the Cadet title of 'the graveyard of Duma legislation'. The hostility of a majority of the State Council to the zemstvo scheme for the western provinces was undisguised. The nobility there might be almost entirely Polish, but nobility they remained and as such they had a prescriptive right, in the view of the State Council, to the privileges of their class. The view was entirely in keeping with the general character of the upper chamber. But did it provide the true source of the opposition to the bill? Or was it not rather a mask for the concerted intrigue of the higher bureaucracy, perhaps with encouragement from influences still nearer the throne, against Stolypin personally?

A peculiar feature of membership of the reformed State Council, half of whose members, it will be recalled, were elected and the other half nominated by the crown, was that a member of the unreformed body might or might not be included by the emperor in the new upper house for the period of a year. This was one means

by which Nicholas maintained a degree of control of the State
Council. The majority against the zemstvo bill included an
extreme right-wing faction. It was to this faction that Nicholas
now addressed himself privately, first urging its members to support the bill and then advising them to vote according to their
conscience. Stolypin was kept in ignorance of this latter recommendation. On 4 March the vote was taken in the State Council
and the bill rejected by a majority of twenty-four. Included in the
majority were several notables of the extreme right, newly
appointed by the emperor and recently received in audience by him.

Anger and obstinacy told upon Stolypin. On the following day
he proffered his resignation to the emperor. He was asked to
reconsider it. His terms for remaining in office were overbearing
and impolitic: he requested the suspension for three days of both
legislative houses in order that the bill might be brought into
force under article 87 and at the same time demanded the suspension from the State Council of his two most hostile critics,
V. N. Trepov and P. N. Durnovo. Nicholas gave only a cold
consent. Stolypin had done nothing to improve his relations with
the sovereign, with the court or the higher bureaucracy, with the
State Council or the Duma. The latter was in no way behind the
rest of the country in condemning him roundly for so dictatorial a
resort to article 87. It was this action of Stolypin's which provoked
the resignation as president of the Duma of the somewhat embarrassed Guchkov, who solaced himself with a long spell of travel
in the Far East.

The clash with the State Council coincided with a renewed and
more serious crisis over the affair of the monk Iliodor. In the
background, more visibly than before, loomed the figure of
Rasputin. It was the evidence of the latter's growing influence
which now sharpened Stolypin's anxieties. Early in 1911 he had
presented a report to the emperor on the notorious scandal of
Rasputin's personal behaviour and had ordered his banishment
from the capital. In so doing Stolypin had drawn upon himself the
unforgiving hatred of the empress.

When the Iliodor episode broke out again in civil commotion
in Tsaritsyn and a fresh crop of ecclesiastical scandals, Stolypin
approved the measures taken by the chief procurator of the Holy
Synod, Lukianov, to end an intolerable situation. At this point,
while under heavy attack from reactionary elements in the hier-
archy, he found himself at odds once more with the emperor, who

proposed to replace Lukianov by V. K. Sabler, a former assistant of Pobedonostsev who was both Rasputin's patron and accomplice. In the end, only a week or two after he had proffered and withdrawn his resignation, Stolypin was required to call off all action against Iliodor. Lukianov's resignation was delayed until the autumn.

On 27 April 1911, when by a large majority the Duma passed a vote of censure on him for his manoeuvre over the zemstvo issue, Stolypin made his last public speech. He was depressed and in indifferent health, increasingly aware of the web of intrigue around him and suspicious with some cause of Witte, who in an effort to restore his political fortunes seemed fully prepared to come to terms even with the forces of reaction. Most of the summer Stolypin spent on his estate in a condition of semi-retirement. Few doubts were left in political circles that he would soon be dismissed. Even in the previous year, when he had gone on holiday to the Crimea, it was bruited abroad that he would not return to duty, and now there were rumours of his appointment as viceroy of the Caucasus, as governor-general in the western provinces, as ambassador. In July he paid a brief visit to St Petersburg and was conscious of being almost completely ignored.

At the end of August, in the midst of summer military manoeuvres in the south, a memorial to Alexander II was unveiled in Kiev in the presence of the emperor and empress. Stolypin was present on the occasion. Three days later, on 1 September, he also made his appearance at a gala performance in the city theatre of Rimsky-Korsakov's opera, *Tsar Saltan*. During the second interval, while standing in the first row of stalls with his back to the stage, two shots were fired at him almost at point-blank range by a young man in the audience. In a slow gesture of devotion Stolypin turned towards the imperial box and made the sign of the cross. He died in hospital four days later, during which time Nicholas apparently made no attempt to visit the dying man. There can be little doubt of the connivance of the secret police in the murder. The assassin, Dmitry Bogrov, was another revolutionary turned police spy. The authorities in Kiev had been forewarned of a terrorist attempt on Stolypin's life, and yet the police chief of the city had himself provided the assassin with a ticket of admission to the theatre. Bogrov was hanged before the member of the Senate deputed to investigate the murder could arrive in Kiev.

As the current of European affairs moves towards 1914 the record of diplomacy of the belligerent powers appears to lose what little rational meaning it might otherwise have possessed. There is, without doubt, a certain consistency in Russian diplomacy from 1905 onwards—the consistency, one is tempted to say, of fatality—but in every other respect the Russian conduct of affairs is at once strangely confused and mechanical.

It was more by accident than design that the Anglo-Russian Convention of 1907 marked a point of final departure in the relations of Russia to Germany. The break with Germany widened only under the impact of the Bosnian crisis of 1909. And even then, perhaps, the prospect of a Russo-German rapprochement directed against Britain was not entirely ruled out. Such an alliance, at any rate, had been the German emperor's considered aim during Russia's war in the Far East. He had found momentary support from a stupefied Nicholas ineptly trying to conduct foreign policy on his own initiative. In search of diplomatic support against the Anglo-Japanese alliance St Petersburg was willing to concede considerable advantages to German trade in the commercial treaty of July 1904. But the original plan of a defensive alliance against Britain which had been proposed by William, to which France was eventually to be asked to adhere, came to nothing. In July 1905, however, when Witte was about to sail to the United States for the peace negotiations with Japan, a second and better German opportunity arose. The two emperors met on Nicholas's yacht in the Gulf of Finland and William produced for the occasion the draft of a very similar treaty of alliance, to which Nicholas secretly appended his signature on 11/24 July. This was the treaty of Björkö, which was meant to come into force after peace had been formally concluded with Japan.

Not until seven weeks later did Nicholas inform the horrified Foreign Minister, Lamsdorf, of what he had done. The cost of imperilling, indeed of being obliged to relinquish, the alliance with France was elaborated by Witte, and Nicholas had no choice but to retreat in confusion. In spite of William's bitter reproaches, a war against France, the ally of Great Britain, was expressly excluded from the operation of the agreement. So ended the treaty of Björkö. The episode became common diplomatic gossip in spite of the dense veil of secrecy which St Petersburg threw over it. It did nothing to prosper good relations between the two emperors or between their respective Foreign Offices.

Izvolsky, who was appointed Foreign Minister in Lamsdorf's

place in 1906, had been ambassador in Tokyo before the war with
Japan. An exuberant character beneath all his elegance, he was
afforded every encouragement to strike out on an exuberant line
of policy. Russian power politics had always oscillated between
east and west, and defeat in the Far East was now a signal for
diplomatic adventure at the other extremity of the empire. This,
in the cross-pattern of European diplomacy in those years, entailed
panslav pressure in the Balkans once more.

First, however, it was necessary to chart a new course between
St Petersburg and Tokyo. It was American insistence on the
principle of the open door in China, promptly expressed in the
financial penetration of Manchuria, which helped to draw Russia
and Japan together. This, in turn, played a small part in tempering
the Russian attitude towards Britain, the ally of both Japan and
France. The conciliatory attitude of the British government at the
time of the Dogger Bank incident had taken a little of the poison
out of the relations between the two countries, though all the
familiar sources of friction and distrust remained. Nevertheless,
prolonged discussion in St Petersburg between Izvolsky and the
British ambassador, Sir Arthur Nicolson, yielded its formal sequel.
On 18/31 August 1907, a month after Russia had concluded a
largely secret agreement with Japan,[1] an Anglo-Russian convention was signed. Ostensibly it sought to guard against conflict
between the two powers in Asia by agreeing upon respective
spheres of influence in Persia, Afghanistan and Tibet.

In point of fact, it was unlikely in the extreme that this narrowly
conceived trading in imperialism would by itself do much to
resolve Anglo-Russian differences in Asia—least of all in Persia,
where Russia had no lasting intention of striking a bargain with
any other power. It tended, if anything, to deepen the risks of fatal
conflict. Nor was it designed to promote Anglo-Russian amity in
Europe, since nothing in this division of Asiatic spoils was meant
to obtrude upon the still shifting course of Russia's relations with
Germany. What St Petersburg was looking for was diplomatic
support in a renewed approach to the historic 'eastern question'—
control of the Straits—and in a reborn scheme of political penetration of the Balkans. What London was concerned with was the

---

[1]This was followed by the anti-American treaty between the two countries
of June/July 1910, by which Outer Mongolia was recognized as a Russian
sphere, and by the more extensive secret Russo-Japanese treaty of 25 June/
8 July 1912.

menace of German competition and the developing symptoms of German bellicosity. It was this bellicosity that transformed the Anglo-Russian convention into something more than a formal diplomatic gesture.

Slav peoples constituted more than half of the total population of the Austro-Hungarian empire. In foreign affairs the nationalist temper of the third Duma, strongly reinforced by the somewhat irresponsible imperialist sentiment of liberals of Struve's type, was focused upon the south Slavs in the Balkans. Izvolsky cultivated Russian projects of a greater Serbia and at the same time pursued more dramatic plans with elegant tortuosity. Arrayed against him in Vienna was von Aerenthal, who had been ambassador in St Petersburg during 1902-6. In September 1907 the two men suggested an exchange of favours: Russia sought a revision of the Straits convention which would open the Mediterranean to the Black Sea fleet, while Austria desired to annex Bosnia and Herzegovina. The famous tragic farce of error or misunderstanding followed at the meeting between the two Foreign Ministers in September of the following year, at which Izvolsky was convinced he had reached agreement on the terms of the deal. A week later, on 23 September/6 October, with only the most cursory private warning to Izvolsky, Austria proclaimed the annexation of Bosnia and Herzegovina. Amid a great outcry in St Petersburg Izvolsky sought the consent of the other European powers to the opening of the Straits to Russian warships. There was no anxiety anywhere, except in Paris, to save him from the consequences of his scheming. The Austrian *fait accompli*, in fact, had provoked acute apprehension in all the capitals of Europe and no Foreign Ministry was prepared to entertain the further risk of establishing Russia in Constantinople.

In St Petersburg, where the dream of a greater Serbia had been shattered in humiliating circumstances, there was intense resentment against Austria. It was partly directed to maintaining nationalist passions in Serbia. But in the crisis that came with Austrian military movements and the intervention of Germany in accordance with the terms of the Dual Alliance, Russia had no choice but to recognize her own military weakness. Capitulation to Germany in the spring of 1909 inflicted a damaging blow to the vanity which entered so largely into Russian nationalist sentiment.

10. On the Eve of World War

In the three remaining years of peace after the death of Stolypin Russian domestic policies underwent little change. Between them the emperor, the nobility and the government saw no reason for change, or at least for none that the opposition would welcome. Both the emperor and the nobility were inclined to weigh the advantages of reducing the Duma to a purely consultative body; Nicholas himself did not wholly abandon the idea, indeed, until the empire was in dissolution around him. For the time being, however, equilibrium had been restored, or so it seemed. The emperor withdrew into even greater privacy at Tsarskoe Selo. The nobility, still active behind the scenes of government, set the stamp of an unteachable class egoism upon the counsels that reached him there. The positive energies of the government were largely taken up with the progress of land reform and with a renewed drive in the expansion of heavy industry which was directed in the first place towards increasing the country's military potential. For the rest, if the government moved slightly farther to the right, conservative society or a part of it shifted a fraction closer towards the centre. Though opposition energies were beginning to revive, the aftermath of failure still clogged the mind and spirit of Russian liberalism.

Stolypin's place as chairman of the council of ministers was taken by the Minister of Finance, Kokovtsev, who had in fact virtually held the position during the last months of Stolypin's life. The Duma did not warm to him. Experienced and intelligent, he was an honourable but not very striking figure, severely orthodox and somewhat clerkly in matters of finance, prudent in all else to the point of pedantry and entirely without imagination. The self-congratulatory strain in his memoirs makes him appear even more incapable of leadership than he evidently was. The Minister of the Interior in the earlier part of the period, A. A. Makarov, another experienced bureaucrat though of a less well-meaning kind, was dense and arrogant. More influential in some ways than either of these was the Minister of Agriculture, A. V.

Krivoshein, able, adroit and a practised charmer, restrained by few scruples but shrewd enough at moments of difficulty to keep his ambition within bounds. More than any other minister he had learned how much was to be gained at the point now reached in Russian affairs by a flattering show of deference to the sentiments of the empress.

Kokovtsev's path as quasi-Prime Minister was beset by several large and embarrassing obstacles, not least by the incorrigible jealousy of the emperor. For all that it was a necessary part of his management of the state finances and of the protection of the country's credit abroad, Kokovtsev's interest in the work of other ministries, and in foreign affairs in particular, provoked strong suspicion on Nicholas's part. The Prime Minister had also to contend with the immovable weight of diehard prejudice of the majority of the State Council, who continued to veto any item of Duma legislation with the smallest tincture of liberalism. In addition, there were the groups of the extreme right in and outside the Duma to whose financial support the government had seemingly been committed by the regular subsidies sanctioned by Stolypin. More vulgar than Meshchersky but no less insolent and blackmailing, the deputy Markov levied tribute on the state treasury on behalf of various reactionary associations and gutter sheets, demanding increased subventions from Kokovtsev on pain of political reprisals. Finally, there was the attitude of the empress. At the outset of his appointment she had requested Kokovtsev to be frank above all else with the emperor and herself. As events proved, it was the frankness of others for which she soon held him responsible. Almost a couple of years before Kokovtsev was dismissed the empress had expressed the opinion that he would be happier as, say, ambassador in Berlin. For by then she was convinced that another chairman of the council of ministers would be able to silence the disgraceful slander of 'the man of God' she had discovered in the person of Rasputin.

Two incidents in the closing phase of the third Duma, one apparently trivial, the other ominous, played a part in later events. Both occurred in April 1912. The first was a duel which the volatile Guchkov fought with an army officer named Miaso-yedov whom he suspected of treachery and who was an intimate friend of the Minister of War, General Sukhomlinov, or of the latter's wife.[1] The other was a strike on a British goldfield

[1]Miasoyedov was hanged as a spy in March 1915.

concession on the river Lena, in Siberia, which ended in grim tragedy. Beginning as a dispute over food supplies and deplorable conditions of management, the strike had lasted a fortnight but had been peaceful enough when the troops who had been summoned to the scene opened fire on a crowd of several thousand. Though there was not a single military casualty, more than two hundred men were killed and as many wounded. In reaction to what appeared to be so wanton a massacre strikes flared up in all parts of the country; in some cities there were attempted street demonstrations. Even the conservative benches of the Duma were shocked by the bland philosophic reflection of the Minister of the Interior, Makarov, on the affair: 'It has always been so— it always will be so'. A Labour deputy named A. F. Kerensky, a lawyer, sent by the opposition on a mission of investigation to the scene, used the occasion to launch a powerful oratorical attack on the government. But the industrial strikes were more significant than the oratory. The strike movement had begun to revive in the previous year, and from now until the outbreak of war it continued to gather strength. In spite of the passions aroused by the Lena goldfield shooting, in spite also of later Bolshevik claims, perhaps it should be made clear that the strikes from 1911 until the beginning of 1914 were primarily economic and not political.

The third Duma completed its term in May 1912. A mood of public indifference born of lost illusions was still evident in the elections to the fourth and last Duma which concluded in the following October. Once more the government took no chances and the election procedure was duly rigged in various ways. The Ministry of the Interior contrived new arbitrary groupings which reinforced the supremacy of the landowners' votes, in still more provinces the clergy were raised to the status of a separate electoral college and the provincial governors resorted to factitious technicalities to strike out the names of opposition candidates. In the result there were about fifteen more deputies of the extreme right in the new Duma, which seemed likely to be even more conservative as a whole than the old. For in the centre the Octobrists, no longer the main element in the so-called government bloc, had lost ground heavily to the candidates whom the government had put up against them. The Cadets were more or less unchanged in strength, as also were the handful of Labour deputies and the combined body of Social-Democrats. The

Octobrist, Michael Rodzianko, an aristocratic landowner of anglophil sympathies, an enormous figure of a man, loud-voiced and self-important, who had succeeded Guchkov as president of the Duma in the previous year, was re-elected to that office. Guchkov himself, possibly through government manipulation of the votes, failed to be re-elected and now led from outside the chamber a party reduced in strength by about fifty seats. He had not long to wait before he was elected to the State Council.

Almost from the opening of the fourth Duma on 1 November the growing pressure of events was reflected in a slightly changed alignment of groups and parties. The three separate groups of the conservative and nationalist right, though at one on broad issues of policy, often found themselves at odds over public questions which involved nothing less than the prestige of the monarchy; while the Octobrists, though they emphasized the position of balance they had secured by switching their votes from time to time to the government, were drawn into still closer relations with the Cadets. From the first, indeed, there was a somewhat more critical spirit in the fourth Duma. It was expressed in what was at times an almost militant solicitude for the constitutional proprieties. Rodzianko himself gave a lead. In his opening speech as president he declared himself 'a convinced supporter of the representative system' and spoke of the need for strengthening constitutional principles and for (in the nearest English translation) 'eliminating an impermissible illegality' (*proizvol*). At these words most of the deputies of the right rose in a body from their seats and left the chamber. But there were others of a less rabid temper on whom Rodzianko's hint was not wasted.

It was certainly wasted upon the State Council. The latest replacements in the upper chamber had served to make it even more right-wing than the government itself, more zealous for the prerogative of the crown and more regardless of public opinion. Conservative deputies in the Duma, particularly those who were active in the zemstvos or municipalities, might unexpectedly echo public opinion in criticizing individual ministers, but the State Council was unperturbed by feeling in the Duma. Throughout the ten years of its existence as a legislature there was only a single law proposed on the initiative of the Duma (not, that is, of the government) to which the State Council gave full approval. Now, in one instance after another, it proceeded to whittle down Duma legislation at will whenever it did not completely reject bills sent up from the lower house. It rejected once more the proposal to create lower units in the zemstvo organization at the cantonal level and on a classless basis and emasculated the plan for reforming the judicial system in the rural areas. The only effective contribution to this latter scheme of reform was the law passed in June 1912 which restored to justices of the peace elected by the zemstvo assemblies the judicial powers exercised by the land captains.

The government policy of russification was maintained by much the same administrative methods as before. One special measure directed against Polish nationalism took the form of carving out from a stretch of the Polish countryside which contained a sizable Ukrainian element the new Russian province of Kholm, the fifty-first province in European Russia. A similar attempt to detach the southern part of the Finnish province of Vyborg and join it to the province of St Petersburg collapsed in face of the resolute opposition of the local population.

Anti-Polish legislation included the special measures directed against the Jewish population of the towns. Throughout the western and south-western provinces an inspired anti-semitism prevailed. Not the least notorious illustration of this official policy during the reign was given in 1913, when the Beilis trial, like the Dreyfus case in France, divided the country into two camps and in the result shocked public opinion in the west. In the spring of 1911 the dead body of a thirteen-year-old boy was found in Kiev and widely spread rumours of a Jewish ritual murder led to the arrest of a Jew named Mendel Beilis. There was prolonged uproar in the press and a final great surge of public feeling before the accused man was brought to trial in Kiev towards the end of September 1913. Hundreds of foreign correspondents were present. As the trial proceeded a damaging weight of evidence was accumulated of official instigation of rumour and the corruption of witnesses. Behind all the plotting and perjury, a policy of diverting criticism from the government to the Jews was revealed. The person responsible was no other than the Minister of Justice for the previous seven years, I. G. Shcheglovitov. Feelings of acute embarrassment had been aroused in conservative quarters by the time the charge of ritual murder was dropped a month later and the accused man acquitted.

One other event of the year 1913 should have been, but failed to be, a landmark in Russian history. The three-hundredth anniversary of the founding of the Romanov dynasty, formally celebrated with immense pomp in St Petersburg on 21 February, provoked scarcely more than a ripple on the surface of national sentiment. Monarchist loyalties, it is true, were still strong among sections of the peasantry and nationalist organizations staged patriotic demonstrations here and there, but there was all too little in the event itself to touch the heart or imagination of the great mass of the tsar's subjects. The popular mood was submissive and incurious. For his part, Nicholas seemed determined to exclude the Russian people from the celebration of the anniversary. His symbolic tour of the historic centres of the Muscovite power—Vladimir, Nizhny-Novgorod, Kostroma, Yaroslavl, Suzdal, Rostov, Moscow—was indeed a Romanov family occasion, designed to commemorate not the achievements of Russia but the past glory and future greatness of the dynasty.

Of the future greatness of the dynasty there were already doubts. The name of Gregory Rasputin, though it was not wholly unfamiliar before then, first appeared in the Russian press in 1910. A year later it was on the lips of almost every literate person in St Petersburg and was spoken with varying degrees of bewilderment and apprehension. Already Rasputin's influence upon the emperor and empress, and through them upon the choice of candidates for office in Church and state, had become a factor of some consequence in Russian politics.

There is nothing to be said for melodramatic versions of Russian or any other history, but it is not easy, in spite of all determinist readings of the events of 1917, to exaggerate the part played by Rasputin in the downfall of the monarchy. 'Scientific' history, since it takes so little count of the will and the passions of the individual, too often destroys the substance of history, and Rasputin belongs to the substance. The details of the story are by this time hackneyed, their crude and coarse extravagance overwritten. Rasputin, it may be granted once more, was a symptom rather than a cause of the cancer which devoured the tsarist regime. But so ugly and startling a symptom could not fail to produce momentous consequences of its own. Next to the fantasies of Nicholas's continued assertion of the rights of autocracy, the intervention of Rasputin in affairs of state was the principal mischief which corroded monarchist loyalties and swept away all means of resistance to the popular forces of revolution. It may be sufficient to observe once more that Rasputin had achieved the reputation of a *starets*, a holy or half-holy man, as a familiar Russian type of wanderer who begged his way from monastery to monastery, that he was illiterate, that in the absence of a surname the one given to him (derived from the word *rasputnik*, a profligate) was meant to distinguish his violent lusts. He differed from others of his vagrant pilgrim kind in possessing unusual peasant shrewdness and a histrionic sense that eventually enabled him to affect hypnotic powers. Coarse and powerful, studiously acting a part and gaining steadily in self-confidence, he preached a dark but oracular doctrine of redemption through sin. In the process he acquired a certain reputation among various assertive figures in the Church and a following in fashionable female society in St Petersburg. In this society, where esoteric religious cults had long been popular, he drew the attention of the two feather-pated Montenegrin princesses who were married to grand-dukes. These, together with the witless Anna Vyrubova, the confidante of the empress, brought Rasputin to the notice of the imperial couple. On 1 November 1905, Nicholas entered in his diary the bald record: 'Today we have made the acquaintance of the man of God Gregory, from the province of Tobolsk'.

A determining psychological factor in what followed was the religiosity of the empress. It was the increasingly superstitious religiosity of an ailing and neurotic woman. Before she had given birth to a son and heir in the summer of 1904, Rasputin had had a predecessor of sorts, himself the latest in a line of miracle-workers, in a French mystico-medical quack named Philippe. Now, after the birth of a son and heir who suffered from the incurable disease of haemophilia, the empress, her own health worsening, was racked by anxiety for his life. Awkward and unhappy in public and resentful of her lack of popularity, she saw scarcely anyone outside her family or the narrowest court circle. From the first she discovered in Rasputin not only an inspired vessel of Orthodoxy but also the embodiment of peasant devotion to the crown. Next came the discovery, which is supported by apparently reliable evidence from several quarters, that he could stop the tsarevich's bleedings when the doctors had failed. It was clear to her that Rasputin could be no other than an instrument of divine Providence. As such the doors of Tsarskoe Selo were open to him.

In 1911 the appointment of Sabler, a close associate of Rasputin, as chief procurator of the Holy Synod opened the eyes of the unsuspecting to the formidable extent of the latter's influence. It had still to reach its astonishing climax. The depravity of Rasputin's mode of life, scandalous enough before then, had become all the more notorious after the monk Iliodor fell out with him and proceeded to add his own testimony; while the unsavoury or sinister character of some of the figures by whom even at this time he was surrounded was likewise common knowledge. The empress, outraged by so many evil reports of her man of God, sought to forbid any public mention of Rasputin. This was too much for the Duma. In April 1912, after Guchkov had publicly denounced the *starets*, Rodzianko secured an audience with the emperor and proffered a solemn warning of the injury that the throne was likely to suffer through Rasputin's access to the imperial circle. Purishkevich followed with a furious attack on Rasputin in the Duma. At this point the press, though no formal ban was imposed, was silenced. From the beginning of the year, thanks in the first place to Iliodor, copies of some of the empress's letters to Rasputin—letters with here and there an almost worshipping phrase though they were otherwise innocent enough—were in circulation in the capital. They added a spice of obscenity to what was already a prodigious scandal. Makarov, the Minister of the Interior, who had gone to some pains in order to lay hands on the originals and had succeeded in buying them up, committed the crude blunder of handing them over to Nicholas. In the last days of 1912 he was replaced by the apparently more dependable Nicholas Maklakov, a brother of the distinguished Cadet, a roguish and rather fatuous diehard.

Kokovtsev's departure was announced on the last day of January 1914. It had long been prepared. He had made no good impression on Rasputin at a meeting which had been thrust upon him in the previous year; while Meshchersky, now in closer correspondence than ever with Nicholas,[1] together with the reactionaries in the Duma were bent on his downfall. Nicholas retained him in office, as years earlier he had retained Witte in similar circumstances, just long enough to enable Kokovtsev to complete negotiations for a heavy French loan. That achieved, he was dismissed immediately after the usual expression of the emperor's complete confidence in him, and was awarded the title of count.

[1] In any estimate of Nicholas's intelligence a fact which cannot be ignored is that almost the only newspaper which he read regularly was Meshchersky's corrupt and vulgar *The Citizen*.

Into his place stepped no other than Goremykin. He was in his seventy-fifth year, no less servile and indolent than before and steeped in an even vaster indifference. But he had the approval of Rasputin.

Amid the stagnation of these years the most creative impulse in the life of the country sprang from economic development. Together with agrarian reform the quickening pace of industrial and technological progress appeared to offer most hope for the future.

The Russian economy was still basically agricultural. The total increase of population during the twenty years from the beginning of the reign until the outbreak of war in 1914 was no less than fifty million, with an annual increase at the close of the period of three million. Only a fraction of the increase, as has been indicated, was absorbed by industry or trade. In 1914 the rural population was still not far short of eighty-five per cent of the whole. The standard of living for the majority was wretchedly low, yet the village shared, however patchily, in the general material advance. The technical level of peasant farming, aided by the expert services of the zemstvos (and by small-scale imports of agricultural machinery) was undoubtedly rising. Perhaps the biggest contribution to the relative prosperity of a section of the peasantry came from the growth of credit and producers' co-operatives, in which once more the zemstvos had played a conspicuous part.

The Russian co-operative movement had assumed great importance by 1914, when it consisted of some thirty-three thousand societies with a total membership of over twelve million. Though the figures might be thought small in relation to so vast a population, they held encouraging prospects for the future. Consumers' co-operatives, which had been introduced as far back as the 1870s, grew rather slowly in the large centres of population after 1905. The growth of credit co-operatives in the rural areas was more remarkable. In 1914 they had a membership of eight or nine million and represented the largest co-operative venture of its kind in the world.[1] Of the total amount of loans of about five hundred million roubles a year the greater part went into peasant purchases of land and livestock. The agricultural pro-

[1] The credit co-operatives held eighty-five per cent of the share capital of the Moscow Narodny bank, founded in May 1912.

ducers' associations similarly developed at a promising rate after 1905. A fair number of the eight thousand co-operatives of this type in 1914 had achieved a degree of peasant affluence for their members.

The evils of the village remained. The most conspicuous was still drunkenness, in which the government had acquired a vested interest. The state monopoly of spirits, rapidly extended to the whole country after an experimental start in 1893, contributed an enormous share of the total revenue. The budget estimate for 1914 allowed for receipts from excise, almost entirely from the sale of vodka, of as much as a thousand million roubles out of a total of three thousand five hundred million. This, the largest single item in the budget, was a hundred million roubles more than in 1913, when consumption of vodka was two hundred and eighty million gallons, representing nearly two gallons per head of population. These 'drunken budgets', as they were called, had evoked a certain crisis of conscience in the third Duma. There was support on all sides for a proposal to permit local authorities to close down liquor shops at their discretion. Kokovtsev resisted it tenaciously, betraying an all too characteristic anxiety for the supreme task of balancing the budget while arguing pertinently enough that the state monopoly was not itself the cause of drunkenness. His intractable attitude in the matter had earned him a further mark of disfavour from the emperor, who had been brought round to the idea of temperance reform.

Drunkenness was similarly on the increase among the industrial workers, together with a variety of forms of gambling. But urban conditions generally, it might be hazarded, were improving to some small extent in the period immediately before the war. The fresh spurt in industry from 1911 onwards brought, most notably, an increase in coal production and expansion in iron and steel and in cotton manufacture. It owed much to a further influx of foreign capital. In 1914 perhaps a third of the total capital investment in Russia was foreign; in mining and metallurgy the proportion may have been a half. The total number of wage-earners in industry and commerce was between eight and nine million; in mining, metallurgy and manufacture it was over three million. If industrial wage-levels, and standards of living with them, were low, that was chiefly because, in spite of the adoption of advanced techniques, the productivity of Russian labour was low. But wages in most industries were rising faster, it would seem, than prices. Statistics in this field, however, are no more reliable than the usual run of Russian statistics, and in any case are not easily translated into household budgets. In the metallurgical industries, where wages were highest, the average monthly wage in 1913 appears to have been between thirty-three and thirty-six roubles. For the whole of industry the average has been estimated at between twenty-two and twenty-four roubles. In purchasing power this was only a little above a meagre subsistence level, though it is hard to generalize on the subject with confidence.

Labour was still plentiful and labour rights were narrowly restricted. Although the legal propriety of forming trade unions had been conceded in March 1906, their powers were at once so loosely defined and so rigidly controlled that the existing unions soon disintegrated or were reduced to almost complete inactivity. For all practical purposes strikes were still prohibited by law. In 1907 unions were forbidden to organize public meetings of any kind—a regulation which was not strictly enforced where approved educational schemes were in operation. Two laws passed in 1912 sought to make obligatory the provision of sick benefit funds throughout industry and to establish the principle of workers' compensation. In the first instance, the scheme was financed by contributions from both employers and workers, and was largely administered by the latter. It was more generally observed than the scheme of industrial compensation, which amended earlier regulations that had been almost entirely ignored and in which the cost of disability payments was intended to fall upon the employers alone. Nevertheless, legislation of this kind afforded evidence of a nascent state paternalism modelled upon German practice. It did not stand in the way of keeping watch upon labour agitators or of arrests and deportations.

Illegal though they were, strikes could not fail to keep pace with the simultaneous growth of industry and of literacy among the urban proletariat. The strike movement had reached its lowest level in 1910, when fewer than fifty thousand workers were involved in some two hundred strikes. But with the renewed industrial expansion in succeeding years the figures rose sharply. If the numbers for two or more strikes in the year in the same enterprise are added together, about seven hundred thousand workers were on strike in 1912, nine hundred thousand in 1913, and from January to July 1914 the total was nearly a million and a half.

Except in the summer of 1914, the revolutionary parties

bore little responsibility for these strikes. Within Russia, indeed, they were in almost total eclipse. The expatriate Social-Democratic and Socialist-Revolutionary leaders led a fevered but dispirited and demoralizing existence, penurious, introverted and more quarrelsome than ever. Underground contact with Russia was difficult and uncertain. In 1913 the amnesty which graced the Romanov tercentenary brought back from exile several revolutionaries of note, among them the Menshevik leader Martov, but their return to Russia brought little immediate advantage to either Social-Democrats or Socialist-Revolutionaries. The Bolsheviks, more especially, seemed to be a spent force; what had been preserved of their organization was riddled by agents of the secret police. Their ranks had been thinned not only by arrests and imprisonment but, more significantly, by desertions. From 1908 onwards, indeed, the membership had been invaded by doubt. Had not the underground role of the party been proved a failure? Among both the Social-Democratic intellectuals and the rank and file the conviction had grown that the cause of socialism in Russia would best be served by 'legal' activities—by trade union organization and the defence of working-class interests in the Duma. Surely, it was urged, the whole conception of a party of professional conspirators was out of date and ripe for liquidation. It was this line of reasoning which distinguished the so-called 'Liquidators', who were strongest among the Mensheviks.

Against them, as against the legal Marxists and the 'Economists' in earlier years, Lenin fought with characteristic virulence. Almost isolated at times among the warring exiles, he could no longer count upon the discipline of the remnants of his following inside Russia. Nor could he look for party funds from men like Savva Morozov, one of the richest of native Russian capitalists, who had committed suicide in 1910. But never during these bleak years of exile did he lose sight of the goal of power. Although more than once during the period he confessed that he did not hope to live to see the revolution, he continued with ruthless single-mindedness to plot the course of revolution. His belief in himself and in his Marxist prescription for power never wavered; a true fanatic, though selfless in the pursuit of power, he acted on the principle that all who were not for him were against him. He was, as Plekhanov, for instance, had come to realize, quite without scruple, a conspirator prepared to jettison every democratic principle of socialism in the name of a socialist revolution.

It was when the Social-Democratic Party in exile was most irreparably disunited that Lenin severed the last slender threads that joined Bolsheviks and Mensheviks. In moral principle—perhaps the crux of all the differences between them—the factions were, in truth, all but a world apart. In January 1912 a small conference which Lenin summoned in Prague of his expatriate following, and which was attended by several delegates from Russia, formally expelled the Mensheviks from the ranks of the party. It elected a new central committee, to which soon afterwards a Georgian Bolshevik named Stalin was co-opted. Although in Russia itself for almost two years afterwards Bolsheviks and Mensheviks still sought to unite their respective factions in a single party, Lenin never abandoned the exclusive claim which he had asserted to the Social-Democratic title.

At Prague, in spite of renewed calls in their midst for a boycott, the Bolsheviks resolved to enter their own candidates for the elections to the fourth Duma. In their electoral campaign they were, unknown to themselves, assisted by the secret police. On the editorial staff of *Pravda* (*Truth*), the legal daily newspaper which the Bolsheviks started in St Petersburg in April, were two police agents. It was the security department of the Ministry of the Interior which arranged for the election to the Duma, among the six successful Bolshevik candidates, of one of its agents, Roman Malinovsky. A delegate from Russia to the Prague conference, where he was elected to the central committee of the party, Malinovsky's speeches in the chamber, which were composed by Lenin, were so vehement and so telling in denunciation of the government that the police department was eventually obliged to withdraw its support from him. His secret role was confided to Rodzianko, and Malinovsky, to the general astonishment at the time, resigned his seat in May 1914 and disappeared abroad.[1] But *Pravda*, with which the police maintained its link, preserved almost to the last a barely disguised seditious character. Constantly closed down by court order, it constantly reappeared under a slightly modified title—*Workers' Truth, Truth of the Workers, Proletarian Truth*, and so on. Not until the outbreak of war was it finally suppressed for defeatist propaganda.

As is evident from the admittedly ambiguous example of *Pravda*,

[1]He returned to Russia after the revolution of February 1917 and was executed in the following year by the Bolsheviks.

the press in Russia in the years before 1914 enjoyed what in the circumstances was remarkable freedom, greater than any it had known before or has known since. In spite of all intimidation by the censorship, there was wide latitude for the expression of anti-government opinion. *Russkoe Znamia* (*The Russian Flag*), the scurrilous organ of the Union of the Russian People, was countered not only by the Marxist journals but by a considerable liberal press. If the popular conservative *Novoe Vremia* (*New Times*) in St Petersburg and the more heavily conservative *Moskovskiya Vedomosti* (*Moscow Chronicle*) carried the big guns, they were challenged to some purpose by the ardently liberal *Russkiya Vedomosti* (*Russian Chronicle*) in Moscow. There was something to suit all tastes among the politically-minded part of the population.

But the public which studied newspaper reports of Duma debates was not, it may be repeated, numerous. Right up to the war the larger part of educated society remained listless and apathetic where politics were concerned. On a given issue it might as before instinctively side with the opposition against the government, but it was not disposed to cherish opposition doctrines. The intelligentsia had lost its bearings, and was very conscious of having done so. Its conservative wing had always been a minority, but now it was those truths of Russian experience which had illuminated the conservative philosophy of a writer like Leontiev that brought home to former progressives the inadequacy of the beliefs they had formerly taken on trust. A famous sign of the times had been the publication in the spring of 1909 of a volume of essays, entitled *Vekhi* (*Landmarks*), by seven authors, among them Struve, Nicholas Berdyaev and Sergey Bulgakov, all three formerly Marxists. What had gone wrong these writers asked, with the liberal aspirations of educated society? Through what failure of faith or philosophy had earlier hopes been disappointed and reaction enthroned again? The answer returned to this question was a chastening one: the guilty men were the Russian intelligentsia. Brought up in the odour of irreligion, they had sought only shallow and 'unhistoric' ends. In pursuing an ideal of the emancipation of humanity they had rejected all spiritual light and leading, all sense of established Russian tradition and of the mystical fraternity which lay at the heart of Orthodoxy. It was not merely an element of intellectual instability in Struve or the somewhat romantic eschatology of

Berdyaev which inspired this judgment upon the rationalist and positivist temper of the radical intelligentsia. Struve and the others were concerned in all sincerity to reconcile Russian liberalism with Russian religious thought.

The established order of the Orthodox Church contributed little or nothing to the spiritual life of the nation, and yet Orthodox doctrine, as it was unfolded in the teaching of Vladimir Soloviev, for instance, held the vivifying essence of a gospel of humanity. It was not ex-Marxists only who felt that the Church might still become a potent factor in national life. In 1909 hope of fundamental measures of Church reform had not yet been extinguished among both a section of the higher clergy and a group of influential laymen. A movement for reform in earlier years, led by several bishops and theologians, had aimed at purifying the Church by freeing it from the fetters of the state. The practical end in view was to restore the patriarchate (abolished by Peter the Great) and to loosen the grip of the civil power upon the Holy Synod, the immediate task to raise the educational level of the parish priesthood and widen instruction in the Church schools. These hopes were canvassed at a conference of ecclesiastical figures in January 1906 which was summoned by consent of the tsar and which was designed as prelude to a full *sobor* (assembly) of clergy and laymen. But there was no sequel. The conference laboured earnestly for a year and produced a voluminous report, but the assembly was not held, the reformers among the bishops and the principals of theological seminaries were translated to more distant scenes, and the Holy Synod grew increasingly servile in support of government policies of reaction. The decline of the Church continued, its authority ever more deeply compromised by association with the Union of the Russian People and by the subservience of several of its princes to Rasputin.

In life and in death the most powerful opponent of the Church was Leo Tolstoy. His rational Christianity was directed not merely against Orthodox dogma and ritual but against the entire order of an established Church. In 1899 the publication of Tolstoy's novel *Resurrection*, though in Russia it was severely mutilated by the censorship, evoked deep and disturbed feelings. The effect of his indictment of Church and state was all the more profound because on this occasion, in order to assist the emigration to Canada of members of the persecuted sect of Dukhobors, Tolstoy went back on his former decision, marking his condemnation of property rights, not to accept payment for newly published work. His excommunication by the Holy Synod in February 1901 produced an even greater stir both at home and abroad. In Russia it did nothing to diminish the force of Tolstoy's teaching. Tolstoy denounced revolution equally with autocracy; but his repudiation of property and the state, not to speak of his idealization of the *muzhik* as the only true representative of humanity, undoubtedly played its part in the rise of revolutionary sentiment. On the other hand, revolutionary violence was in no way mitigated by his doctrine, essentially a protest against the tradition of violence in Russian social development, of non-resistance. Significantly, amid the national mourning at his death on 7 November 1910, when the Duma (though with some protests from the right) broke off its sitting in heartfelt tribute, the government preserved an embarrassed and eloquent silence.

Tolstoy's was by far the most pervasive influence in the literature and thought of the reign. (Russia's 'evil genius', Nicholas called him.) Few other Russian writers, indeed, could wholly escape it. The force he exerted was in the first place of a moral character. His work, as Chekhov put it, justified all the hopes built upon literature. Through every difference of imaginative purpose in the work of other writers, every rejection of Tolstoyan argument, his moral authority is apparent. Something even of the argument is visible in the crystalline depth of Chekhov's art. It is no less evident in the somewhat leaden realism of Gorky's maturity, in the coldly poetical realism of Bunin, in the esoteric realism of Andreyev. Gorky's didactic impulse, indeed, owed more to Tolstoy than to Marx. Of all the imaginative writers of note of the period Gorky was the only one to identify himself, even though he kept at a certain distance from it, with the Bolshevik faction. Drawn into Marxist agitation at the triumphant start of his career, arrested in 1900, his election to the Academy of Sciences annulled by the government in 1902, arrested again after Bloody Sunday of 1905, active in support of the Bolshevik insurrection in Moscow in December, in exile in Capri he remained in touch with Lenin and was the most constant financial stay of the Bolsheviks in exile.

From the later Tolstoy, who renounced art, to Gorky, Russian literature follows a 'social' or 'civic' tradition. It remains to note a wholly different aspect of literature and art during the twenty years or more before the revolution. The realist writers of varying hues represented only one of two main streams of achievement. In the last decade of the empire, when realism flowed into backwaters of eroticism and cerebration, it was much the narrower stream. The genuine creative power in verse and prose came from the Symbolists, who drew upon the aesthetic revival inaugurated in the 1890s by Merezhkovsky and freed it of spuriousness and preciosity. In turning their back on civic ideals and echoing Mallarmé's saying that poetry is written with words the Symbolists brought superb resources of language and craftsmanship to their metaphysical preoccupations. The greatest names among them are Viacheslav Ivanov, Andrey Bely and—the supreme poet of the movement—Alexander Blok. From the Symbolists, during the last year or two of peace, derived several other movements, among them the Futurists—extravagant and posturing, yet candid in rejection of the cults which had failed their generation.

With the rebirth of poetry went the brilliant flowering of painting, ballet and music in the new century. This drew its inspiration from Diaghilev's wonderfully creative *Mir Iskusstva* (*The World of Art*) and was most closely associated with the names of Benois, Fokine and Stravinsky. Even more strikingly than literature, the 'pure' art of Russian painting and music from 1907 onwards, much of it the work of voluntary expatriates, illustrates the response of cultivated Russian society to the collapse of its political aspirations.

In art and literature, as in learning also, Russia held its own with the west. The advance of Russian industry marked a similar approach to the material basis of western society. More than all else, however, the distance that separated Russia from the west in these years before the European catastrophe was being narrowed, it seemed, by the rate of progress in education.

The concern for education at all levels in the latter part of the reign ran parallel with other utilitarian projects of Russian development. On the government side it implied no conversion to enlightened social principles. Yet in spite of the reactionary temper of the Ministry of Education, the government exerted itself to striking effect. In higher education the greatest advance was in technology, where the special institutes supervised by the respective ministries, among them the celebrated Polytechnical Institute in St Petersburg, Witte's favourite child, expanded from year to year. In the universities, where in the humanities standards were in every particular as high as in the west, the number of students rose from fifteen thousand at the beginning of the reign to some thirty-five thousand in 1914. In that year there were in all about ninety thousand students in the higher educational institutions, including twenty-one thousand women. The development of higher education for women had been late and conspicuously rapid in Russia.

No concessions of substance were made to the principle of university autonomy. Whatever theoretical rights the university authorities might enjoy in making new appointments, the important chairs were more often than not filled at the instructions of the Minister of Education, who similarly exercised rights of dismissal and the right of expulsion of students for political offences. The minister from 1910 until 1914, L. A. Kasso, a Bessarabian landowner of furious temperament, was commonly described as a bull in a china shop. He had met the student demonstrations at the time of Tolstoy's death with mass expulsions and arrests and a ban on all meetings within university precincts. In the highly charged atmosphere of Moscow University the intrusion of the police at the opening of term in January 1911 culminated in the enforced resignation of the rector and vice-rector. About a hundred members of the academic staff resigned in protest, among them the great historian Kliuchevsky and the no less eminent scholar Paul Vinogradoff. The remarkable thing is that learning flourished and the opportunities for university education prospered in so wintry a climate.

There was a similar expansion in secondary education, where it proved impossible to restrict entry to the *gymnasium* to the children of the gentry or of officialdom. The syllabus of the *gymnasium* was modernized, that of the *realschule* broadened.

But the main advance, and the most encouraging prospect of all, was in primary education. Since the early years of the reign, when the census of 1897 had revealed that only one person out of every five of the population could read and write, the zemstvos and the more progressive municipalities had had the support and aid of a host of voluntary agencies in their efforts to grapple with illiteracy. By far the biggest single item in most zemstvo budgets was expenditure on the maintenance of the local primary schools. Though these were steadily increasing in number, rapid expansion was beyond the unaided resources of the zemstvo boards. Any national scheme of promoting literacy clearly required the adoption by the government of the principle of compulsory school attendance and the co-ordination of the school systems of the state, the Church, the zemstvos and municipalities. The abortive project of compulsory school attendance submitted to the government by the second Duma was taken up by the third Duma, and on 3 May 1908 a law was passed for the gradual introduction of free education for all children from the age of eight to eleven. For all its conservatism the third Duma had gone farther in 1911 and secured a majority for a bill which would have brought all primary schools, those of the Church included, into a single system administered by the agencies of local self-government under the supervision of the Ministry of Education. This was rejected out of hand by the State Council. Yet the extension and the reform of primary education were not halted. Much the greater part of the cost fell on the treasury, since the government would in no circumstances permit the zemstvos and municipalities to levy a higher rate. From a state expenditure on education of forty-four million roubles in 1906 the figure rose by about twenty million roubles a year until the revolution.

In 1908 it was hoped that universal education would be achieved in 1922. At the best this was an optimistic calculation. The estimates of numbers of the school population during the early part of the reign vary considerably, partly because of indeterminate figures for the national minorities. But at the turn of the century there may have been in all seventy thousand schools, more than half of them Church schools, and a school attendance of four million. The school census for January 1911 gives the number of schools as over a hundred thousand, of which nearly two-thirds were maintained by the zemstvos and municipalities, and a school population of over six million. In 1915 there were a hundred and twenty thousand schools and over eight million schoolchildren. This was a long way short of the goal which had been set for that year. War or no war, there could plainly have been little prospect of establishing universal education by 1922. At the outbreak of war, at any rate, almost exactly half the number of children between the age of eight and eleven did not go to school. And the standard of literacy achieved by the great majority of those who did, most of whom would never read a page of print afterwards, could scarcely have been high.

Yet the forward stride in popular education in Russia in the years immediately before the revolution remains impressive.

The achievement as a whole should not be underrated. How formidable were the obstacles to the liquidation of illiteracy in a country as vast and as ethnically diverse as Russia, where immense areas were sparsely populated by scattered communities and climatic conditions so often restricted movement outside the cities, is evident from the repeated withdrawal of Soviet claims in the 1930s to have accomplished the feat. The period 1908-14 was too short for educational reform in tsarist Russia, as it was too short for the realization of agrarian reform. But the hope and the promise were there. The outbreak of war in 1914 put a stop to both.

As late as 1913 Lenin dismissed the prospect of war between Russia and Austria, which would be 'a very useful thing for revolution', as a daydream. Like all the other Great Powers, Russia blundered into world war. Yet in its concluding phase Russian diplomacy reveals few fine shades of doubt or hesitation. From the window of St Petersburg all the essential elements of the crisis of 1914 had been starkly apparent since the Bosnian crisis of 1909. Little had occurred in the interval to modify the pattern of European rivalries or the competition of Russian and Austrian pressure in the Balkans. The desire to maintain friendly relations with Germany was still strongly in evidence among both the tsar's entourage and the government in St Petersburg; besides mere distaste for the alliance with the western democracies, there was still a certain active anglophobia at the Russian court. Thus in spite of mounting alarm at the rising scale of German ambitions and of fears for Russian interests in the Near East, agreement had been reached with Germany in 1911 on the Berlin-Baghdad railway. Nationalist tensions in the Ottoman Balkans, however, which still drew Russian eyes towards Constantinople and the Straits, admitted of no such accommodation with Austria. And, after Russia had played her part in forming the Balkan League, the Slav sympathies of St Petersburg in the Balkan wars of 1912-13 were countered by the manoeuvres not of Austria only, patently seeking 'the great solution' in war, but of the other member of the Dual Alliance. Only the common alliance with France against Germany finally brought Russia and Britain together. The French had concluded a secret naval convention with Russia in the summer of 1912; in June 1914 the visit of a British squadron to Kronstadt was designed with a similar end in view.

A day before the assassination on 15/28 June 1914 of the archduke Franz Ferdinand at Sarajevo by a Bosnian Serb terrorist, the session of the Duma had closed. The strike movement in St Petersburg had spread rapidly to other parts of the country and reached menacing proportions. In the capital and in the south it had assumed an openly political character; at the beginning of July Social-Democratic and Socialist-Revolutionary agitators were once more active. On 8/21 July, when President Poincaré arrived in St Petersburg, barricades were going up here and there in the city. Two days later, when Poincaré left Russia, the Austrian ultimatum was delivered to Serbia.

In the tragic flurry of diplomacy which followed not the least of Russia's misfortunes was that Sazonov, Foreign Minister since 1910, was singularly lacking in force of character. He was not the man to surmount a crisis. Related by marriage to Stolypin, he had risen all too rapidly in the ministry and had little to offer beyond industry and the fatal gift of good intentions. Always anxious to please, after Stolypin's death he felt too insecure to press his own point of view against the militant Russian representatives in Belgrade and Sofia, both of whom enjoyed powerful patronage, or against Izvolsky, who as ambassador in Paris was thirsting for revenge for his diplomatic defeat in the Bosnian crisis. It may well be that no other Russian Foreign Minister could have done better, but certainly Sazonov had chosen to acquiesce in the extreme and fatalistic view that the clash of the powers in the Balkans must end in war. Nevertheless, it was he who, in response to the Austrian ultimatum to Serbia, first urged no more than partial mobilization of the Russian army—that is, mobilization in the south only, where it would be directed against Austria but not against Germany. This would have been a gesture of some significance in the formal exchanges of European diplomacy of the era which ended in 1914. But in the course of the rapid changes of mind in St Petersburg during the next few days the Russian Foreign Minister exerted all too little influence. No doubt the technical military case against partial mobilization under a non-territorial system such as the Russian was sound. Yet the fact remains that Sazonov permitted himself to be overridden in a political decision of the greatest magnitude by the intimates of the chief of staff, General Yanush-kevich. On 17/30 July, two days after the Austrian declaration of war against Serbia, Russia decreed general mobilization. Forty-eight hours later Germany declared war upon Russia.

11. *Defeat and Dissolution*

For none of the belligerents was the first world war so catastrophic or so costly as it was for Russia. The ordeal of war brought to her people vast and profitless tragedy. Russian official statistics of killed and wounded are almost always an under-estimate, and it is probable that there were close on two million dead in a total casualty list of between seven and eight million. To these losses must be added enormous material destruction and an immeasurable toll of human suffering. The cost of defeat was paid even more heavily in a cataclysmic aftermath of revolution which bred a still greater and continuing ordeal. The experience of the Russian masses between 1914 and 1917, eclipsed in the scale of tragedy only by their experience a quarter of a century later, has its place in the political background of much that has happened in the world since.

None of the belligerent powers was less prepared for war than Russia. In the interval after the shock of defeat by Japan some progress had been made in the reorganization and technical equipment of the army and in the development of military-industrial potential. At the last moment a heavy loan from France had been allocated to railway construction in the strategic western areas. But the interval for recovery was all too short. Even if it had been longer, the Russian system of government, so little changed in substance by the semi-constitutional dispensation of 1905, ruled out any prospect of the country being effectively organized for war, least of all against so formidable and technically advanced a power as Germany. Russia was, indeed, no match for her principal enemy. Superiority in manpower could not make up for a crushing inferiority in armament manufacture, for the poverty of Russian communications, the defective Russian commissariat or the shortcomings of Russian military leadership. The western belief, at the outset of the fighting, in the weight of 'the Russian steamroller' bore witness only to a profound ignorance in the west of Russian realities. It ignored, in any event, the inveterate Russian habit in war of prodigally wasting human lives.

In contrast with popular sentiment at the outbreak of the war with Japan, Russia's entry into the world war moved the nation to a religious fervour of patriotism. All differences, it seemed, were forgotten in an impulse of devotion to 'faith, tsar and country'; all national distinctions were obscured and the empire of the tsars was united once more by war. The strike movement in the cities dissolved in the flood of popular emotion. All parties and groups in the Duma, or almost all, pledged their support to the government at a special one-day session of both chambers on 26 July/8 August. Alone among the socialist factions the tiny Bolshevik group in the Duma, together with a handful of Mensheviks and the extreme wing of the Socialist-Revolutionaries outside, cautiously held out against the prevailing mood. The Bolsheviks refused to vote war credits; most of the Mensheviks and the Labour group under Alexander Kerensky qualified their support of the war effort only by approving a 'defensive' as distinct from an 'imperialistic' purpose in the struggle. But for the country as a whole the war in which Russia was engaged was indeed a defensive war. With 'society' in the foremost ranks, the nation was resolutely bent on victory.

The patriotism of the masses in the early days of the war was wholly spontaneous. But it had, as might have been suspected in so shallow an order of society, only shallow roots. It dwindled almost at once into the negative sentiment of the substitution of Petrograd for the German-sounding St Petersburg on 31 August/13 September and the anti-German riots in Moscow some weeks later. In the countryside there was little to match the imposing demonstrations and religious observances in the cities. After the initial stir of mobilization the village remained ominously mute and self-absorbed.

It was from the village that the millions of the Russian army were largely drawn. Illiterate and untaught for the most part, they were, in effect, an army without a cause. Faith, tsar and country notwithstanding, at no stage of the war had the Russian peasant-soldier any real comprehension of the issues at stake or any enthusiasm for the fighting. He fought bravely, with the fatalistic courage he had always shown, although in retreat from the invader of the western borderlands with something less than his customary endurance. Ignorant of what he was fighting for, he was nevertheless made aware amid the holocaust of the early defeats how badly as a rule he was led. With few exceptions, the generals of the imperial army were of mediocre quality, many of them holding high command through mere seniority or, worse still, as with the youthful and incompetent chief of staff, General Yanushkevich, through influential connexions at court. And lower down the chain of command the crippling losses in the first months of the war among the regular junior officers, perhaps even more among the N.C.O.s, were of disastrous consequence in the fighting that followed. British experience in the war was not entirely dissimilar, but the scale of Russian losses in those early months was so much greater that the disaster was of an altogether different order.

A decision taken even before the outbreak of fighting was destined to have profound and deadly results. On 16/29 July, largely on the initiative of Sukhomlinov, Minister of War, a law was issued on the administration of the army in time of war. It conferred sweeping and all but unrestricted powers upon the commander-in-chief not only in the immediate zone of military operations but in a geographically undefined rear. In effect, over enormous and almost limitlessly extensive stretches of territory the civil administration made way for a purely military regime. The law did not so much as mention the council of ministers, which in the event was powerless to intervene in military measures of control of the civil population and which was often left in complete ignorance of them. By the spring of 1915 the whole of Poland, the Baltic provinces, Finland, the Caucasus and Petrograd itself had been brought under military rule.

Another measure of a different kind adopted at the outset of the war had similarly weighty consequences. In the atmosphere produced by years of uneasy debate on the ethics of the state monopoly of liquor, the temporary closing down of the liquor shops was promptly extended to a complete ban on the manufacture and sale of vodka. For almost a year Russia was virtually teetotal. Though the country did not remain so, the legal ban continued in force. It deprived the state of its principal source of revenue and at the same time contributed in no small degree to the accelerating pace of inflation.

It is possible here to note only the salient episodes in the disastrous military course of the war and their bearing upon the circumstances and temper of the home front. The appointment as commander-in-chief of the grand-duke Nicholas Nikolayevich, an uncle of the tsar, after the latter had been dissuaded with some difficulty from himself assuming supreme command, was popular with the army and with the country. But neither in his capacity as a soldier nor in

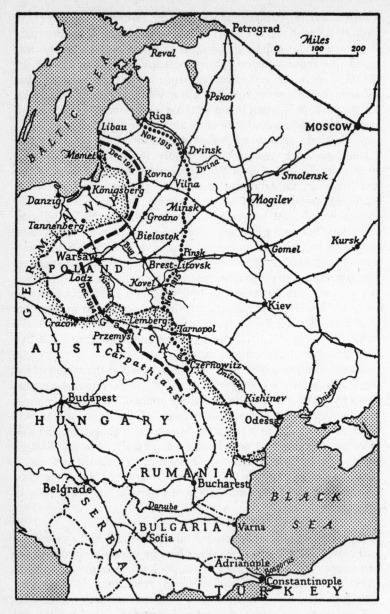

The Eastern Front, 1914–15.

any other way did the grand-duke merit confidence. Certainly he confided little of strategic or moral inspiration to his subordinate generals. Their failings were immediately demonstrated in the appalling defeat at Tannenberg, after the Russians, in accordance with the terms of the secret military agreement with France which required them to assume the offensive within twenty days of the beginning of mobilization, invaded east Prussia and, in response to the urgent appeal of the hard-pressed western allies, attempted an ambitious enveloping manoeuvre against the German forces. During the last fortnight of August the two armies of General Rennenkampf and General Samsonov, powerful in numbers but in little else, fumbled their opportunity, were outwitted by the enemy, failed to effect a junction and were cut up separately. Two entire Russian army corps surrendered; Samsonov committed suicide.

Tannenberg instilled in the Russian high command and in the ranks of the army a lasting sense of inferiority. It inflicted a grievous shock upon public opinion in Russia and dismayed the western allies. Yet it may be repeated once more that it was this hastily improvised pressure in the east which secured the withdrawal of German divisions from the critical battle on the western front and thus played its part in the miracle of the Marne.

Simultaneously with the invasion of east Prussia came the offensive, on which Russia's strategy had originally been based, against Austria-Hungary, the weaker enemy. Long prepared in detail, after a critical opening phase it met with striking success. The attack across the frontier into Galicia (its population almost entirely Polish and Ukrainian) was launched on a broad front and was rewarded on 21 August/3 September by the capture of Lemberg (Lwow) and, a little later, of Czernowitz. The entire Austrian position was imperilled. The German counter-stroke, on 15/28 September, came in southern Poland.[1] Amid savage fighting the German armies drove forward towards the Vistula and almost succeeded in capturing Warsaw before they were driven back. Lodz fell at the beginning of December, but when the depth of

[1] At the beginning of hostilities a proclamation to the people of Russian Poland, drawn up by the council of ministers but issued by the commander-in-chief, had held out the prospect of the unity of the Polish lands and autonomy under the Russian crown. But nothing was done to further this pledge. Although the Polish nationalists under Roman Dmowski at once sided with the *entente* powers, from the beginning the leader of the Polish Socialist Party, Josef Pilsudski, was engaged in organizing a Polish Legion to fight for Austria against Russia.

winter brought the fighting to a halt the Russian armies still
covered Warsaw.

Though they had suffered enormous losses, the military prospect
as yet did not appear critical. A great part of Galicia had been
gained and held, and the withdrawal from western Poland had at
least brought a considerable shortening of the Russian line. Yet
the military nakedness of the land had become all too evident.
These first months of fighting had disclosed in the most disturbing
fashion the basic inadequacy of supplies, and with it the deficiencies
of lines of communication, of transport and of Russian staff work.
There were acute shortages of everything, from artillery to rifles,
from boots to medical supplies; there were as yet no Russian aero-
planes at all. Even rations were short. Most threatening of all at
this early stage was the shortage of shells. Russia had accumulated
what were relatively insignificant reserves only, and against an
estimated monthly expenditure of a million shells current production was no more than a hundred thousand.

There was as yet little thought of defeat. Beyond all question,
however, something of the will to victory had already perished in
the traumatic shock of Tannenberg. Doubt of Russia's allies began
to make itself felt. With too little understanding as yet of trench
warfare (which did not settle on the eastern front until the beginning of 1916), convinced that Russia alone was bearing the real
burden of the fighting, a section of public opinion had already begun
to protest that Britain would fight to the last drop of Russian blood.

Nor can the effect of the pro-German element in ruling circles
be ignored. It had the vehement backing of Witte, who did not
trouble to conceal his opposition to a war which he was convinced
would ruin Russia,[1] and a more insidious ally in elements close to
Rasputin. Early in the war Nicholas received a memorandum,
drawn up with the aid of the Minister of the Interior and the
Minister of Justice, which urged the necessity of bringing hostilities
to a close at the earliest possible moment, since the association
with the western democratic powers involved the Russian empire in
mortal peril. The existence of this memorandum eventually became
known in Duma circles. Meanwhile, however, the Russian-British-
French declaration of 23 August/5 September, by which each of
the powers undertook not to conclude a separate peace, had brought
some measure of satisfaction to all.

[1] Witte's death on 27 February/12 March 1915 brought much relief to the
allied embassies in Petrograd.

Throughout the first winter of the war 'society' as a whole sought zealously to preserve national unity. Opposition to the government, and with it the prospect of achieving a democratic parliamentary regime, waited upon victory. Liberal opinion, which had always indulged panslav sympathies with Serbia, was particularly ardent in support of Russia's righteous cause. In the last year or two before August 1914 it had once more cultivated cautious ties with the parties of the left, but now it washed its hands of the taint of collaboration with socialists who were defeatist or even conspicuously 'defensist'. For the rest, the educated public of all shades of opinion cast around for practical means of aid in prosecuting the war. The government claimed their loyalty, but it was clearly improvident to rely upon the government alone.

The zemstvos took the lead early in August in founding a union for the relief of the wounded and sick and elected as president the amiable, energetic but not very practical-minded Prince G. E. Lvov, who had guided the earlier Red Cross organization set up in 1904. A week later the municipalities followed suit with a union of towns for the same purpose. On 29 August/11 September official approval was given to the association of both unions in a Red Cross organization which became known as Zemgor. There was work enough for them to do in the provision of hospital trains, ambulances, canteens and so on, and beyond this lay a wide field of further voluntary aid within the means of local bodies. The only question at issue was how much they would be permitted by a jealously bureaucratic government to do.

Hindered as they were at every turn by the Minister of the Interior, it was to the Duma that the zemstvos and municipalities looked for support. Dismissed after the one-day session on 8 August, when it had been coolly proposed by Nicholas Maklakov at the Interior that the chamber should not meet again until the autumn of the following year, the Duma had chosen not to disappear from sight but to function as it were unofficially. More than five months passed before it was in fact summoned again, but during the interval all the members present in the capital met regularly as an informal relief committee, over which Rodzianko presided. In this capacity they maintained close contact with the union of zemstvos and the union of towns. And, since even in the throes of a crushing military setback such as Tannenberg the existence of the Duma as a legislative body continued to be ignored, inevitably they went on to the discussion of more vital matters.

The situation in which the active members of the Duma found themselves during these months was indeed anomalous. The powers of the chamber, restricted enough in time of peace, were still more drastically curtailed in time of war. In peace the Duma had exerted most influence upon government policy through its financial commission. But, as a matter of constitutional principle, it had no right to submit criticism of a war budget. In any case, with the Duma in recess, ministers had gone ahead with legislation under article 87 over an enormous field and often to dubiously legitimate purpose. The government seemed bent, indeed, on ignoring the Duma as an act of considered policy. Here, amid solemn affirmations of the union of tsar and people, was the un-exorcized ghost of absolutism. The most conspicuous and the most pernicious feature of the wartime method of government, in fact, was the extreme assertion of the prerogative of the emperor. In the last resort, it was this that precipitated the fall of the monarchy.

With disaster in these conditions facing the country, the Duma refused to submit. Far from being eclipsed by a revived absolutism, it in fact became, on the eve of its extinction, of greater consequence than before. There were men of high character and ability in its ranks, liberals and conservatives, and there was perhaps nothing remarkable in their attempt to rise to the occasion. What was remarkable was that, in collaboration with newly created agencies for assisting the war effort, they were able to enlist almost every section of public opinion in an eleventh-hour bid to save the regime from itself.

The Duma witnessed without regret the expulsion of the five Bolshevik deputies. Early in September Lenin had published in Berne his 'Seven Theses on the War', in which he urged the workers in every belligerent country to transform the imperialist war into a civil war against the government at home. Shortly afterwards the Bolshevik deputies were arrested on a charge of treasonable conspiracy.[1] It was with less composure that the main body of the Duma attended the two-day session, eventually summoned in response to anxious requests, which opened on 27 January/9 February 1915. Though the appearance of unity was somehow preserved, it was with consternation that members listened to the negligent reassurances of the chairman of the

[1]They were tried by a civil court, found guilty and in February 1915 were deported to eastern Siberia. In spite of government fears to the contrary, there was no serious protest from the industrial proletariat.

council of ministers, Goremykin. Already, at a private meeting of the military and naval commission two days earlier which was addressed by Sukhomlinov, the levity of the Minister of War had struck a chill into the heart of almost every member present. The sacred unity of the tsar's government and the representatives of the people was in fact already breaking down.

In March the Russian campaign in Galicia was resumed. It met with prompt success when the great fortress of Przemysl, besieged during the previous four months, capitulated and a hundred and twenty thousand prisoners fell into Russian hands. The victory, which promised the conquest of the whole of Galicia, provoked a remarkable display of Russian imperialism. Except for the fixed resolve to gain Constantinople and the Straits and the trickery that until the last moment went with it, nothing is more indicative of the temper of Russian imperialism even in the empire's struggle for existence than the immediate attempt to assimilate Galicia to the Russian Orthodox Church and crown. The ruthless ecclesiastical dragooning of the Ukrainian Uniats (Orthodox in observance but owing allegiance to Rome) was met everywhere by violent resistance.

To mark the triumph in Galicia, towards the end of April Nicholas made a tour of inspection of the captured territory. On 1/14 May, hard on the heels of his departure, the tremendous German-Austrian offensive opened on the eastern front. Reinforced by German divisions withdrawn from France, Mackensen broke through on a crucial sector of the Galician front. The Russians fell back in total confusion, entire divisions surrendered, and by the end of June the Russian forces had been almost completely driven from Austrian territory. Meanwhile there had been heavy probing German attacks along the entire front, particularly in the north. In July came the great offensive in Russian Poland. On 4 August Warsaw fell, then Kovno and Brest-Litovsk. On 18 September Vilna was captured. On the northern sector, covering Petrograd, the Germans took Libau, the only Russian warm-water port on the Baltic. When the fighting died down after four months of continuous retreat, the Russians had lost all their western fortresses and had withdrawn to a line running from Riga to Dvinsk along the Dniester to the Rumanian frontier. In the centre they had fallen back well into strictly Russian territory.

The rout was in every way intelligible. The Germans had

transferred the full weight of their military operations to the eastern front. By the summer of 1915 there were twice as many German-Austrian divisions in the east as there were German divisions in the west. In theory, the Russian forces were still numerically superior. In point of fact, the active units were heavily depleted, and the total number of effectives at this time was probably smaller than at the start of the fighting. There was no shortage of men in Russian uniform. Far from it: by the late summer of 1915 Russia had called up as many as ten million men. But already her losses were staggering. The official statistics, it may be repeated, are by no means reliable, and it seems reasonably certain that the total number of dead and wounded already exceeded two million, while the figure for prisoners of war, notably under-estimated even by the military and naval commission of the Duma in its report to the emperor in August 1915, was very nearly as great. From the beginning of the German-Austrian offensive in May Russian losses in captured may have averaged about two hundred thousand a month—a drain of manpower all the more calamitous because of the sketchiness and confusion of training arrangements in the rear.

Still more serious at this stage was the continued shortage of munitions of war. The German breakthrough on the Galician front had been achieved in the first place by a brief but devastating artillery bombardment, to which the Russian batteries, because of the lack of shells, were unable to reply. Throughout the retreat there were numerous sections of the line where the guns were rationed to two or three shells a day. And not shells only were lacking. Again and again a second line of infantry was ordered to advance empty-handed against the enemy with instructions to pick up a rifle from among the dead fallen in the earlier wave of attack. In the light of these grim commonplaces of the fighting on the Russian side in 1915, the marvel is that the Russian soldier fought as tenaciously as he did, that the number of prisoners and missing was not vastly greater and that the army was not destroyed as a whole.

Since the peasant soldiers of Russia were the people of Russia, their experience of war filtered through to the rest of the population. To their testimony was added the tragic story of the masses of refugees streaming eastwards in the rear of the army. As the Russian armies retreated the zone under the direct control of the military authorities was enormously enlarged. While the fighting was still confined to the western borderlands, it was largely the 'unreliable' Jewish population which had been ordered, at twenty-four hours' notice and under penalty of death, to vacate towns and villages for distant but unspecified areas farther east. Now, in the name of military necessity, the entire civil population of great areas was summarily evacuated by military order. With this obligatory withdrawal went a blind imitation of the scorched earth strategy of 1812. As a result, several million people, helplessly bound for nowhere in particular, were herded eastwards along the scanty roads after their houses had been burned down, their grain destroyed and their cattle driven off or slaughtered. There was no organization, no thought for the human misery involved. Only after a heavy crop of deaths from starvation or typhus was an attempt made to plan and supervise the withdrawal. Meanwhile the effect on public opinion everywhere in Russia was calamitous. To panic was joined despair. The celebrated report at a meeting of the council of ministers on 4/17 August 1915 made by the Minister of Agriculture, Krivoshein, tells its own story: 'The great migration organized by headquarters is leading Russia to revolution, to perdition and the edge of an abyss'.

As these elements of catastrophe accumulated and popular anger and apprehension mounted, the hand of the government grew still more nerveless. The ministers themselves, most of them thoroughly alarmed by this time at the indifference of Goremykin, were at sixes and sevens. The members of the Duma raged bitterly; from the start of the Galician rout they had continued to direct a barrage of criticism against Sukhomlinov as the minister responsible for war supplies and thus the chief author of the country's misfortunes. In June Guchkov delivered a fierce attack upon him and representatives of industry and the municipalities of Moscow and Petrograd added their censure, while leading Duma figures began to plan a parliamentary alliance to voice the demand for a trustworthy government.

In face of a growing volume of criticism the council of ministers had set up a special body early in June to co-ordinate measures of supply for the army. It was already plain that changes in the government could not long be delayed. They came later in the month, after a visit by the emperor to military headquarters. Much against his will, and to the extreme chagrin of the empress, he parted with Sukhomlinov, for whom they both cherished unusually warm feelings. In his place Nicholas appointed General Polivanov, an able and conscientious officer, who was strongly supported by Guchkov and a considerable section of the Duma. Nicholas Maklakov had been dismissed from the Ministry of the Interior a week earlier in favour of the less violently conservative Prince N. B. Shcherbatov, and the odious Shcheglovitov, Minister of Justice, and the despised Sabler, chief procurator of the Holy Synod, went in the first week of July. The new Minister of Justice was A. A. Khvostov, an honourable man, though something of a diehard, while the new chief procurator, A. D. Samarin, was a conservative but respected churchman of an eminent slavophil family.

With this infusion of fresh blood and a somewhat less reactionary spirit in the council of ministers, hope revived in Duma circles. On 19 July/1 August a new session opened. The Cadets, the Octobrists and the moderate right, soon to be leagued in a Progressive bloc, promptly secured a large majority for a resolution favouring the appointment of 'a government enjoying the confidence of the country'. The phrase echoed ever more loudly in the chamber and corridors of the Tauride Palace during the next year and a half. At the same time Rodzianko, Guchkov, the union of zemstvos and the union of towns, and representatives of the business community set about the task of preparing for the mobilization of industry. What they had in mind was an unofficial war industries committee, with local committees throughout the country, which would work under the guidance of the Ministry of War in setting up new plants, evacuating threatened factories and placing contracts. On 17/30 August Guchkov was permitted to attend a meeting of the council of ministers at which his proposals were endorsed and special councils were simultaneously set up for national defence, transport, fuel, and food supplies. A fortnight later a fifth special council was instituted for the care of refugees. The councils were composed of representatives of government departments, of the Duma, the State Council, Zemgor and the central war industries committee.

The labours of these new agencies undoubtedly produced results, though at considerable expense. Vast sums of money from the treasury were put at their disposal; there was enormous waste; the initial bungling, the duplication of effort and the growth of a new bureaucratic caste exempted from military service sometimes reached a pitch of scandal. Yet the evidence of a change for the better soon became apparent. Under the direction of Guchkov, the central war industries committee effected a relatively speedy improvement in military supplies. The committee included, in a startling and wholly successful innovation, representatives of both management and labour. Both the central and the local committees set up in this manner gave strong support to the Duma in its increasing pressure upon the government.

For it was now that the entire system of legally constituted authority in Russia began to fall apart. Amid the tension of war the peculiar hold of Rasputin upon the imagination of the empress grew more powerful and in the process cast its spell upon the ruler of Russia. What Miliukov in later years called the 'dynastic monomania' of the imperial couple worked havoc upon the whole order of state. Prompted by the empress, who in this matter was incited not only by Rasputin but by jealous fears that the commander-in-chief was exercising authority which belonged to the tsar alone, Nicholas decided to assume supreme command of the army. In one sense the step might appear a mere formality, since General Alexeyev, the studious and experienced officer who had replaced Yanushkevich as chief of staff, would be in effective command. In another sense, the decision, designed though it was to remove the perilous confusion arising from the dual authority of government and military headquarters, was clearly dangerous. With the army in headlong retreat and Petrograd itself threatened, it seemed madness on the emperor's part to assume formal responsibility for the military conduct of the war and at the same time to remove himself from the advice of ministers who were wholly dependent on his will. The decision, communicated to them in advance, filled them with alarm and foreboding. Reluctantly, the emperor listened to their objections and was unmoved. In despair, all but one minister besides Goremykin signed a letter to the emperor imploring him to reconsider his decision. Never before had the tsar's ministers presumed so greatly.

Their daring made no difference. On 24 August/6 September 1915 Nicholas took over at the new *stavka* (military headquarters) at Mogilev. The grand-duke Nicholas Nikolayevich faded out as commander on the Caucasian front. The empress was thrilled at the prospect which her consort had thus opened up of writing 'a glorious page in the history of your reign and in Russian history'. She herself, in his absence at headquarters, was resolved, she wrote to him, 'to wake people up, to put order into all, and unite all forces'. Already she had a new and better candidate in mind for the Ministry of the Interior, someone approved by 'Gr' [Gregory], 'our Friend' and the man of God.

With the emperor's departure from the capital a militant mood fell upon the Duma. For the newly formed majority, and indeed for most of the ministers, the immediate obstacle to 'a government enjoying the confidence of the country' was Goremykin. But though the worst was not yet known, it was impossible to doubt the accession to power of the empress and Rasputin. Rodzianko was not alone in suspecting—incorrectly—that the empress had secretly been designated regent.

The Progressive bloc in the Duma had been in the making all through the debates in July. It was composed of six of the main parties, from the Cadets on the left to the moderate nationalists on the right, and included some three hundred of a total of four hundred and twenty deputies. Three groups in the State Council gave it their support also. The motives of the conservative elements in this parliamentary alliance, who were provoked in the first place by the 'dark forces' near the throne, bore a curious likeness to those of the conservative-minded gentry in the English Parliament on the threshold of the civil war. They had not been converted to a belief in popular sovereignty, but desired only a government which was prepared to end corruption and illegality. It was, in fact, a government enjoying their own confidence that they looked for. Even the liberals on this occasion demonstrated an unusual realism. Late, all too late, Miliukov had begun to suspect that a system of parliamentary democracy in Russia might not be all gain.

It was he who had led the opposition to the demand within the ranks of his own party for a government responsible to the Duma. At the end of that road, he was at last convinced, lay the undisciplined power of the masses.

The programme of the Progressive bloc was announced on 21 August/3 September 1915. Besides the reconstitution of the government, it sought to remove all harmful restrictions upon the exercise of public initiative in the critical tasks before the nation. To this end it proclaimed the need for maintaining strict legality in administration and for imposing agreed limits upon the supersession of the civil authorities by the military. For the rest, it proposed the introduction of many of the liberal measures which 'society' in general had long advocated—the abolition of various religious and other forms of discrimination, the withdrawal of regulations directed against labour unions, the repeal of the restrictive legislation of a quarter of a century earlier on the powers of the zemstvos and municipalities and the establishment of zemstvos at the cantonal level.

Although the conservatives were inclined to baulk at a statement of liberal remedies which might obscure the overriding need for harnessing the energies of government to the task of victory, the programme was clearly well designed to conciliate public opinion and to enlist popular enthusiasm in the national cause. As such it made a strong appeal to ministers like Krivoshein and Sazonov. Most of the other ministers, indeed, were prepared to parley with the Duma on these terms. But for Goremykin, their chairman, so challenging an alliance of parties in opposition to the government was an affront to the tsar's prerogative. On 2/15 September, after he had been received in audience by the empress, Goremykin reported to Nicholas at headquarters. He returned with instructions from the emperor to the council of ministers to attend to their duties and with an order for the prorogation of the Duma. No date was fixed for summoning it again. This, perhaps, marked a turning-point in the fate of the monarchy.

A renewed shock of anger ran through the Duma. Among both Cadets and Octobrists there were some whose instinct was to defy the order of prorogation, while other members wished there and then to transform the Duma into a constituent assembly. One of the most forceful speakers on the Cadet benches, A. I. Shingarev, voiced an unmistakable warning when he declared: 'After the thunder of Sevastopol Russian slavery ceased. The war with Japan sowed the seeds of a Russian constitution. Out of the torment of this war will come freedom for the nation and our liberation from old forces and instruments of power'.

The Duma dispersed. The talks with ministers were broken off. But the anger and the excitement did not die down. For many people the demand for a government enjoying the confidence of the country now became, in truth, a demand for a government responsible to the Duma. What other end, indeed, could a sincere patriot of any political shade pursue? In the new chapter of affairs that now opened, in which ministers and high officials were dismissed and appointed in ever more rapid and bewildering sequence, only Alexandra's will was law: Russia, as the conservative deputy Shulgin put it, was an autocracy without an autocrat. From Rasputin divine guidance flowed to the empress, who in turn exhorted and advised the emperor at military headquarters. Again and again in her loving, vehement and preposterous letters to him, in ill-spelt and ungrammatical English, she urged him to assert himself, to be more autocratic, to impose his will upon all without exception. 'Be firm, remember you are the emperor!' was the burden of all those daily letters in which with a mingling of artless-ness and hysteria she communicated the advice tendered to her by Rasputin. He had heartened her by discovering in her a likeness to Catherine the Great; for her own part, it had been borne in on her that Rasputin was 'like Christ'. 'Follow Gr', she wrote. 'Think more of Gr.' It was for her child's sake as well as her husband's sake that she drank in Rasputin's words. For there was 'Baby', the tsarevich, heir to the autocratic power. Russia was the tsar's inheritance and the inheritance of 'Baby' after him. For herself she longed to send the traitorous Duma packing. Rodzianko, the president, ought to be hanged; Guchkov also deserved hang-ing—could not a convenient railway accident be arranged for him?; the place for Polivanov, the Minister of War, for Prince G. E. Lvov and for Miliukov was Siberia. Russia, she was to write later, loves to feel the whip.

It was Rasputin's nominees, recommended to the emperor by the empress, who received the emperor's command. Nicholas would sometimes demur to her requests, would even question Rasputin's infallibility, while she for her part would anxiously excuse herself for her boldness, but her will as a rule brooked nothing more serious than delay. She had marked down the signatories of the letter to Nicholas seeking to dissuade him from assuming the supreme command, and one by one they were re-placed. Since the new men required the approval of the *starets*, only the most doubtful types were candidates for appointment. In October the Minister of the Interior, the chief procurator of the Holy Synod and the State Comptroller were all dismissed. In the following month the Minister of Agriculture, Krivoshein, was astute enough to withdraw from the political scene. Power re-mained with the empress, sick and half-frantic though she was, until the end. Since the Duma met at long intervals, it was never in a position effectively to challenge her domination of a fond and equally blind husband.

For 'society' the year 1915 closed in a mood of grim resolve touched by bleak apprehension. In spite of all the injury and loss that Russia had sustained, the war was not yet lost; as events proved, the Russian armies had reached the virtual limit of their retreat. The military prospect had indeed brightened, since war production was rising and the calm on almost the entire front in the winter months afforded the Russian armies an interval for recuperation.

But one bitter disappointment had marked the close of the year. The allied withdrawal from Gallipoli in September had finally wrecked the hope of establishing short sea communications with Russia. Turkey's entry into the war on the side of the Central Powers in October 1914 had opened another Russian front but had otherwise caused little military damage; after the initial Turkish success in the Caucasus the Russians had more than held their own. But the failure of the Gallipoli campaign was heavy with consequences for Russia amid the ruinous civilian shortages of 1916.

It was the Turkish choice in favour of Germany, however, which once more kindled Russia's 'historic mission'. There was never a moment while hostilities continued when the government in Petrograd swerved a hair's breadth from the resolve to annex Constantinople and the Straits. This, indeed, was Russia's principal war aim. It had the enthusiastic backing of nationalist and liberal alike. From the start Sazonov pursued it tenaciously. Goremykin, in an unwonted spurt of rhetorical energy, was the first to speak openly of it, saluting 'Russia's glowing future, decreed by history—there, on the shores of the Black Sea, by the walls of Tsargrad'. Russian diplomatic pressure on Britain and France was such that their consent could not be withheld without grave risk of splitting the alliance. It was given in a secret treaty endorsed by both countries in March and April 1915 respectively. Even then the Russian Foreign Office on at least three separate occasions afterwards urged the high command to undertake independent operations against Constantinople in order to make assurance doubly sure.

Though there was no apparent reason why the emperor should not have retained him in office indefinitely, in January 1916 Goremykin was at last retired; he had lost the confidence of Rasputin. In opposing an invincible cynicism and inertia to the demands of the Duma he had played no inconsiderable part in reducing the constitutional machinery of government to impotence and in bringing the country to the very edge of defeat. In that role he was now superseded as chairman of the council of ministers by Sturmer. The appointment of Sturmer, coarse, thick-witted and infinitely contemptible, outraged even extreme conservative opinion. A former provincial governor and assistant of Plehve, a notorious toady and almost certainly corrupt, he had only a close association with Rasputin to recommend him.

Illiterate Siberian peasant though he was, Rasputin had reached a zenith of power which even at this time of day startles the imagination. He had no specific policy other than to buttress the influence he had gained with the imperial couple. Even now it is not certain whether and to what extent he was used by others. What is certain is that all political doors in the capital were open to him or to his emissaries. There were mysterious comings and goings at his daily receptions, where he received petitions and conducted business. Anna Vyrubova, infatuated as ever, was still his intermediary with the empress. The other members of an inner group close to him at various times during this lunatic period of Russia's fortunes consisted of a right-wing deputy, Alexis Khvostov, nephew of the Minister of Justice, an unprincipled careerist who for a time became Minister of the Interior; the chief of the department of police, Beletsky, who was appointed assistant to Khvostov; an adventurer named Prince Andronikov; a scoundrelly journalist by the name of Manasevich-Manuilov, formerly an associate of Meshchersky; a charlatan of the occult, Dr Badmayev; a high officer in the gendarmerie, Komissarov; and always Rasputin's own man of affairs, an all too human rogue named Simanovich. Sturmer also was Rasputin's man, though until the very end he pretended to have no more than a bare acquaintance with him.

Before the Duma was convened again on 6/19 February 1916, Sturmer sought to pledge the deputies to silence on the subject of Rasputin. The request was unceremoniously refused. At this meeting of the Duma the emperor, taking his cue from Rasputin, for the first and only time attended in person. The Progressive bloc was in no mood to be swayed by the mere presence of the tsar. Public criticism of the government, and of Sturmer in particular, was loud and uncompromising. A note of desperation even in highly placed circles mingled with it. The news of the dismissal on 13/26 March of General Polivanov, the Minister of War, was received with the utmost incredulity. He had been almost the only member of the government to command general confidence— a confidence which, because of his tendency to panic, he did not altogether deserve. General Polivanov, Nicholas explained, stood too close to Guchkov's war industries committee, 'whose activity does not inspire me with confidence'. Into Polivanov's place stepped an elderly military nonentity, General Shuvayev. From this time the visits of the empress to military headquarters became more frequent.

In March, at the urgent request once more of the western allies, the Russian high command, which had not planned to resume the offensive until the following June, launched a heavy attack in the area east of Vilna. It was thrown back with considerable losses. In May, when the Austrian offensive against Italy threatened the collapse of the Italian front, Alexeyev reluctantly undertook to bring relief by way of a major campaign against Austria. The famous offensive directed by General Brusilov opened on 1/14 June. Fighting continued until the beginning of September. Relatively well nourished, the onslaught achieved swift and dramatic gains on both flanks. Brusilov's feat, assisted in part by the half-heartedness of the Slav elements in the enemy ranks, was indeed remarkable and demonstrated in striking fashion the Russian power of recovery. The Russian armies penetrated deeply into enemy territory and captured in all some four hundred thousand prisoners. Lacking staying power once more, their advance was halted by the German reinforcements thrown into the battle and the offensive petered out. In the final reckoning, the Russian victory, which was achieved only at the cost of appalling casualties, brought greater gains to Russia's allies than to Russia herself.[1] It reduced German pressure in the critical western battles of Verdun and the Somme and gave sorely needed relief to the Italian army, but the failure to win any broad strategic advantage in the east brought only deepening discouragement and an increase of war weariness. Criticism of the high command mounted.

It was drowned, however, in the increasing volume of protest against the government and against the visible domination of Rasputin. Even now, it should be said, the protest was largely confined to the relative handful of people, mainly in the capital, who constituted public opinion in Russia. Among the masses as

[1]Though the staggering blow suffered by Austria-Hungary contributed largely to the disintegration of the Dual Monarchy, it was also the principal factor which brought Rumania into the war on the allied side. And the effect of Rumania's feeble showing in the war was to add two hundred miles to the length of the Russian front.

the blood-letting continued and hatred of the war sharpened there was growing unrest, but apart from this all that they shared with educated society was the suspicion that the empress, 'the German woman', favoured the German cause. Sturmer was similarly suspect, and probably with as little reason.

On 20 June, after a long session in which deputies were noticeably irregular in attendance, the Duma had been prorogued. Some three weeks later, while Sazonov was on holiday in Finland, he learned that he had been dismissed. To the consternation of the allies' representatives in the capital, he was replaced at the Foreign Office by no other than Sturmer, who had coveted the post as an imposing sinecure and who remained chairman of the council of ministers. Only a little time before, in view of the patent instability of the government, General Alexeyev had proposed to the emperor that a 'dictatorship' be established at headquarters with authority over the council of ministers. Nicholas had rejected the idea and instead had enlarged Sturmer's powers to deal with departmental conflicts.

From the summer of 1916 the whole system of government in Russia began to disintegrate. In the celebrated phrase of Purishkevich, there followed the period of 'ministerial leapfrog', when ministers personally chosen by Rasputin and the empress, each more incompetent or of more doubtful character than the last, succeeded one another in dizzy and grotesque succession. Between the autumn of 1915 and the autumn of 1916 there were no fewer than five Ministers of the Interior, four Ministers of Agriculture and three Ministers of War. During the last months of all, when not a single figure of note was left to whom those of good will in the Duma could rally, the sequence of change was even more kaleidoscopic.

It is necessary to distinguish between two related aspects of the closing phase of the Russian monarchy. One involves the progressive breakdown of the machinery of government and administration. The other projects the specific character of mass unrest in a society which could neither continue to function under the old dispensation nor progress towards parliamentary democracy.

First and foremost among the causes of breakdown were the economic consequences of the war. Like the war itself, the dislocation of economic life and the pressure of inflation were felt much more acutely in Russia than in the other belligerent countries. The initial problem arose from the vast scale of Russian mobilization and its effect upon peasant agriculture. With a standing army in peace-time of less than a million and a half, by the end of 1916 Russia had mobilized an additional thirteen or fourteen million men. More than one out of every three men of military age were thus serving in the armed forces. Because of 'over-population' in the village in peace-time and the existence of reserves of female labour, productivity on peasant land did not greatly suffer; indeed, increased demand and higher prices provided incentives to higher production. But on the large estates, which produced for the market, the effect of the severe and sometimes all but total shortage of labour was drastically to reduce the area under cultivation. And to this loss was added the loss of agricultural output in the enemy-occupied western regions. Thus much of the responsibility for feeding the country was thrown directly upon the peasant allotments, where most families ordinarily consumed all that they produced. Since exports of grain had now virtually ceased, war-time resources might have seemed adequate for the needs of the nation as a whole. But three major obstacles stood in the way of ensuring the distribution of food supplies to the population in the towns.

There was, first, the drain on available supplies represented by the much higher consumption of the millions called up into the army. Next—and increasingly important—was the reluctance of the peasantry to part with their grain, even for higher prices, because there was so little they could buy with the money they received in payment. By the beginning of 1916, when the effect of the enemy blockade had been reinforced by the loss of the industrialized western provinces, the output of consumer goods had been reduced to a mere trickle through concentration on war industry. Production for civilian purposes was starved of both raw materials and skilled labour, and the basic requirements of the village, from iron nails to cotton piece goods, could be obtained only with extreme difficulty or not at all. Finally—and this, in the last resort, was the key factor—the whole system of food distribution to the towns was threatened by a growing paralysis on the railways. Notoriously inadequate in peace-time and more than ever inadequate through the loss of the main western network, hopelessly burdened by the volume of military traffic and the movement of refugees, crippled by depleted and deteriorating rolling stock, the railways were the most vulnerable sector of Russia's war economy.

It was chaos on the railway system which brought crisis to the mechanism of urban supply.

In the villages the war grew more and more unpopular. From the summer of 1916 there was a marked increase in the number of men of military age who went into hiding in the forest in order to evade military service. The cities had even more cause for discontent. Among the industrial workers complaints became more articulate, strikes more frequent and more stubborn. For with food shortages went spiralling prices in an inflationary process stimulated by declining revenue and mounting expenditure. The rise in wages could not keep pace with the rise in prices, which was powerfully assisted by unrestricted speculation. It has been estimated, and the estimate is probably not greatly exaggerated, that against an average increase of wages of one hundred per cent by the autumn of 1916 must be set an increase of prices of three hundred per cent. Certainly there is no reason to doubt that for the majority of workers in Petrograd real wages at that time were lower than at the outbreak of war. The price of flour in the capital had almost doubled, the price of meat had trebled, the price of salt had risen fivefold. And fuel was virtually unobtainable. The government had made only half-hearted attempts to control the distribution of food and did not address itself to the control of prices until the close of the year. By that time it was all but impossible to enforce price restrictions.

The strike movement had come to life again in the spring of 1915. It could not afterwards be halted. More than half a million men came out on strike in 1915, more than a million in the following year; in January and February 1917 the proportion was higher still. The strikes, which until almost the last sprang from wage disputes only, met with scant sympathy from the Ministry of the Interior. Agitators were arrested and considerable numbers of strikers were conscripted into the army, while many of those employed in the armament factories were kept at their job under conditions of military discipline. Labour unrest nevertheless grew. From the summer months of 1916 the underground revolutionary factions became active once more, particularly in Petrograd, the largest and hungriest centre of population in the northern 'consuming provinces'. There, as the bread queues lengthened, so did the revolutionary oratory. With its population of two million, its giant industrial plants and revolutionary tradition, Petrograd, as in 1905, was inevitably the centre of the storm.

For mass revolt was undoubtedly in the air. The threat of what was to come paralysed the mind and will of those in authority. And not of those in authority only. 'Society' itself, vainly searching for solid ground under its feet, shrank from the spectacle of a revolution which would sweep away more than the monarchy. Russian liberals were now, in truth, frightened liberals. For the pent-up bitterness of the masses had turned to hate and rancour; across the gulf that divided them from their betters they recognized only the enemy. The government, the Duma and educated opinion as a whole all sensed the wrath to come. Nowhere is the presentiment of unimaginable disaster more vividly communicated than in the famous report of October 1916 by the department of police in the capital. Town and country alike, it said, were in ferment. The report, drawn up with the help of spies planted in the patriotic labour group of the central war industries committee, gave warning that in Petrograd 'a fearful crisis' was on the way. With the menace born of hunger and hardship, it noted, went a longing for peace that grew stronger daily. It foresaw 'uncontrollable riots', 'chaotic, elemental and catastrophic anarchy'.

The irony of the Russian situation at the time was that, from a strictly military point of view, the country was in many ways better equipped for waging war than at any time before. Domestic production of war supplies and munitions had soared—the output of heavy artillery, for instance, had been quadrupled—and substantial quantities of munitions from abroad were arriving not only at Vladivostok and Archangel but also at Murmansk, which towards the close of the year was linked to Petrograd by a new seven hundred-mile railway built (largely by prisoner-of-war labour and at heavy cost in life) across mountain and swamp in little more than eighteen months. Yet none of these gains outweighed the progressive demoralization of the country. It was not the civil population alone who were demoralized. Defeatism was now widespread in the rear of the army. However dutiful the troops at the front continued to be—and the astonishing thing, in spite of all later denials by the Bolsheviks, is that the front-line troops, a small trickle of desertions notwithstanding, were still amenable to strict discipline—behind the lines, in barracks and depots and training centres, revolutionary propaganda was making rapid headway.

The Duma had been summoned again for 1/14 November. 'It will be rotten', the empress had written to her husband before the event. In an agitated chamber, which might well have displayed more violence of feeling if it had been aware of more than a fraction of the truth concerning Rasputin which was revealed after the fall of the monarchy, or if it had known that in her letters to Nicholas at headquarters the empress had been asking for information and dates of future military operations, Miliukov led off with a rhetorical attack upon the government and upon the dark and 'pro-German' forces behind it. Having mentioned both the empress and Sturmer by name, he listed the recent actions of the government and concluded each item of denunciation with the phrase, 'Is this stupidity or is this treason?' There was not a shred of tangible evidence for the implied accusation, but it came with bombshell effect. Through the intervention of the censorship the speech occupied a large blank space in the newspapers. But it was circulated in the capital in thousands of duplicated copies, as also was the speech a fortnight later in which Purishkevich vehemently denounced Rasputin and his camarilla.

In between the two speeches, on 9/22 November, Nicholas, over the objections of the empress, dismissed Sturmer, who was replaced as chairman of the council of ministers by the Minister of Transport, A. F. Trepov, a colourless conservative of the old school though no friend of Rasputin. But a mere change of personalities at this hour could do nothing to clear the air. The empress was as interfering as ever, the Duma was still powerless, while the politically-minded public could only gaze helplessly at the abyss opening at their feet. Panic spread among all those who stood to lose most from the dissolution of the monarchy. The State Council, the Council of the United Nobility and the grand-ducal clan all added their warnings to the vain pleas of Rodzianko.[1] But Nicholas could not be approached, or, if a means of access to him was found, proved imperturbable as well as blind. At military headquarters he was all but ignored. He had rejected the entreaties of his personal staff to come to terms with the Duma, he had turned aside the overtures to the same end made to him by the British and French ambassadors, he had rebuffed the dowager empress. Trivially occupied, obstinate and fatalistic, in a letter to the empress at this time the autocrat of Russia subscribed himself, with something of pathos, 'your poor little weak-willed hubby'.

[1]Rodzianko, in truth, had not helped matters by interfering in everything, including military affairs, when the Duma was not in session and he had therefore no political standing.

For the past month or two confused and somewhat artless schemes had been discussed in exalted quarters for saving the dynasty. There was talk of murdering Rasputin, uneasy chatter of the palace revolutions of the eighteenth century. New plots and conspiracies were hatched at court in fine profusion: they included several different schemes for exiling or even murdering the empress, even for doing away with the emperor himself. Out of it all on 17/30 December came the murder of Rasputin. This was the work of a trio consisting of Purishkevich, a youthful grand-duke and Prince Felix Yusupov, who was married to a niece of the emperor. Invited to the latter's palace, the man of God swallowed cyanide of potassium in his cakes and wine without visible effect and was then dispatched with revolver shots.

There was instantaneous relief in political circles, even something of jubilation, although on the mistrustful masses the effect, characteristically, appears to have been a dawning suspicion that the *starets* may after all have been the friend of the people. Rasputin's body, recovered from under the ice of the Neva, was buried in secret at Tsarskoe Selo in the presence of the emperor and empress. Sorrow reigned in the imperial family. But for the rest once more nothing was changed, except that almost the last flicker of loyalty to the person of the emperor was extinguished. The process of swift decay in the body politic was resumed under the aegis of the empress and of the minister who now stood closest to her. This was A. D. Protopopov, Minister of the Interior since the previous September and the most futile and ridiculous of the servants of autocracy in its death-throes. An Octobrist in the Duma with some reputation as a liberal and one of the begetters of the Progressive bloc, in the summer of 1916 he had led the formal and somewhat foolish Duma delegation to Britain and France with Miliukov as his virtual adviser. His reputation for liberalism had been shattered when he accepted office under Sturmer and thereby established his connexion with Rasputin. Effusive and mentally unstable, inept to the point of absurdity but addicted to grandiose paper plans, Protopopov was exposed to the contempt of former colleagues and the mockery of the press and in the result appears to have lost what little reason he had left. Part of his time as mainstay of the regime was apparently spent in spiritualistic *séances* with the empress in which the two of them sought to summon the shade of Rasputin. After the latter's death Nicholas was dissuaded from dismissing Protopopov only through the earnest intervention of the empress. The visibly unbalanced Minister of the Interior was the prop and stay of the empire when the revolution erupted.

While Protopopov continued to play the part allotted to him the fearful decline in almost every department of state continued. Still apparently robbed of will and energy, the Duma looked on. In December the public announcement, made with the consent of the allies, of the secret agreement for the annexation of Constantinople and the Straits stirred scarcely a ripple of interest. As chairman of the council of ministers Trepov stayed the course for five weeks. Before the end of that period the empress had bethought herself of Prince N. D. Golitsyn, the aristocratic figure-head of a committee for assistance to prisoners of war under her patronage. On 27 December/9 January 1917, much to his own astonishment, that elderly and inexperienced gentleman succeeded Trepov. Golitsyn was equipped with the customary blank forms, already signed by the emperor, which he had inherited from Trepov, who had inherited them from Sturmer, for the dissolution of the Duma. Only the date needed to be filled in.

Amid strikes, food queues in the capital and anti-war agitation, the last desperate attempts were made to save Nicholas from himself. All was quiet on the eastern front. The emperor was with his family at Tsarskoe Selo. In the absence of General Alexeyev, who was sick, the deputy chief of staff, General Gurko, had vainly urged Nicholas to make his peace with the Duma and dismiss Protopopov. At this point a further attempt at conciliation was made by the French ambassador, Maurice Paléologue; while on 30 December/12 January the British ambassador, Sir George Buchanan, greatly daring for all his stilted phrases, drew the emperor's eyes to 'the abyss' and 'the parting of the ways'. There was no response other than a curt show of resentment.

At a late hour the Progressive bloc roused itself so far as to prepare for the eventual abdication of the emperor. He would be required to abdicate, it was agreed, in favour of his son, the tsarevich Alexis: the tsar's younger brother, the grand-duke Michael, would serve as regent. To this end a list was drawn up of the members of a Russian 'cabinet' which would function in the emergency. How near was the emergency few of the designated cabinet ministers suspected, since even now nothing went farther with them than words. Yet events were moving fast towards a decision. On 29 January/11 February, on the day an inter-allied conference opened in Petrograd to concert plans for a simultaneous offensive on the western and eastern fronts in the spring, in a spasm of authority Protopopov ordered the arrest of the labour representatives on the central war industries committee. The workers in the capital, who three weeks earlier had saluted the anniversary of Bloody Sunday with fresh strikes and demonstrations, responded with protest meetings and more strikes. On 14/27 February the Duma reassembled. There had been widespread fears that the occasion would provoke renewed mass disturbances, and extra precautions had been taken by the police and security forces. But the event passed off quietly. Before the Duma met Rodzianko had had his last official audience with the emperor. He made no greater impression upon Nicholas than before. But four days later, in a desperate speech in the chamber, Kerensky declared: 'The tsar must be removed—by terrorist means if there are no other'. To this last expedient had the Duma majority been converted by a sense of impending catastrophe.

Both the timing and the circumstances of the rising in the capital took everybody by surprise. On 22 February/7 March the emperor left Tsarskoe Selo for military headquarters at Mogilev. Conditions in the capital appeared no different from what they had been for the past three or four months. Though the wage strike at the great Putilov works looked somewhat more threatening, though in the industrial suburbs the queues outside the bakers' shops were longer and more sullen and the Duma at the time was engaged in fierce criticism of the government's food policy, the centre of the city wore its wonted air of order. On the following day, 23 February/8 March, a Tuesday, the first disturbances broke out.

They were wholly unorganized. The remnants of the revolutionary groups and factions, still small and secret, remained only dimly in the background of events. There were no notable Socialist-Revolutionary or Social-Democratic survivors of an earlier phase of revolutionary struggle to lead the masses. Lenin, an unknown or barely remembered name, was in Switzerland, and the other ideologues and strategists of the extreme left were equally far from the scene. Driven by elemental passion, by hatred of the war, by feelings of rancour and revenge which could no longer be endured passively, the mass moved of itself.

Without form or shape, the surge of violence against the existing scheme of things was necessarily aimed in the first instance at the throne and the occupant of the throne.

On the opening day of what could not yet be recognized as the Russian Revolution mobs invaded the bakers' shops. More factories came out on strike. Among more trivial events, women threw stones at the police. Next day some two hundred thousand workers were out on strike in Petrograd and in the first serious clashes with the populace between twenty and thirty police were injured. No troops had been used so far, since the police appeared confident that they had the situation generally under control. They were less confident on the following day, when vast crowds filled the streets, strike processions formed, slogans were shouted, red flags flew, shots were fired, houses and shops were looted, police stations and other public buildings set on fire and individual members of the police murdered. With the appearance on the streets of mounted Cossacks came rough but not ill-humoured exchanges between the demonstrators and the troops; here and there incidents occurred which came near to fraternization. On the evening of that day, Nicholas, imperfectly informed at head-quarters of the course of events, telegraphed an order to the commanding officer of the garrison to suppress the disorders immediately. The order was unrealistic in the extreme. The garrison of some two hundred thousand men consisted largely of reserve battalions of raw peasant recruits and the sick and convalescent, who in their barracks had for some time been subjected to an increasing weight of revolutionary propaganda.[1] There was, in fact, little real attempt to use army units to put down the disturbances. This was mass revolution, elemental and unorganized, it is true, but revolution none the less.

On Sunday the crowds moved forward from the suburbs into the centre of the city, filling the Nevsky Prospekt and the great squares and embankments running off it. The firing, desultory until now, became heavier; in a few instances, troops armed with machine-guns fired directly at the crowds and some forty or more

[1]The danger in the capital had been recognized by the authorities. Besides the detailed plans drawn up for the security troops and police in the mainten-ance of order, it had been proposed to strengthen the garrison with seasoned and loyal troops by recalling from the front the greater part of the Guards cavalry division. But, among other objections, there was no room for the troops in the winter barracks of Petrograd and the neighbourhood, and General Gurko allowed the proposal to drop.

people were killed. But always the crowds formed up again and the troops withdrew. So matters stood on Sunday. The climax came next day, 27 February/12 March, when the few detachments of troops still thought to be reliable were sent against the insurgents. At once the men of a reserve battalion, having killed their officers, joined the demonstrators and themselves opened fire on patrols of mounted police. On that Monday morning the floodgates opened. One by one the garrison units, many of their officers murdered, went over to the side of the insurgents. Vast crowds roamed the streets, looting, shooting, setting buildings alight, emptying the prisons, seizing the arsenals, murdering here and there, tearing to pieces every member of the police they met and taking ministers and high state officials prisoner. Towards nightfall virtually the whole of the civil population of the capital and almost the entire garrison of their own accord had taken their stand against what little was now left of the forces of constituted law and order. The revolution had been secured in five days at the cost of perhaps a thousand casualties and a few hundred dead.

On 25 February/10 March the government had prorogued the Duma. (Two days later, at the height of the insurrection, the council of ministers had persuaded a speechless and plaintive Protopopov to resign and had formally proposed to Nicholas that a new head of the government be appointed who would command 'general confidence'.) But the members of the Duma had chosen not to retire from the scene. On the following day they elected from their midst a 'provisional committee' of twelve, which was vaguely charged with responsibility for restoring order. Headed by Rodzianko, it consisted of precisely those leaders of the Progressive bloc who had earlier been named as a 'cabinet', together with Kerensky and the Menshevik leader Chkheidze as representatives of the left. In this fashion the 'Provisional Government' of revolutionary Russia entered upon its brief spell of power.

It was on the same day that the Petrograd Soviet of Workers' Deputies came into existence out of the chaos of revolution. Made up of various left-wing members of the Duma, members of the labour group of the central war industries committee who with other prisoners had been released from the Kresty gaol, and a number of representatives chosen almost at random from the rank and file in the factories, the Soviet promptly took over a wing of the Tauride Palace while the new provisional committee were in disturbed session there. That evening many thousands of the population of the capital who had made a revolution almost without knowing it put in a clamorous appearance at the first session of the Petrograd Soviet. Two days later, when the Provisional Government formally assumed office, the Soviet became the Soviet of Workers' and Soldiers' Deputies and the repository of military power in the capital.

What, meanwhile, of the autocrat of all the Russias? Still unperturbed and still irresolute, Nicholas waited until no choice was left. At headquarters he received without visible emotion the advice tendered to him from all sides to abdicate in favour of his son. General Alexeyev, who had returned to duty, had consulted all the commanding generals at the front, and all, including the grand-duke Nicholas Nikolayevich, had declared that abdication was imperative if the monarchy was to be saved. Yet although apparently willing to abdicate, Nicholas proposed to delay action until he was back at Tsarskoe Selo. On 28 February/ 13 March he left by train for Petrograd. He was not permitted to reach the capital: the imperial train was halted and diverted to Pskov, the headquarters of the northern army. On 2/15 March, a few hours before the two loyal conservatives, Guchkov and Shulgin, arrived in Pskov to add the persuasions of the provisional committee of the Duma to the rest, Nicholas signed the act of abdication in favour of his son, only to change his mind immediately afterwards and bequeath the throne to his brother Michael. Impassive to the last, to all appearances resigned to whatever fate might send but meanwhile still absorbed in the trivialities that had occupied him throughout the reign, he retains a melancholy and ineffectual dignity until the brutal moment of revolutionary reckoning in the summer of the following year.

Not the reign of Nicholas II only was at an end. The monarchy itself had been overthrown and could never be restored. Certainly there was no power in Russia which could put a Romanov on the throne again. For in the space of five days the order of centuries which rested on the monarchy had dissolved as though by itself. There was no resistance outside the capital to the violence, like that of some elemental force, of the upheaval. Petrograd, Peter the Great's city, the source and centre of the absolutist-bureaucratic state, made the Russian Revolution; Moscow and the other cities only followed Petrograd's example, while the countryside tacitly endorsed what the factory workers and peasant soldiers of Petrograd had decided. But Petrograd spoke and acted for an empire in revolt, and in the popular acquiescence in so vast a disturbance lay explosive forces that had still to be released. It was what lay beyond the fall of the monarchy that mattered. Like the people of the capital, the country as a whole remained watchful and expectant, the evil passions of revolution mingling in millions of men and women with a simple and half-barbarian idealism.

Revolution had been long predicted in Russia. For at least a couple of generations in one form or another it had served as a faith and a cause for a doctrinaire and intransigent intelligentsia. The faith had its martyrology, the cause its historic gains and reverses. Liberal, Narodnik and Marxist, each in his own fashion, had tended the sacred flame, all three with a characteristically Russian excess of devotion. But the revolution of 1917, accomplished without leadership and almost without conscious aim, was like nothing that had been predicted. The loss and suffering of war had inflamed deep-lying discontent, while the literate or half-literate among the masses had recaptured something of the vision of freedom and justice which had shone in the false dawn of 1905. Yet the crude paradox of the Russian Revolution remains: for all its spontaneity it sprang not so much from the will of the people as from the mere decomposition and collapse of the tsar's government. As such it had still to discover itself. The long night of tsarist despotism was over: so much was cause for unconditional rejoicing. But the centuries had moved slowly over the vastness of Russia, and 'jumps' in history are seldom what at the time they appear to be. All the evidence of our distracted modern period, indeed, suggests that there are no real 'jumps' in history, Russian or any other. The lingering autocracy of the tsars had died a natural death, but what was to come was beyond all imagining.

The Bolshevik Epilogue

Though successful revolutions have their own momentum, the momentum does not always come from within. How did the Bolshevik faction, notoriously a small minority within the minority in Russia who were socialist by conviction or sympathy, capture power from the provisional guardians of a popular revolution and, against all apparent odds, retain it? What happened between February/March and October/November 1917 that enabled a relative handful of revolutionaries *a outrance* to impose upon an inchoate ideal of democracy the dictatorship of a single party and thus to perpetuate, though in a transformed ideology, the tyranny of the tsars and the inhumanity of the absolutist-bureaucratic state?

History, it may be repeated once more, is what succeeds. But what succeeds in the guise of innovation seldom fails to reflect the continuity of the present with the past. In one sense the Bolsheviks triumphed because, in pursuit of power and the burning desire to create a new heaven and earth, they alone were prepared to resort to traditional methods of Russian rule. Given the sum total of the instruments of power, a revolution from above, as Russian history had always proved, opens wider vistas than a revolution from below. This was the gist of Lenin's socialist faith. The road from tsarist autocracy to a democratic order of things was perilous and uncertain, though not completely impassable; it was a shorter road which led from tsarist autocracy to the so-called dictatorship of the proletariat. And it was one much more easily negotiated. Amid the conspicuous failure of all other groups and parties to foresee what was involved in this choice between opposite courses, the determination and ruthlessness of the disciplined Bolshevik faction were a powerful instrument of victory. A genius of opportunism in Lenin and the brilliant resource of Trotsky were elements in the continuing revolutionary drama which contributed much more than a hypothetical dialectic of history to the *dénouement*. Inspired by a philosophy of social change, the Bolshevik *coup d'état* was not a mere conspiracy.

But it was effected by wholly conspiratorial means. And since in politics no victory is won except through the errors of the other side, it was the Provisional Government, unfailingly blind to the conditions of its survival through every successive phase of reconstruction, which in the last resort encompassed its own defeat.

Duma hopes, liberal hopes more especially, had been all too confidently built upon the prospect of parliamentary rule in a constitutional monarchy with a boy of eleven as monarch. But the Provisional Government set up on 2/15 March had secured provisional recognition from the Petrograd Soviet—all was as yet provisional—only on the condition that a constituent assembly to be elected by universal franchise would be summoned in the near future to establish a permanent form of government. A constituent assembly, it will be remembered, had once been the liberal dream. Now, again too late, Miliukov protested against an appeal to the illiterate millions that would shatter liberal calculations. For at once it was made plain beyond all argument that the masses in revolt would never accept a constitutional or indeed any other form of monarchy. The grand-duke Michael's gesture in consenting to leave the issue of his accession to the will of the forthcoming constituent assembly was an empty formality.

What was even more formidably plain was that no more than the seat of power in the emergent revolutionary order was held by the Provisional Government. The source of power was the Petrograd Soviet of Workers' and Soldiers' Deputies, which alone had its roots in the life of the masses and alone had at its disposal a popular force of coercion. Already, on the previous day, the soviet had issued its famous Order No. 1 to the garrison. While urging them to maintain discipline, the order called on the troops to form representative committees in every unit to control the distribution of arms and to assume much of the authority hitherto exercised by their officers, enjoining them at the same time to obey no government order which was inconsistent with the soviet's own instructions. Government orders notwithstanding, indeed, Order No. 1, which was observed not in the capital only but throughout the country, destroyed military discipline at a blow and set in train the complete disintegration of the Russian army. Although even now the revolutionary logic of this dual power was not apparent to the socialist parties, the as yet leaderless Bolsheviks among them, the Provisional Government itself could scarcely fail to recognize the limitations upon the exercise of its authority. Crowding the halls and corridors of the splendid Tauride Palace, rude and unceremonious in the home of the Duma, breathing hard down the necks of the newly appointed ministers, were the direct representatives of the masses, rough, vociferous and patently to be reckoned with.

The Duma itself had almost ceased to count for anything at all. It had never been, and was not now, in any genuine sense representative. A restricted franchise and partly rigged elections had established only the slenderest ties between the Duma majority and the people. Middle-class in composition and outlook, the liberals, not to speak of the doubtfully converted conservatives, enjoyed in 1917 not much more than the support of their own class in the country. The local soviets that sprang up everywhere on the model of the Petrograd Soviet were as close to the peasant masses or to the urban proletariat as the deputies of the Duma for the most part had been remote and almost alien.

In the capital the Provisional Government was under relentless pressure from the Petrograd Soviet. For a month, however, it still enjoyed the conditional support of all the left-wing parties represented on the soviet, among whom Mensheviks and Socialist-Revolutionaries predominated. No thought arose in the minds of the left-wing parties of claiming power for the soviet itself; by all the Marxist rules, the phase of bourgeois revolution had still to develop. In this attitude of mind the Bolshevik handful were scarcely to be distinguished from the Mensheviks and Socialist-Revolutionaries. Timid and indecisive at the moment of destiny long predicted by their leaders, they also were largely content to salute the era of bourgeois democracy. But with the arrival of Lenin, after the historic journey by sealed train across Germany, at the Finland station in Petrograd on 3/16 April, the whole situation was astonishingly transformed. Lenin's call to his followers and to the country was to prepare to overthrow the Provisional Government. An end to the imperialist war, the land to the peasants, freedom for the people—these aims could be achieved only by an immediate proletarian revolution, which would light the way for world revolution and the universal triumph of socialism. Accordingly, down with the Provisional Government! The prescription for victory followed: the tactics of the second and crowning phase of revolution were embraced in the slogan of 'All power to the soviets!'

It took the Bolshevik rank and file some little time to recover from the shock of this bold and supremely confident programme. But the shock passed, and the tireless energy, drive and demagogic passion of their leaders were harnessed to the devotion and discipline of the rank and file of the party. Bolshevik propaganda at the front, in the rear, in the soviets and above all in the factories, where it promptly told upon the newly formed factory committees, gathered irresistible momentum. In peace and in the ordinary circumstances of tsarist rule, however weak, the naked summons to seize power from the government of the day would have had little effect. In a time of military defeat, social anarchy and economic chaos it kindled fresh hope and a reckless excitement. Since from the start the slogan of 'All power to the soviets!' masked an appeal to the masses for the exclusive support of his own faction, Lenin waged war implacably against the rival socialist parties who almost everywhere were in the majority in the soviets.

From the Provisional Government in its earliest version Lenin had little to fear, since day by day its link with the revolutionary masses grew more tenuous. The chosen Prime Minister, Prince G. E. Lvov, who had headed the union of zemstvos, was infinitely well-meaning. But the reality of the situation for him was lost in clouds of rhetoric. Miliukov as Foreign Minister and Guchkov as Minister of War maintained only a slightly clearer understanding of events—and both, Miliukov more especially, were anathema to the more militant wing of the Petrograd Soviet. The only popular figure in the government was the Minister of Justice, Kerensky, who appeared to ride the storm with complete assurance and who held audiences captive with his tinsel oratory. It was Kerensky—significantly, a vice-chairman of the soviet—who at this climax of Russian history wore the likeness of a man of destiny. He saw himself, indeed, to quote one of the acutest Russian observers of the events of 1917, as 'a bit of a Bonaparte'. As Minister of War in place of Guchkov, who with Miliukov resigned after a couple of months, he was the dominant figure in the coalition government formed on 5/18 May, in which six representatives of the socialist parties (other than the Bolsheviks) in the Petrograd Soviet, among them the Socialist-Revolutionary leader Chernov as Minister of Agriculture, sat with nine non-socialists. Already the revolutionary tide was turning sharply towards socialism.

From now onwards the tide flowed fast and yet almost until

the end the Provisional Government, however constituted, chose to ignore the fearful force of events. The government failed in all else because it failed in courage and clarity of mind. Of the two cardinal blunders which brought it down the first was the refusal to acknowledge the bitter necessity for ending the war. As early as May it had proclaimed its desire to conclude 'a general peace without annexations or indemnities'. That gesture having been made, nothing more followed and the government prepared to resume the fighting. The dilemma which confronted the Provisional Government was plain: however deep the people's longing for peace, what would be left of either Russia or revolution in the event of occupation by the German armies? (That dilemma was not resolved even for the Bolsheviks until after the allied defeat of Germany.) Yet more than anything else it was the continuation of the war which drove the urban masses into the arms of a faction in no way inhibited either by 'bourgeois' patriotism or by political responsibility. However hard the decision, however small the aid or comfort of Russia's allies in her predicament, there was, in truth, no choice but to negotiate an armistice and sue for peace if the democratic order in the making was not to be submerged in revolution. How could the government, while continuing the war, simultaneously create order out of chaos, restore a shattered economy and satisfy the immediate demands of the people?

Perplexed and irresolute in this situation, the Provisional Government thrust an enormous advantage into the hands of its adversary by observing all the rules of the parliamentary game. In the midst of the conflagration it fiddled distractedly, repeating on every possible occasion the same constitutional tune. Law was its watchword, liberty its guide. That such courtesies on the part of the government were wholly alien to Russian practice in a crisis of state is perhaps immaterial; the relevant thing is that the government allowed itself to be paralysed by legalistic niceties into 'democratic' tolerance of the forces which were openly seeking to destroy it. From this textbook parliamentarianism sprang the second crucial blunder of the Provisional Government in the period between the two revolutions—the temporizing and inertia over the 'agrarian question', which was relegated, along with much else, to the constituent assembly. The socialists who remained in the government, it should be noted, were even more guilty in this respect than the non-socialists.

For in the end it was the peasantry who were the means of destroying the Provisional Government. Nothing had worked more strongly in them from the moment revolution broke out in the capital than the long-nurtured desire to carve up the private landed estates. So far as the peasants were concerned, a solution of the 'agrarian question' in the circumstances of the fall of the monarchy could not mean anything except the distribution among them of all the land still in private ownership. For the government the penalty of delaying this solution should have been unmistakable. The landowning interest, it is true, was well represented in the earlier versions of the Provisional Government, but it was not far short of madness to wait until the peasants, ignoring the newly appointed commissars in the rural areas, of their own accord began to take possession of the private estates. That indeed was social revolution. It was the peasant, in short, whether he wore a sheepskin jacket or an army greatcoat, who enabled the Bolsheviks to seize power. The army had begun to disintegrate the more rapidly because the peasant-soldier's first thought was to hurry back to his village in order to share in the spoils; he voted for peace, in Lenin's phrase, with his legs, and in the same process voted for expropriation. Until the late summer, except for the bitter war which had broken out between the peasants still attached to the commune and the richer peasants who had separated themselves from it as individual farmers (and who were often forced back into the commune), the village was relatively quiescent; the private estates as yet suffered not much more than the normal depredations of individual villagers. But from September onwards, plunder, arson and expropriation were in progress everywhere in the countryside. Once more, as in 1905, thousands of manor houses were ransacked or burned down and nothing left undone that would make it impossible for the landowner to return. For the peasants would not wait upon the Provisional Government or upon the constituent assembly either.

With this pitiless war against the landowners went an intensified silent war against the government. More completely than before the peasant was master of the food situation. In the towns the renewed strikes which marked the progress towards 'workers' control' in industry had done nothing to prevent one factory after another from closing down and had indeed brought production virtually to a standstill. For the peasants there was less incentive than ever to sell their grain. In Petrograd and other large cities the prospect of famine drew near. And still the Provisional Government, ridden by legalistic-liberal obsessions, postponed the formal transfer of land to the peasant communities.

'Peace and bread' was the simple and reiterated Bolshevik slogan. From the beginning it alone made sense to the war-weary and the land-hungry. The offensive on the Galician front launched in June under the political direction of Kerensky proved a fiasco; after the first few small gains, entire units refused to stir and the enemy counter-offensive rolled over the Russian positions. Not the smallest doubt remained that the army would not continue the struggle, and yet peace did not seem to be a day nearer.

The longer peace was deferred the greater the Bolshevik opportunity. The reverse suffered by the party in the 'July days', when it headed a doubtfully spontaneous demonstration in the capital in support of the transfer of power to the soviets, was more apparent than real. Lenin was obliged to go into hiding, but the Bolsheviks had tested their strength to some purpose. Nor had the cause of socialism suffered any set-back: there were eleven socialists among the eighteen members of the new government over which Kerensky formally presided. And in the crisis of confidence in the Provisional Government which followed next month, when in a bid to restore order both in the army and in the civil administration the new commander-in-chief, General Kornilov, attempted a military-political *coup*, it was not Kerensky who prevailed. Without a shot being fired, Kornilov's advance on the capital was blocked by the industrial proletariat only because it was to the Petrograd Soviet that the Prime Minister had appealed in defence of the revolution. In doing so he had for all practical purposes signed away his authority.

For although even now Lenin almost alone among the Bolshevik leaders was confident of the summons of history, the Bolshevik accretion of strength in the soviets and in the principal cities could no longer be doubted. At the beginning of the revolution the party membership had totalled twenty-four thousand; in August it was two hundred thousand. On 12/25 September a third coalition government was formed under Kerensky. It was no more realistic than its predecessors; perhaps, indeed, the time for realism other than Bolshevik realism had already passed. Lenin's confidence proved contagious. What was now in sight as he directed the party's strategy and Trotsky, who had assumed complete control of the Petrograd Soviet, organized the forth-coming armed insurrection was not the transfer of power to the soviets but the seizure of power by the Bolshevik faction. On 25 October/7 November that historic seizure of power was achieved with relative ease.

Under the ordeal of war tsarism had collapsed from within, its backward and repressive order of society broken, its inert and anomalous system of government totally discredited. At the moment of revolution there was nothing at hand to take its place; an alternative scheme of government and society had still to be discovered by trial and error. If in the revolutionary out-come authority in the state passed, with the tacit consent of millions, to the so-called vanguard of the proletariat, it did so for one further reason of profound psychological significance. This was the long tradition in Russia of anti-bourgeois sentiment. For generations the spectacle of the gulf between the masses and the classes, between the illiterate millions and educated society, had evoked together with socialist sentiment the denunciation of what Herzen called the 'bourgeois pox' in Europe. All the high-pitched idealism that attended the overthrow of tsarism, as well as all the accumulated hate, was intensified by the violence of Bolshevik propaganda against the *burzhui*.

Of the events that immediately followed the Bolshevik seizure of power only a few need be mentioned here as a commentary on what had gone before. The significant thing is that the Bol-shevik victory led by swift stages to the complete destruction of a democratic socialist ideal. In spite of misgiving and alarm in the Bolshevik ranks, in spite even of opposition in the leading party cadres, not the non-socialist parties only but all the other socialist parties and factions were ruthlessly shut out from the new scheme of government in the making. The Bolshevik *coup d'état* was the prelude to one-party rule. And one-party rule was enforced only by terror. On 7/20 December 1917, Lenin set up the Cheka (*Chrezvy chainaya Commissiya*, or extraordinary commission) for the suppression of counter-revolution, and in so doing re-created in a new and more dreadful guise the tsarist system of political police. On 6/19 January 1918, the day after it had at last met, the constituent assembly, which had a Socialist-Revolutionary majority, was dismissed by the Bolsheviks without compunction or ceremony. On 3 March 1918, after two months of armistice, the Bolsheviks put their signature to the disastrous and humiliating treaty of Brest-Litovsk. And in the following May the civil war, which for months past had smouldered amid these and other shocks and outrages, burst into flame.

Against the fearful background of horror and cruelty which the Russian civil war presents the fate of Nicholas and the imperial family falls into a minor scale of evil. Placed under arrest, after the act of abdication, for his own safety, Nicholas joined his wife and children at Tsarskoe Selo, was removed with them in August to the Siberian town of Tobolsk and, after the Bolshevik accession to power, suffered progressive hardships and humiliations. In April the family were dispatched to Ekaterinburg, in the Urals, a city where hatred of tsarism flourished rankly in the memory of the old possessional serf factories. On the following 16 July all were hideously done to death in the cellar of a merchant's house in the city.

Among the many pronouncements on the Bolshevik epilogue to the Russian Revolution, that of George Plekhanov, the founding father of Russian Marxism, is to be remembered. He had returned to Russia after the great upheaval, a dying man, and had fought with all his remaining strength against Lenin and against the Bolshevik strategy of a party dictatorship in the name of socialism. In the Bolshevik rejection of a democratic ideal he foresaw both a betrayal of the revolutionary ethos and the horrors of the civil war. Before Plekhanov's death on 30 May 1918 Russia had indeed been plunged into a renewed and in many ways darker nightmare of despotism. In this there was surely nothing predetermined. Political liberty is admittedly a western concept and the bias of the Russian centuries has been towards authoritarianism, but all the history of our own time demonstrates the necessity of political liberty if revolutions are to be saved from the revolutionaries. Before 1917 the Russian liberals had squandered their opportunity not through upholding the claims of political liberty but through demanding in so backward and regimented a country and so vast an empire too much liberty too soon. In October 1917 the Bolsheviks found the ground largely prepared for their experiment in Communist autocracy not only by tsarist rule but also by the liberal error. It may be true that the era of European liberalism came to an end in 1914, but it is certain that in Russia the prospects of a liberal experiment were shattered by the liberals themselves.

Bibliography

(Revised and brought up to date for this edition.)

ARKHIV Russkoy Revoliutsii, 22 vols, Berlin, 1921–37.
AXELROD, L. I., Etiudy i vospominaniya, Leningrad, 1925.
BADAYEV, A., The Bolsheviks in the Tsarist Duma, New York, 1929.
BLACK, Cyril E., (Editor), The Transformation of Russian Society: Aspects of Social Change since 1861, Cambridge, Mass., 1960.
Bolshaya Sovietskaya Entsiklopediya, 66 vols, Moscow, 1926–48.
BUCHANAN, Sir G., My Mission to Russia, 2 vols, London, 1923.
CHERNOV, V. M., Rozhdenie revolutsionnoy Rossii, Paris, 1934.
Pered Burey, New York, 1953.
CURTISS, J. S., Church and State in Russia: The Last Years of the Empire, 1900–1917, New York, 1940.
DAN, F. I., Proiskhozhdenie Bolshevizma, New York, 1946.
DANILOV, General Y., La Russie dans la guerre mondiale, Paris, 1927.
FLORINSKY, Michael T., Russia: A History and an Interpretation, 2 vols, New York, 1953.
The End of the Russian Empire, Yale University Press, 1931.
GOLOVINE, General N. N., The Russian Army in the World War, Yale University Press, 1931.
GURKO, V. I., Features and Figures of the Past: Government and Opinion in the Reign of Nicholas II, Stanford University Press, 1939.
HAIMSON, LEOPOLD H., The Russian Marxists and the Origins of Bolshevism, Harvard University Press, 1955.
HANBURY-WILLIAMS, Sir J., The Emperor Nicholas II as I Knew Him, London, 1922.
IZVOLSKY, A. P., Memoirs, London, 1920.
KATKOV, G., Russia 1917, London, 1967.
KATKOV, G., OBERLANDER, E., POPPE, N., and VON RAUCH, G., Russia Enters the Twentieth Century 1894–1917, London, 1971.
KEEP, J. L. H., The Rise of Social Democracy in Russia, Oxford, 1963.
KERENSKY, A. F., The Catastrophe, London, 1927.
KIZEVETTER, A. A., Na rubezhe dvukh stoletiy: vospominaniya, 1881–1914, Prague, 1929.
KNOX, Major-General Sir A., With the Russian Army, 1914–1917, 2 vols, London, 1921.
KOKTOVTSEV, Count V. N., Iz moego proshlogo: vospominaniia, 1903–1919, 2 vols, Paris, 1933.
Krasny Arkhiv, 104 vols, Moscow, 1922–41.
KRUPSKAYA, N., Memories of Lenin, London, 1942.
LIASHCHENKO, P. I., Istoriya narodnogo khoziaistva S.S.S.R., 2 vols, Moscow, 1947–48.
MAKLAKOV, V. A., Vlast'i obshchestvennosti zakate staroy Rossii: vospominaniya sovremmenika, Paris, 1932.
Pervaya Gosudarstvennaya Duma, Paris, 1939.
Vtoraya Gosudarstvennaya Duma, Paris, 1946.
MARTOV, L., MASLOV, P., and POTRESOV, A., Obshchestvennoe dvizhenie v Rossii v nachale XX veka, 4 vols, St. Petersburg, 1904–14.
MELGUNOV, S., Na putiahk k dvortsovomu perevorotu, Paris, 1931.
Legenda o separatnom mire (Kanun revoliutsii), Paris, 1957.

MILIUKOV, Paul, *Political Memoirs, 1905–1917*, ed. by Arthur P. Mendel, Ann Arbor, Michigan, 1967.

MILIUKOV, P. N., *Istoriya vtoroy russkoy revoliutsii*, Vol. 1, Sofia, 1929. *Vospominaniya*, New York, 1955.

MILIUKOV, P. N., SEIGNOBOS, C., and EISENMANN, L., *Histoire de Russie*, Vol. 3, Paris, 1933.

MOSSOLOV, A. A., *At the Court of the Last Tsar*, London, 1935.

NAUMOV, A. N., *Iz utselevshikh vospominaniy 1868–1917*, 2 vols, New York, 1954.

NICHOLAS II, *Dnevnik Nikolalya II, 1890–1906 (Krasny Arkhiv,* Vols 20–22 and 27), Berlin, 1923.
The Letters of the Tsaritsa to the Tsar, 1914–16, London, 1923.
The Letters of the Tsar to the Tsaritsa, London, 1929.
The Secret Letters of Tsar Nicholas, London, 1938.

OLDENBURG, S. S., *Tsarstvovanie Imperatora Nikolaya II*, 2 vols, Belgrade, 1939.

PALÉOLOGUE, M., *An Ambassador's Memoirs, 1914–1917*, tr. by Frederick A. Holt, London, 1973.

PARES, Sir B., *The Fall of the Russian Monarchy*, London, 1939.

PIPES, R. E., *Struve: Liberal on the Left. 1870–1905*, Cambridge, Mass., 1970.

POBEDONOSTSEV, K. P., *Moskovskiy sbornik*, Moscow, 1896.
Pisma Pebedonostseva k Alexandru III, 2 vols, Moscow, 1925–6.
K. P. Pobedonostsev i ego korrespondenty, 2 vols, Moscow, 1923.

PUSHKAREV, S. G., *Rossiya v XIX veke (1801–1914)*, New York, 1956.

RADKEY, Oliver H., *The Agrarian Foes of Bolshevism*, New York, 1958.

ROBINSON, G. T., *Rural Russia under the Old Regime*, London, 1932.

RODZIANKO, M. V., *The Reign of Rasputin: An Empire's Collapse*, London, 1927.

ROMANOV, B. A., *Rossiya v Manchzhuriy (1892–1906)*, Leningrad, 1928.

SAZONOV, S. D., *Fateful Years, 1909–1926*, London, 1928.

SCHAPIRO, L., *The Communist Party of the Soviet Union*, 2nd ed., London, 1970.

SEMMENIKOV, V. P. (Editor), *Monarkhia pered krusheniem*, Moscow 1927.

SETON-WATSON, G. H. N., *The Russian Empire 1801–1917*, Oxford, 1967.

SHECHEGOLEV, P. E. (Editor), *Padenie Tsarskago rezhima*, 7 vols, Leningrad, 1925–7.

SHIPOV, D. N., *Vospominaniya i dumy o perezhitom*, Moscow, 1918.

Short History of the Communist Party of the Soviet Union, Moscow, 1939.

SHUKMAN, Harold, *Lenin and the Russian Revolution*, London, 1966.

SLIOSBERG, G. B., *Dorevoliutsionny stroy Rossii*, Paris, 1933.

SPIRIDOVICH, A. I., *Velikaia voina i fevral'skaia revoliutsiia, 1914–1917 q.q.*, 3 vols, New York, 1960–62.

SUKHANOV, N. N., *Zapiski o revoliutsii*, 7 vols, Berlin, 1922–23.

SUMNER, B. H., *Tsardom and Imperialism in the Far East and the Middle East*, London, 1942.

TAUBE, Baron M. de, *La Politique russe d'avant querre et la fin de l'empire des tsars, 1904–17*, Paris, 1928.

TREADGOLD, Donald W., *Lenin and His Rivals. The Struggle for Russia's Future*, London, 1955.
Twentieth Century Russia, Chicago, 1959.

ULAM, Adam B., *Lenin and the Bolsheviks*, London, 1966; published in the U.S. as *The Bolsheviks*, New York, 1965.

BIBLIOGRAPHY

WALKIN, JACOB, *The Rise of Democracy in Pre-Revolutionary Russia. Political and Social Institutions under the Last Three Czars,* London, 1963.

WITTE, Count S. Y.,*Vospominaniya,* 3 vols, Berlin, 1922–23.

WOLFE, B. D., *Three Who Made a Revolution,* New York, 1948.

WOYTINSKY, W. S., *Stormy Passage,* New York, 1961.

ZEMAN, Z. A. B., *Germany and the Revolution in Russia. Documents from the Archives of the German Foreign Ministry,* Oxford, 1958.

ZENZINOV, V., *Perezhitoe,* New York, 1953.

Index